POLAR POLLUTION

OUTDOOR MEMOIRS of POLARFLEECE

Doug Hoschek

Introduction

In this book I want to share what I believe are very important facts and conclusions gained from my forty-five years of selling, developing, and marketing fibers for clothing here in America for American fabric mills, garment makers, retailers, and consumers. Most notably, I am credited as the creator, co-inventor, and marketer of Polarfleece fabric and the Polarfleece technology.

Despite my past success, I am a solitary man in outdoor textiles today because of my opposition to sending textile manufacturing offshore. Beginning in the 1980s, outdoor brands have closed textile factories in America and sent those jobs to China and other Asian countries. The result has been major job losses in America and catastrophic pollution in the offshore countries—pollution that is also affecting America.

I have written this book to share the rich history of outdoor textile manufacturing in America, the devastation caused by the move to offshore, and my call to action to all of us to restore jobs and save the environment by bringing those manufacturing jobs home. In July of 2011 Greenpeace completed a year long investigation into toxic water pollution in China. The report challenges clothing brands like those named in this book to eliminate releases of hazardous chemicals from their supply chain and products. The exact quote from Greenpeace in the July 13,2011 EcoTextile publication says,"now we have scientific evidence confirming that hazardous chemicals are being released into China's rivers to make clothes worn by people around the globe." If anyone doubts that toxic chemicals to make textiles have ever been released into rivers you need only to read this book.

Chapter One:

Outdoor Textiles in America

Between the mid-1800s and the early 1900s, textile production, and especially outdoor textiles, evolved from homemade clothing into apparel made with machine-age technology. This period of time is commonly called the Industrial Revolution. That revolution, based in Europe and mainly England, was carried across the ocean to America by educated and family minded folks seeking the democracy and frontier where they could build a new life.

One hundred years ago, Oregon became the most powerful and profitable textile market for outdoor apparel. Oregon-raised wool was the best in America, and revenues from wool fiber were second only to steel in the U.S. economy. A 1913 *Portland Commerce* newspaper tells how wool fibers created the finest woolen fabrics and clothing in America. In Salem, Oregon, the Thomas Kay Woolen Mill was an important part of the legacy of outdoor textiles. Today, the mill is an intact historic site, open to the public as a museum and activity center.

From Jantzen swimwear and White Stag skiwear, to Pendleton classic woolen outerwear, sportswear, and its famous trading blankets with native art designs, the textile industry made Portland, Oregon, and its sister city of Seattle, Washington, the manufacturing center for the great American outdoors from the early 1900s through the 1970s. By providing tens of thousands of jobs and enabling the economic success of cities like Portland and Seattle, American manufacturing helped people realize the American dream of recreation and owning their own homes. The land of central Oregon—once simply called *Shaniko*—produced the famous wool that traveled by rail to the Portland area, as well as across America to eager textile mills in the Northeast.

In the 1960s, synthetic fibers of nylon appeared in fabrics such as the famous patented quilts of Eddie Bauer down clothing and sleeping bags. REI founder and President Jim Whittaker's success in climbing to the top of Mount Everest in 1963 signaled the start of using nylon fabrics in outdoor clothing manufactured for skiing, hunting, fishing, hiking, and camping. As a result, Oregon and Seattle textiles went through a makeover, switching from wool and woolens to down and nylon outdoor clothing. Oregon brands such as White Stag and Jantzen added cotton and acrylic fibers to their sportswear lines, and expanded the apparel and styles beyond outdoor clothing. Also during the 1960s, polyester fiber became a blending fiber for cotton in sportswear and bedding, and a new technology of nonwovens called fiberfill began to replace wool and down for insulation.

During this period of change, nylon fibers produced by DuPont were woven into fabrics, mostly on the East Coast of America. As a result, the process of manufacturing outdoor textiles changed. Where there used to be one harmonious mill, such as a woolen mill that bought fiber and used its machines to make yarn, fabrics, and finished products, now there were mills for each function of the manufacturing process.

My role in fibers and textiles for outdoor products made in America started in New York City in 1967 at a public corporation called Celanese Corporation. I was given the responsibility of selling polyester fibers as fiberfill materials to makers of skiwear, outerwear, quilted robes, sleeping bags, and bedding products. It was at this time that Celanese and other very powerful chemical companies, such as DuPont and Monsanto, began to make synthetic fibers out of their chemicals, rather than sell chemicals to a mill to make its own fibers, textile yarns, and fabrics. To get consumers to use the chemical fibers of nylon and polyester, instead of the natural fibers of wool and cotton, these companies marketed directly to the consumer via print media and television commercials.

I moved from New York and the Celanese fiber chemical company to Seattle, where my former boss and I developed new types of fiberfill in our factory and sold it to outerwear and skiwear makers. We made our own sleeping bags, pillows, comforters, and dog beds for retailers, especially L. L. Bean. The success of fiberfill led me to develop a fabric that functioned just like nonwoven fiberfill for insulation in skiwear and outerwear. Partnering with Malden Mills, a privately owned East Coast pile-fabric mill, Polarfleece® was created. Rather than offer Polarfleece as a sportswear fabric to mainstream retailers, it was sold exclusively to outerwear makers that sold to specialty retailers.

The Evolving Outdoor Marketplace Today

Since the creation of Polarfleece as a 100 percent polyester fabric and the use of Gore-Tex® to make nylon-fiber fabrics waterproof and breathable, brands that use fibers and chemical enhancements such as moisture wicking and antimicrobial technology have become an industry that does marketing but no manufacturing of its own. The manufacturing is sent offshore to companies in China.

With wholesale revenues in the billions of dollars, Oregon, and especially Portland, finds Nike ($19 billion), Columbia ($3.4 billion), Adidas (more than $3 billion), and many others, such as Ice Breaker from New Zealand, headquartering in Portland and taking advantage of an experienced workforce and a history of textile manufacturing dating back a hundred years. Each major brand has a flagship store and/or retailing location downtown and in the suburbs.

As of 2011, global production of cotton and of oil-based fibers such as nylon and polyester face critical supply issues. Fibers made from wood pulp, such as rayon and viscose, have seen double-digit increases in orders, and natural fibers such as hemp and bamboo have found their way into clothing. During my forty-five years of experience, I have seen this kind of supply problem strangle the biggest brands, while providing innovators a chance to bring out new fibers and products. Eddie Bauer did it with down over wool; Patagonia took my Polarfleece and did it with polyester over both wool and down, as well as fiberfill. A mid-1980s Patagonia newsletter says the company was holding back growth to 35 percent while it got business controls like inventory management in place and kept dealers happy with supplies.

To sum up, whenever a unique new fiber has entered the outdoor-textiles marketplace, a start-up brand was involved in bringing that fiber to market. The most direct reason I can give from years of observation is that textile brands get so big and so overloaded with inventory and financial budgets, they simply cannot take the risks they did as younger start-ups.

Today, makers of outdoor products bring to the market not only a unique product with a system of patent rights, but a vision of new fibers for outdoor clothing. Members of the third generation of Bishops at Pendleton like to refer to the fiber changes as perfect storms of things coming together.

Columbia Sportswear took the innovation of polyester fibers in a fiberfill called Thinsulate™ from 3M, the nylon fibers in Gore-Tex, and the polyester fibers in Polarfleece to an all-out marketing campaign and a business plan that shut down their factories in Portland and Missouri, and led to Columbia chasing the Nike express to Asia. Columbia's core was hunting and fishing clothing, which Mother Boyle always told me was its profit center. In my opinion, Columbia built its brand into sportswear and footwear and a game of Scrabble over outerwear vs. activewear with its cross-town rival, Nike. Fibers play a critical role in the technology that drives the Wall Street indexes.

Myself being among the earliest, if not the first, to develop an outdoor textile technology with polyester, Polarfleece has literally created a layer of clothing that stands alone and does not compete with the other five basic layers: jacket, shirt, pants, socks, and shoes. The brands that built the outdoor textiles of today received unlimited amounts of marketing funds from the fiber producers, of which I was a part, building polyester into a leader of a market controlled by wool and cotton for more than a hundred years.

But marketing is not one of the functions of today's offshore manufacturers of fibers and almost all textile materials. Rather, the money being sent to Asia to produce fibers and textile technology is creating catastrophic issues resulting from environmental pollution.

Today, billions of dollars are needed to save China's clean drinking water. The Ministry of China reports that 90 percent of the country's groundwater is polluted, and more than 320 million citizens have no safe drinking water. Seriously impacting China's economic growth, this pollution issue is the main focus of outdoor textile brands, as evidenced by the Sustainable Apparel Coalition, co-headed by the U.S. Environmental Protection Agency (EPA).

On the positive side, today there exists a new waterless dyeing technology known as AirDye®. Not since the opportunity to take polyester fiber into fiberfill and then Polarfleece have I seen or heard of a technology using a polyester fiber that has the ability to change the mainstream textile apparel. AirDye technology has created a new system for adding color and prints to synthetic fabrics that anchors the reality of making textile fabrics once again in America.

My Goal for the Future of Outdoor Textile Production

Textiles business has for centuries brought wealth and comfort to all places on the globe. Trade among countries has seen natural fibers such as wool, cotton, and down sent from country to country to complete the processing of fibers into fabrics, clothing, and gear. For most of the past sixty years, synthetic fibers of polyester and nylon have dominated the textiles world. From an investor's standpoint, there is much more money to be made by a mill or finished-product maker using high-grade goods than there is in manufacturing cheap, low-grade goods. It's time to return textile manufacturing to America. It's time to give our country the advantage of goods (fabric and product) labeled "Made in America," to give purchasers the assurance that all fiber and benefits are just as represented.

There are no better conditions in the world than in America for the manufacturing of first-class goods, and our country is entitled to let the world know of our beautiful lands and resources, including our climate and water, which are protected by law and by the convictions of our citizens. The health of our climate and water cannot be diminished. This assures each of us the reality of personal health as we daily look after ourselves and our loved ones, friends, and associates.

I trust the day is not far off when some practical men and women who understand the manufacturing of really first-class goods, both natural and manmade, will establish mills and assembly factories in our country to manufacture such goods. Then our well-dressed citizens—men, women, and children—will find it to their benefit to demand American resources that are made into fabrics and finished products in our own country, thus building up good, sustainable industries, as well as giving America the fame it deserves as a country noted for the manufacture of superior fabrics and finished products. This also will help us develop another industry, namely sustainable natural resources as raw materials.

I wish we had a commitment from our citizens, for our citizens, supported by our laws and constitution, to label goods from outside America for what they really are. To support my wish, I have written my story of working in American textiles for my entire career since I graduated from college in 1965. My story involves relationships bonded in resources, machines, buildings, lands, people, and technology, melding and riveting me to "Made in America."

But before we jump into today's world of textiles, where the bounty is far beyond the minds of any of us who started it with synthetics fifty years ago, let me share the story of an authentic civilization recorded in history for more than ten thousand years.

Widely known is the old civilization of domesticated animals and primitive man of the Mesopotamian plain. More closely connected to the Northwest and the marketplace of outdoor textiles presented in this book is an area along the narrow mainland coast of southeast Alaska, inhabited for the last ten thousand years by Native Americans named the Tlingit people. The Tlingits shared a deep belief that we descended from beings who could metamorphose from animal to person. They believed the forces that animated the life of people also animated the life of the sea, the forest, and the waters, that only a thin veil separated the mortal world and the spirit world.

Much of my book presents the developing history of textiles, which began with natural fibers of wool and down and evolved with modern science into synthetics of polyester and nylon. I call you first back to the beliefs of the Tlingits when they lived and dressed in the same woods and waters that are now home to the biggest players in activewear and outdoor textiles, back to the words of Chief Seattle, "We are webbed in blood to the land; whatever we do to the land, we do to ourselves."

I believe he is saying that all things possess their own individuality, or spirit, and are capable of independent action with other spirits, that we come together webbed into whatever belief we have in creation. To fully understand the symbolism of this, I think you must go back in time and immerse yourself in a different world view. Go back to an era when you would adjust your thoughts to the seasonal flow of time, when each season required a different kind of protection from Mother Nature, and each season offered nature's gifts to be used without the taking of living things.

For the Tlingits, we find cedar being peeled from fallen branches and trees and from the stronger trunks of older trees, leaving the trees to stand for hundreds more years. Cedar made their baskets for food and water. It also made their protective clothing, including headgear, worn to protect them from the rains of the Northwest. Cedar being peeled from trees is like wool being sheared from the body of the sheep. In neither case is their life ended, and the next year brings more cedar for peeling and more wool for shearing.

Outdoor climates have stayed much the same for thousands of years, allowing greater numbers of humans to populate the Earth. As these populations come together, humans are living longer. This requires increasingly more of what nature has created and what nature wants to give to us. As populations increase and nature's resources are discovered and used, again that thin veil appears that separates what we need from what we want.

More than any other textiles, outdoor and activewear products participate in the natural world, relying on nature's climate for their purpose and profit. On the outdoor lands of America, lands far from the biblical records of the development of human beings, a metamorphosis occurred and continues on a cradle of some of the world's largest glacial ice fields—referred to in our times as the Alexander Archipelago.

Somehow tied to today's words of global warming and wilderness, the meanings are spoken out in brands of textiles. Today the thirst of modern textile machines joins in a mass consumption of oil-based fossil fuels that lie under the ground of once-sacred lands. In my lifetime, this thirst pushed me to create polyester fiberfill and then Polarfleece fabric.

Suffering through sludge and pollution from these often-toxic chemicals, our country righted the wrongs, creating the Environmental Protection Agency in the 1970s, and assuring that manmade and natural resources would survive without destroying our lives, nature, and our planet.

Sadly today, with manufacturing shifted to offshore countries, the EPA regulations have been ignored. Now almost forty years later, the reality includes massive human casualties, as well as destruction of natural resources and nature's creatures. That veil is once again drawn between the mortal world and the spirit we call nature.

Chapter Two:

1960s to Present Textiles

For whatever reason, I have been ahead of the curve in my career in textiles ever since I started in 1965. The famous line from the movie *The Graduate* about plastics being the future stuck to me when I graduated from the University of Montana and returned home to Long Island and New York City, I took a job selling cotton yarns for one of the oldest American yarn spinners, Aberfoyle. The offshore takeover of cotton had begun, and both America and England were destroying thousands of machines and moving on to synthetic fibers—acrylic, nylon, and polyester.

The technology for making synthetic fibers was controlled by American chemical companies such as DuPont, Celanese, and Monsanto. These companies created the chemical chips that were melted and extruded into synthetic fibers in their own fiber factories, which they called plants. I think the name plants, rather than factories, was used to somehow create a tie-in to the natural cellulose fiber of cotton plants, which the new synthetics were replacing. As cotton-sourced textile manufacturing moved offshore, these polyester, nylon, and acrylic fiber plants became substitutes for cotton plantations in the South.

Moving from Cotton to Polyester

After a year with Aberfoyle, I was offered a job at Celanese Fibers Marketing. An older sales rep at Aberfoyle, Bruce, had moved to Celanese and helped me get the introduction for the job. I was hired to sell and market polyester fiberfill made with Fortrel® polyester fibers. A division of the Celanese Corporation (a Fortune 500 public corporation), the Celanese Fibers Marketing Company was unique in the fiber business at that time; its biggest competitors—DuPont, Monsanto, and Eastman Kodak—used only a direct selling approach for the manufacturing of the fibers. Celanese broke away from that tradition by selling directly through Fiber Industries—the division of Celanese that did the manufacturing. Invoicing went to customers from Fiber Industries; Fiber Industries gave marketing funds to the Celanese Marketing Company. This structure allowed marketing to follow the most productive and profitable fiber areas. It also allowed the parent company, Celanese Corporation, to remain a chemical-based manufacturer of the raw materials used to produce polyester fibers.

The name Celanese came from the words *cellulose* and *easy care*. The company started out as a maker of acetate fibers from cellulose plant fiber—thus the "Cel" part of the name. Acetate made it easier to care for fibers made from cellulose—hence the "an ese" at the end. The fiberfill area that I was hired into was developing polyester fibers to move on from the acetate fiberfill fibers. Meanwhile, companies like DuPont were bringing out superior fibers for fiberfill in polyester, branded as Dacron® 88.

Celanese had a patent on a technology called a tow spreader and threaded-roll processing, initially created to make cigarette filters from acetate fibers. My boss, Claude, used the technology to set up polyester-pillow processing machines across the United States. In particular, he organized the purchase of a fiberfill and quilting customer in Seattle, JenCelLite Corporation. This business was a large customer for Celanese acetate fibers, which they used to make fiberfill batting for quilting of outerwear fabrics. Under the company's outdoor-minded founder, Harry Jensen, JenCelLite became one of the first leading-edge makers of acetate fiberfill and shipped the acetate batting all over the United States to other quilters for outerwear garment fabrications.

It was very important to me that this arrangement was established when I began the plan to sell polyester fibers for fiberfill. I realized that with JenCelLite's success at selling acetate across the country and with exclusive patent rights for the tow spreader, the best approach to sales was to sell the fiberfills—not the fibers. After I developed the sales of a nonwoven fabric that used only fiber, not yarn, I saw the potential to make finished fabrics—not just an inner liner covered with woven fabrics—using fibers without yarn.

Following the Thread of a New Idea

Five years later, in 1973, my boss at Celanese, Claude, bought the JenCel-Lite Company. I moved to Seattle to manage the sales of fiberfill and quilting for a very large customer base of outerwear and skiwear companies between Seattle, Portland, and Denver. These companies were well-established in down-quilted and woolen outerwear and included Eddie Bauer, Pendleton, White Stag, Pacific Trail, and a host of others that made private-label outerwear for Sears and J. C. Penney. Since nylon fabrics were the cover fabric for down and fiberfill, Blank Textiles gave me the sales rights to a market that placed tens of millions of yards of fabric orders twelve months a year.

Commissions from these sales gave me a healthy living until the production of nylon fabrics was sent offshore in the late 1970s, wiping out the American mills in the 1980s. My barrel was not empty because, also in 1973, I was hired as an independent sales rep for Malden Mills, a leading maker of pile fabrics. Focusing on fake furs for stuffed toys and knockoffs of real fur coats, the technology of making pile fabric used a fiber fabrication called "sliver knitting." The face of the fabric was all fiber, not yarn, and the backing was a stitched-yarn knit that used yarns like the ones I had briefly sold when I worked at Aberfoyle. Year after year, I studied the products Malden made from fiber fabrics, trying to figure out how to make my nonwoven, high-loft, lightweight fiberfill into a real fabric for outerwear. It proved impossible; the polyester and acrylic fibers could not be held together like wool fibers are held using water and a fulling type processing.

Then offshore caught up with the nylon and polyester fabrics and the fiberfills. In 1979, I faced losing my lucrative sales of three fabrics and being left with nothing. While offshore manufacturing took the down, nylon, and fiberfill to Asia, I became determined to take the famous woolen Hudson Bay trading blanket, reduce its weight to that of fiberfill, and create a new technology.

After nearly two years and many trials with my woolen needle loom, which made nonquilted fiberfill at JenCelLite, I, along with Malden Mills, created the fabric, using the Malden baby bunting and sweatshirt fabrics. It was almost too late. When I attended a September 1981 sales meeting in New York City, Malden told me they had just filed for Chapter 11 bankruptcy protection and were not going to keep the pile and sweatshirt fabrics business going. The pain in both myself and Malden's owner connected, and he agreed to give my double-faced polyester fleece, branded as Polarfleece, a chance to get Malden out of bankruptcy.

Before I get into that story, however, let's look at the current status and reality of making cotton and synthetic textiles offshore without any respect for compliance with the type of EPA environmental regulations that have governed textiles made in America since the early 1970s.

Catastrophic Pollution Offshore

How the government of a country like China abuses its own environment and citizens to profit from the desires for clothing, footwear, and gear for U.S. citizens is a story I truly believe we all need to begin to take action to change. Previous stories of child-labor issues were dismissed with a simple, "They have a right to run their economy and labor as they see proper for their country."

The calling to protect the air and water is a global call. Necessary conformance to environmental protections allows us to survive on this planet, which we are borrowing from our children. We must protect the health of natural resources and humans to ensure healthy survival for both.

Present behaviors and conditions—especially those involved with offshore textile manufacturing—simply defy any reasonable consideration of living on this planet. Popular American companies purchase their textile materials from water so polluted it has tainted 90 percent of the groundwater in China. According to the World Health Organization, water pollution causes a hundred thousand deaths a year and 75 percent of all the health issues in China, and leaves 320 million people (equal to our entire population) with no clean drinking water.

This situation has arisen from the manufacturing of billions of dollars of textile products offered in America by brands that knew the pollution was occurring. They knew because they all started here in America, using textiles produced under EPA regulations, before running offshore. They ignored the truth and their responsibility to protect the environment, no matter where they sought a supplier. In addition to American-owned polluters, large Hong Kong trading companies such as Li & Fung (which reported 55 percent profits in 2010) line the racks of retailers with clothing from the worst water-pollution processing in the history of the world. They cover themselves up with assorted brands to not be identified.

This kind of water pollution makes the last oil spill in the Gulf of Mexico look like a mistake in a bathtub. Overall, reports say textiles use 2.4 trillion gallons of water per year. China produces 24 percent of the world's textiles, which means that one-quarter of the water used by China—600 billion gallons—is polluted and sent back out into rivers and groundwater.

That doesn't have to happen. In chapters of this book, I will demonstrate that my work with polyester fibers, which led to recycling the same fiber from plastic bottles, is mostly ignored by outdoor textiles and general textiles in favor of the current water and air pollution in Asia. Cheap prices do not justify the destruction of water and air quality. The solution still exists to bring textiles back to America to use safe water and healthy air and to clean up our landfills. Bringing manufacturing back will break up the monopoly being created by billion-dollar textile brands manufacturing in Asia, especially China.

Right now, this monopoly is using older American brands now owned by investors and American public corporations. One example is the Field & Stream brand, which began manufacturing outerwear in 1871. The clothing brand is not associated with the magazine of the same name. Field & Stream outerwear was based in the Minneapolis area, making mostly woolen outerwear in their own factories through the 1970s. Woolen mills were a key part of textiles in the Midwest, starting with the Great Lakes trading routes and the popular woolen blankets known simply as Hudson Bay trading blankets, or point blankets.

After textile outerwear production moved offshore, the owner of Field & Stream outerwear decided to increase the use of its famous brand by licensing its name for many outdoor products. This led to a few serious legal issues, agreements, and court filings to sort out product licensing rights been F & S outerwear and the Times Mirror *Field & Stream* magazine. In 2006 the owner of the outdoor textile Field & Stream sold to a group of investors. By then, all the licensed apparel and other outdoor-related products were manufactured offshore. At some point, the investors will develop an exit strategy or go public, as others have done. An exit strategy could easily result in the brand being owned by a company in China. In that case, the sales to citizens in America would be made via retailers such as Dick's Sporting Goods (a current customer of F&S) by a Chinese company working out of China. The only money brought into the American economy would be from the retail sales dollars consumers pay the retailer,

The "Brand-It" Game's Winners and Losers

Top officials in China are now admitting that catastrophic pollution—especially water pollution, as we will see in the next two chapters—has occurred sooner than they expected. For China to survive, that pollution must be cleaned up. The cost of cleaning up water pollution is enormous. It can only come from charging higher prices and/or cutting folks out of the supply chain. Since the U.S. policy with China is founded on trade agreements that include the United States borrowing huge amounts of money from China, the leverage is going to prove out on the side of whichever country is doing the manufacturing. Yet when a 140-year-old American outdoor icon such as Field & Stream gives up "Made in America" to offshore production and then sells many licenses of its brand in outdoor products to investors who are not financially capable of setting up any manufacturing, it seems likely those brands will ultimately be sold to a supplier in China.

This "brand-it" game is also clearly happening at Columbia Sportswear, and at some point, that public company might be sold to Chinese owners, leaving retail markups to the customer as the only economic gains for America. What's more, because retailing is part of Columbia's business and future, even those profits would go to China should they acquire Columbia. Other retailers, such as REI, are also swamped by Chinese suppliers and face the same reality. North Face wants to sell more than a billion dollars of their outerwear in China, and Timberland is opening110 retail stores in China.

All of this fuels what I call "polar pollution"—allowing the hundreds of billions in products consumed in America to be produced in horrific pollution that melts the poles of the planet and fouls water beyond reason. Spread this trend to electronics and anything else made in a country like China, and America is reduced to a labor world of flipping burgers with genetically altered food supplies that leave almost half the population facing issues like diabetes.

How can we stop this from happening? Most companies all started in America under EPA regulations, then ran offshore to get out from under the cost of following the regulations.

There is a four letter word for the biggest offender: Nike. As of January 2011, Nike listed $19 billion in sales and was reporting to its investors that it will double that figure to $38 billion by the end of 2015. The hometown area where Nike built its headquarters campus has struggled for most of the years Nike has been building its business. In fact, the entire state of Oregon has followed with disappointing results in economic growth. In January 2011, the real estate in the Portland area showed one in five homeowners were negative in their equity. A more alarming fact: seven hundred fifty thousand of the state's citizens are on food stamps.

Oregon obviously needs jobs—real jobs that pay a middle-class wage and will be around for many years to come. Recent reports say that within offshore textile brands in Oregon such as Nike and Columbia, the average income of workers is eighty thousand dollars a year. Obviously it pays well to produce offshore and neither own manufacturing nor hire the workers to run it.

The total market share of textiles exported from China in 2010 was $200 billion. That comes close to one trillion dollars in retail sales to the consumer. I think it's safe to say that with Nike operating hundreds of factories in China, most of the $200 billion in exported textiles from China is coming to America.

These numbers please Wall Street and the insider traders that believe selling textiles has more value than manufacturing them. What makes these offshore-manufactured brands worth so much to investors? The companies have no machinery, only land for offices and retail spaces. They have patents to protect their designs.

Consider, however, that Chinese-owned textile companies are also importing their products to America. For example, China is sending $10 million to America from a company based in China, Li Ning, which offers sports shoes, clothing, and equipment. Both Nike and Li Ning believe they can sell even more textiles in America. The simple truth is, a company based in China comes to America, employs twenty people in Portland, and opens a retail store. In China, that company's sales are $600 million to the Chinese population. They hire top American professional athletes, just as Nike and others do, to endorse their shoes and apparel. So what good are the patents owned by the American brands?

Meanwhile, the president of China dines in the White House, drinking healthy water, while 320 million people in China have no safe drinking water. The second-largest water polluter in China is textiles, especially dye houses.

China talks about building commercial airliners—obviously a threat to Boeing, which is across the river from Portland and a three-hour drive up the interstate. Are the citizens of America so dead that this doesn't matter? Is the business of electronics, of "pads" and "pods" and social networking, going to maintain the equity lost in manufacturing in America?

China wants for its people what we have here in America. However, for China to get it, we the citizens of America have become the mice in their tank, running around looking for jobs that do not pay enough to live and eat and maintain our health. Obesity is the concern in every type of house in America, from the White House to the average citizen's house.

A Solitary Man

I lost my seat at the table in textiles by staying focused on making textiles here in America. Today, after creating one of the finest fabrics on the planet—Polarfleece—I am looked at as a solitary man for not wanting to make things offshore. This is my story of being happy when products were made here, and my new reality of being alone and no longer wanted.

At this time, I believe the most to lose have done the least. They are not paying respect to the thread and fabric of life. Sewing this thread—whether shorn from a sheep (wool), grown from the ground (cotton), or raised from under the ground (fossil fuel oil/polyester)—into outdoor fleece is a social adhesive, as well as a way to make clothing for comfort and protection. Fleece has, for thousands of years, provided a voice for love, for education, for healing, and for welcome and farewell. Fleece provides a link to the environment, to other people, and to our spiritual essence.

My only reason for developing Polarfleece while employed by Malden Mills was to protect the made-in-America textile industry, which was being taken off the shores of America on the wave of a new global economics policy.

Polarfleece birthed 100 percent polyester fabrics for outdoor and activewear textile apparel. A horrible fire destroyed the Polarfleece made-in-America mill, and the ashes allowed surviving Malden customers to move its manufacture offshore without the costs of building their own manufacturing mills and sewing factories. The unedited news wire story and photo below describe what I believe is the last stand of making textiles in America.

BY TROT-DRAPER—THE HUNCHBACK.

Amid the smoldering ruins

Heavy smoke and fires were still visible yesterday morning at the Malden Mills complex in Methuen.

PM-MA--Mill Fire, 8th Ld-Writethru,1200
ls: ADDS witness comments, grafs 5-7; ADDS emergency declaration
declared, graf 11; UPDATES patient names, conditions, grafs 45-50
AP Photos and AP Graphic
By ROBERT W. TROTT
Associated Press Writer

METHUEN, Mass. (AP) — An explosion of fire that raged through a
textile mill complex, injuring 33 people, was declared under
control this morning, and officials began turning their attention
to dealing with the hundreds of people who lost their jobs.
The initial explosion, possibly in a boiler, was so powerful
that it blew out the sprinkler system of the Malden Mills complex,
leading to the destruction of four of the five buildings in the
complex.
Workers in some of the buildings said that after the explosion
they were told to stay inside.
``The next thing we knew, the building we were in caught on
fire,'' said a worker who would not give his name.
Eight of the injured were listed in critical condition, state
Fire Marshal Stephen Coan said. Hospitals were appealing for blood
donations to help some of the victims.
Malden Mills owner Aaron Feuerstein vowed to rebuild on the same
spot, if possible, or elsewhere in the Methuen/Lawrence area.
``It was a terrible thing, but I didn't dwell on the tragedy. I
was only thinking of how to rebuild and how to get jobs back to
people as soon as possible,'' Feuerstein said.
A state of emergency was declared by Gov. William Weld for the
cities of Lawrence and Methuen. Under the emergency declaration,
the governor can send National Guard and state police to help the
community without requesting a special appropriation from the
Legislature. Weld said he also would seek to waive the two-week
wait for unemployment benefits.
Malden Mills, which makes everything from upholstery fabrics to
fleece for Patagonia jackets and pullovers, was the area's biggest
employer, providing $10-$12 per hour jobs for blue collar workers.
Sales were about $500 million yearly.
The company, which filed for bankruptcy protection in the 1980s,
made a turnaround with its development of Polartec, a synthetic
warming material used by products sold by many of the most popular
outdoors stores.
``We were really quite astonished and devastated by the loss,''
said Catharine Hartnett, a spokeswoman for L.L. Bean, which uses
Polartec material for vests, pullovers, hats, gloves, parka
linings. ``Obviously it will have an impact on our business.''
More than 1,400 people worked at the mills; in all, the company
employs 3,100 people.
``All of those jobs are in jeopardy,'' Methuen Mayor Dennis
DiZoglio said.
DiZoglio was joined at the site by state and federal officials,
including U.S. Sen. Edward M. Kennedy, D-Mass. All promised to seek
government emergency assistance.
Weld said he would probably declare an emergency at the state

20

level and would be talking with federal officials about a federal
disaster declaration.

Weld said the state would try to help find other space for the
company. He said he already had decided to allocate an additional
$100,000 in the area for job training for dislocated workers and
additional personnel would be assigned to unemployment offices in
the area.

``I've been there two years now. Two weeks before Christmas it's
all gone,'' said Chris McRae. ``This building has been here for 100
years, and now there's nothing left there.''

The mayor said he watched executives of the company, the largest
employer in Methuen, as the fire burned.

``You could see it in their faces,'' he said. ``They knew that
their business was now being destroyed.''

Coan said his office and the federal Bureau of Alcohol, Tobacco
and Firearms were investigating.

``For a fire to move this quick, and consume this much property,
it is a very major fire in the history of the commonwealth,'' Coan
said.

Shaun Hamilton's friend Louis Melendez was working in the first
building when the boiler exploded.

``It started in the boiler room. It was absolute panic,''
Hamilton said. ``People were running all around. He (Melendez) took
a few people out himself.''

Officials said they were still investigating and could not
verify it had started in a boiler.

One of the people Hamilton's friend pulled out of the fire was
unrecognizable, said Hamilton, who was standing outside: ``He was
in sad shape.''

Sixty-one area residents who were evacuated into the
sub-freezing cold remained at the Knights of Columbus Hall and St.
Monica's Church. Water poured on the fire turned to ice on the
ground.

Icy winds of 45 mph, and a water shortage caused by building
walls collapsing on the fire lines, hampered firefighters' efforts
to bring the blaze under control.

Huge cinders of burning wood rained down on nearby businesses
and homes, causing at least one other fire. Two blocks from the
mill, the wooden roof of New England Furniture Stripping and
Refinishing caught on fire, and firefighters were hosing down the
homes around it to keep them from going up in flames as well.
Several houses also had small roof fires caused by cinders.

Malden Mills' four buildings and a warehouse are located in an
industrial area on the north side of the Merrimack River, near the
Lawrence border, about 26 miles north of Boston.

Thick black smoke spread across Methuen, Lawrence and North
Andover, and the sound of sirens filled the air for miles around,
as firefighters and ambulances from at least 30 cities and towns in
New Hampshire and Massachusetts came to help fight the
conflagration.

Coan was unable to confirm initial reports that an 8 p.m. boiler
explosion started the fire, which quickly engulfed the first
building. It collapsed a little more than an hour later, as the

| Printed By: PKA | Slug: PM-MA--MILLFIRE | Time: 2:40:39P |

..re spread to a second building, causing a series of explosions
and sending acrid black smoke and chunks of burning debris into the
frigid air. The third and fourth mill buildings went up before
midnight.

``Malden Mills is a mill building. It has all the hazards of a
mill building — lint, and chemicals, and hazardous materials of
that nature,'' said Methuen Fire Chief Ken Bourassa.

Bourassa said ``the initial explosion was so intense that it
blew out the sprinkler system.''

This morning, about 12 hours after the fire began, he said the
flames were contained.

``The guys took a beating, God bless them,'' he said.

Workers said about 600 to 700 people would have been working the
7 p.m. to 7 a.m. shift.

Early on, employees who had been evacuated gathered at The Front
Row, a sports bar about a block away with a clear view of the
burning mill. Several said their supervisors told them the fire had
been contained in the first building, and they should shut off
their machines but remain inside. Then smoke began to fill their
building.

``There was smoke ... We started going outside, the roof (of the
next building) was up in flames,'' said Dave Arlitt, a foreman.

Officials evacuated some nearby residents after the winds
shifted toward a populated neighborhood, full of one- and
two-family homes and an elderly housing complex. Authorities shut
: electricity to the surrounding area.

One neighbor, who refused to give her name said, ``I was
upstairs cleaning up my son's room. All of a sudden, everything
went pow.''

Firefighters and ambulances came from as far away as Boston's
South Shore suburbs and Nashua, N.H. A sea of ambulances waited in
the mill parking lot in case of further casualties.

Nine victims were treated at Lawrence General Hospital; three of
those were sent to Boston hospitals while the others were treated
and released.

Three unidentified victims were admitted to Holy Family Hospital
in Methuen, where they were in guarded condition with burns and
smoke inhalation; four others were transferred to hospitals in
Boston and Worcester.

Six victims were taken to Hale Hospital in Haverhill; one was
admitted in fair condition, while the other five — including a
firefighter — were treated for smoke inhalation and released.

Dr. Ron Walls, chief of the department of Emergency Medicine at
Brigham and Women's Hospital, said the facility's four patients —
Manuel Heredia, 54; Felix Diaz, 34; Brian Beasley, 27; and Jerry
Barnes, 42 — all were listed in critical but stable condition early
this morning, with significant burns and smoke inhalation.

At Mass General, two men were in critical condition: Alvaro
Rosario, 39, and an unidentified man. A third patient, 24-year-old
Andre DesRosiers, was in serious condition.

At the University of Massachusetts Medical Center in Worcester,
liam Dobens and Abel Reyes were in critical condition, a
spokesman said.

Chapter Three:

Black Magic Fibers

For more than four decades, I have turned the twentieth century's "black magic" fossil fuel into synthetic fibers and fabrics, creating a gold mine and a landfill of petroleum-based nuggets known as polyester and nylon, knitting and weaving and carding them from what was once thought to be an unlimited supply of black lakes and streams under the earth's surface. On a per-pound basis, textiles from these fibers have no equal in consumption. Almost 50 percent of the world's fibers for textiles are synthetic—plastic—while only 40 percent come from cotton.

The global textile industry is the third-largest consumer and polluter of water. The World Bank estimates that 17–20 percent of industrial pollution comes from textile coloring and treatment. Of the toxic chemicals in our water from textiles, seventy-two come solely from textile dyeing. It is believed that thirty of these chemicals cannot be removed using purification processes.

One carpet manufacturer deeply involved in sustainable business practices in America and around the globe reports that they use ten thousand pounds of virgin nylon (synthetic) fibers per hour. They truck thirty tons of garbage to landfills per day. They admit to sending 2.3 million pounds of carbon dioxide into the air per week. Yet their scorecard on the plus side shows that, from 1996 to 2009, they reduced energy consumption by 43 percent and greenhouse gas emissions by 44 percent in absolute terms, while increasing sales by more than 25 percent.

Unlike this carpet mill, the industry that applies the science of "warmth without weight" to polyester and nylon fibers for outdoor fabrics and fiberfills does not report waste reduction, renewable energy, carbon emissions, water and energy usage, or percent of recycled and bio-based materials in products. Far too many products are produced offshore by brands that do not own the factories or control the waste and pollution anywhere close to that of the American carpet mill.

A further thirst for dumping the black magic results in more than 72 billion plastic (polyester) bottles a year heading into landfills after a mere one-time use. Confessions are written and preached in the pews of nature by many activewear and outdoor brands of clothing, gear, and footwear. However, as with most religious confessions, they are not followed by the cleanup of landfills. The above-ground sea of black-magic textile processing pollutes waterways, seriously impacting groundwater and public health.

At the end of the twentieth century, leading carpet mills confessed to their dumping and pollution. They were among the first to recycle fibers from plastic bottles, use more natural fibers of wool, and recycle used nylon carpets. Whatever their intentions, nylon-carpet manufacturing has remained in America probably because of the in-line process of taking fiber and making the finished product in one location. Also, the outdated sweatshop-labor-icon, the sewing machine, does not play a major role in making carpets—unlike clothing and footwear makers that use nylon fabrics made from similar nylon fibers.

Beyond Water Pollution

Textile manufacturing does use sewing machines. The sewing machine allowed for cheap, underage, and in some cases, slave labor to produce textile fibers, fabrics, clothing, and gear outside America. Numerous reports on the Internet address this issue, reporting that workers are trained up to age sixteen and then considered top performers until their midtwenties, when the factory owners declare them over the hill and burned-out. With all the detailed stitching in today's outerwear, I can only wonder how those sewers' fingers feel and what kind of life is ahead for them when they hit their mid-twenties and are let go for being worn out.

A 1990s presentation in Seattle called If Tired Hands Could Talk detailed the stories of sewing-factory workers there during the 1970s. Thousands of sewers went to work each day in the Seattle Pioneer Square industrial area, running sewing machines to stitch nylon fabrics for outerwear and skiwear for famous brands such as Eddie Bauer, Pacific Trail, Far West Garment, Roffe, Tempco, Sportscaster, and THAW (REI). The story told how the children of those sewers, while getting help with schoolwork evenings, would rub their mothers' fingers to help relieve the pain and numbness from trying to stitch the straight lines of channels and box and diamond designs for down jackets. Of course, under China law, the sewers there are required to be single, and many will never have children to help and love them through the rest of their lives.

Before the big push offshore, even before there was a Nike, millions of yards of nylon fabrics consumed in amounts well over ten thousand pounds a day were made in American-owned textile weaving mills and sent to American-owned dye houses for processing the color into the fabric. A simple example is a bimonthly order I would get from Pacific Trail while I lived and worked in Seattle. The company made popular down outerwear from 1974 through 1979. Rick, the purchasing manager, was ordering one million yards at a time from me. The order would request five hundred thousand yards of navy nylon fabric, three hundred thousand yards of red, and one hundred thousand yards each of rust and electric blue. The weight of the fabric was 1.9 ounces per yard; thus that one million yards of fabric represented two million ounces of nylon fiber that were processed into fabric and dyed.

Keep in mind that these years followed the EPA regulations established in 1972–1973. Textile mills had spent millions of dollars creating healthy process-ing, especially for fabric dyeing, to limit water and air pollution to zero emissions as required. Updated machines saved energy and improved fabric quality as well. Twenty years later, in 1996, when American carpet mills took the environ-mental call further, as described above, these American weaving mills and dye houses were out of business or left to sell only to the U.S. military.

In the first decade of the 2000s, the offshore era was established, and the "polar pollution" was getting into the media via reports of ice melting in the glaciers of Montana's Glacier National Park and at both the North and South Poles, including Greenland and other cold land areas.

Black Magic Burns

Beyond the issue of closing weaving mills and dye houses, the black magic spins another web from the spinneret that creates its fiber and fabrics. Today's popular polyester knits and nonwovens—made from the black magic—melt when flame comes in contact with them. This raised concerns about children's sleepwear in the late 1960s, and in the early 1970s, laws were passed to make changes. It is well documented that synthetic fibers—especially polyester—melt and can cause second- and third-degree burns. Within seconds, the flame ignites the fibers and fabric, and even when the fire is put out, at very high temperatures, the melting continues.

Today our country's military does not allow these black-magic wonders of warmth without weight, moisture management, and wind resistance outside the wire of training camps. In other words, it can't be worn in combat. See YouTube videos of myself demonstrating on Seattle public TV popular polyester tee shirts used in all outdoor activities and featuring brands from the biggest makers and retailers that supply American citizens.

When the melting issue became a big concern for troops in combat, Under Amour became a big seller to the military. Yet, the federal government refuses to require a warning label about the flame and melting to the public at large. In addition, there are no standards to regulate either the materials involved or the processing techniques such as laminating and bonding, which go by the name of TPU, or thermoplastic polyurethane. Biodegradable TPU addresses concerns about the solvent used and time to decompose, but ignores warnings about flame and melting. Popular outdoor fabrics called soft shells come under this review.

In addition to the military, electrical and smelter workplaces require fire-resistant materials for workers' clothing. With this knowledge in the open, at least warning labels or stated time for exposure to flame and melting should be required to help the consumer understand the difference between natural fibers that do not melt and synthetics that do melt.

Success in life is a journey, not a destination. Opportunities are not given by our parents, but are lent by our children. During the last four decades of the twentieth century, using the surname Polar, I marketed and helped develop Polarguard fiberfills, and created and marketed the fabric and technology of Polarfleece. Before I was able to address the flame and melting issues, the manufacturing was moved offshore, and the issues were quietly ignored by the offshore textile mills.

By the end of 2010, the reality of my polar products has shown the truth of the black magic: "polar pollution" in landfills, air, and water, and an undisclosed issue of flame and melting to the general consumer. Melting and polyester go hand in hand with our frozen lands and our bodies.

Polarfleece, as the first outdoor fabric to challenge wool and nylon-fiber woven fabrics, has become the abused technology of horrific offshore environmental catastrophes. It is presented with an attitude of conservation for recreation. It is promoted by billions of dollars from brands that sell outdoor clothing, shoes, and gear—retailers, as well as the makers of the products. These brands deny the truth about pollution caused by their fabrics and fibers, and even leave open the question of tainted fabrics and fiber. A Greenpeace investigation of Disney children's textiles led to Denmark banning Disney children's clothes produced in places like China.

Is it healthy to wear synthetic-fiber-based fabrics processed in factories that would be shut down here in America by the EPA? A long list of potential health hazards is published by the EPA and ignored in the offshore factories.

The temperature of our earth climbs as the polar ice caps melt from the emissions of the black magic. Landfills continue being created here and in the offshore countries, where the makers of products under branded corporations in America wall themselves into the security of public trading and investors. Donations of one dollar on Facebook inspire check-ins that pitch the science of synthetic soft shells against the sustainable resources of natural fibers such as wool and cotton. Today, the technical outdoor brands overdose the consumer with claims about chemical fibers and treatments trying to make us believe that for thousands of years before them humans simply could not survive in any form of comfort without them. This soft-shell outerwear is really the most recent attempt to clone the natural fibers of wool and cotton by stabilizing nylon panty hose with double-knit polyester. It does not stabilize polar pollution or global warming. Nor does it create jobs in America to replace those taken offshore to the cheap-labor, black-magic fumes of offshore textile factories.

The air from Asia rises into streams of pollution that travel, jet-stream first-class, to America. Some 30 percent of air pollution in California comes from China and other Asian sources. Radiation from Japan's nuclear plants, victims of a gigantic earthquake and tsunami, shows how fast things travel from Asia to America.

American outdoor brand names swell in ancient lands, on mighty rivers, and on the most difficult faces of the earth's mountains. They will come out of the black-magic bottle as you read this book. None of them created the fibers or fabrics they use, and only natural fibers of wool and cotton—not brands of synthetics—have been given enough time in the wardrobes of America to be called vintage or "made in America." Today, L. L. Bean cotton chamois shirt designs from 1933 are appearing once again, setting a record for one-day sales in December 2010 for this legendary outdoor clothing and shoes.

The Baggage of Greed, Illusion of Supply

Think Marco Polo about what you are going to read. Not just the man but also the game. The pace of global business is running faster, and supplies of all fibers for textiles—natural and plastic—are showing the baggage of greed and illusion of supply. The year 2011 saw cost increases in fibers of almost 80 percent for cotton and 27–30 percent for polyester, nylon, and down. Yet all we hear about are the prices of oil per barrel and gas per gallon. Make no mistake: oil byproducts known as chemicals fuel textiles. Our reliance on offshore textiles is creating the same kind of challenges we face from using offshore oil. Water is drying up or becoming too polluted to drink or use for processing textiles in dye houses in Asia. Man-made fibers of polyester and nylon blew out the candles of cotton in Europe and America during the 1960s. These plastic fibers come from fossil fuel (oil) and have a limited time on the planet.

Today we hear a lot about "authentic this and that" from the leading brands of outdoor textiles, which were once companies created by an owner with a passion for living in and working close to the outdoors. These brands include makers of skiwear, sleeping bags, outdoor clothing, and activewear, and certainly many of them are major players in footwear and gear. They owned their own factories to make their products here in America, some starting above other ground-floor merchants—REI was a walk-up, as was JanSport. Until the early 1990s, the outdoor company was a privately owned authentic maker of products sold to specialty retailers, many of which were near outdoor recreation areas and in smaller towns outside popular vacation areas across America.

From garages and cottage workshops, these companies created icons of such products as backpacks, tents, sleeping bags, outwear, ski pants, and ski parkas. They turned these crafted products into an assembly line of production, all with American workers and materials produced in America. Even a classic drive-in theater screen in Jackson Hole, Wyoming, hosted a sewing factory for Powderhorn Skiwear. Custom clothes have always inspired textiles, and most home sewers are designers wanting to get into the business. Besides the drive-in sewing factory, shops along the main streets of Jackson Hole featured designs created in the back and offered for sale in the front windows. One company started by Frannie as Black Sheep (later changing its name to the safer Wyoming Woolens) with a patent for designing Polarfleece socks demonstrated the possibility of going from a drive-in and store front to a protected technology using American labor and innovation.

At the same time, the bigger skiwear brands were shifting to offshore production and selling out to investors and public corporations. It was not financially possible for a single-owner business to carry that much inventory of assorted apparel items and make products here in America. For example, sweaters made offshore today are not from the authentic sweater manufacturing mills and brands that started it all.

A good example is Roffe, which, during the '60s and '70s, made their own skiwear and famous stretch woolen ski pants in their six-story building in downtown Seattle. Coordinating with Diemetre sweaters, which also had their own sweater mill in Seattle, the Roffe ski outfit matched in colors and patterns to make the leading fashion statement on the slopes. Adding the hat maker Smiley, based in Nevada, ski show retailers lined up to see the complete outfits. Today, hopes of making things here in America are dashed when a company like Columbia uses offshore makers for ski and general outerwear and bundles the business under one public trading brand.

How Consumer Trust Was Built

Consumers today trust a brand's quality of materials and labor based on when it was made first in America. The switch to offshore seems like a double-faced tactic to get more designs and bigger production runs to retailers, while sacrificing the healthy production required by American EPA codes.

What distinguished the original American-made clothing, shoes, and gear in outdoor retailing channels was the quality of both the materials used and the craftsmanship in making them. Loyal customers buying made-in-America products were treated to lifetime warranties like Eddie Bauer's, which ensured that returns would be fixed or replaced at no charge. That creed became the law of the land for all who followed in the outdoor products industry after World War II.

I saw this in action while making sales calls to the Eddie Bauer factory in Seattle. Products were returned for any of a number of reasons—the zipper broke, the fabric tore, the down blew away. The factory production line would stop at the station to do the repair until it was completed and on its way back to the customer. As the company grew, a special repair area was set up to handle all returns and repairs to allow the production line to keep going. Every outdoor company that followed Eddie Bauer did the manufacturing and repairs the same way.

Fabric testing labs were added, as well as quality control for down before it went to the cutting room or sewing floor to be assembled. North Face, at its Berkeley factory, inspected fabric yard by yard before sending it to the cutting-room tables, where patterns were placed over stacks of fabric and cut into pieces for the sewing area. Part of my job was to visit the factory monthly and stand and watch the fabric being inspected. Those visits also included time in the testing lab, where machines checked fabric under the watchful eye of educated engineers. Waterproofing, color fastness, tear strength, down proof ratings were all handled in one lab and covered the fabric flow to the production lines that made the sleeping bags, tents, backpacks, luggage, and apparel.

Wool Pulled Over the Eyes

Since the early 1990s, after sheep were put to rest in favor of polyester and nylon, the wool began to be pulled over the eyes of those lifelong consumers who trusted the brands that are marketed as authentic today. By moving the manufacturing offshore, the same brands today are doing business under public stock, marketing from bell to bell on Wall Street. They achieve billions of dollars in sales without using anything made in their own factories and few, if any, materials made in America. As a result, the quality-control checking is unknown on a day-to-day basis. Greenpeace photos from China on the Internet clearly show the truth of pollution and labor quality control.

It has all come down to one simple plan: pledging to investors to double those billions within five years, while not speaking of a single new job because of how investors feel about the cost of jobs vs. profits in business today. Instead, marketing uses the loyalty of decades of American citizens to assure the Asian community—especially China—that the authentic brand from America is going to be sold to the citizens of China. Wall Street investors see doubling of sales in five years, while the economy and retirement pensions of too many Americans have been destroyed without manufacturing and a middle-class workforce here.

Recent public statements include Timberland bragging about the sustainable efforts of their own facilities, which are really offices and warehouses. They point out light bulb usage, reduction in air travel, and energy usage based on weather conditions getting to and from their facilities. They admit they have little to no control over their present supply chain in terms of reporting on pollution, energy, and waste. These disclosures mirror other companies that remain more protective of their real sustainable standings—

Meanwhile, the unemployment rate in Oregon (home to two of the biggest in the global outdoor textile brand game) has stayed above 9 percent for too many years to count, and the newly elected governor said, "Oregon is in a death spiral" and needs to return to traditional businesses and products. Yet the doubling of sales forecasts at Nike and Columbia does not mean jobs will be created. Their quotes in local Oregon publications about Oregon speak to improving schools and building more bridges, while questioning the business climate as nothing more than a hometown thing. Little to nothing is done by the offshore Oregon brands to create more jobs that will bring in funds for the schools and bridges..

A bit south in California, the authentic, Berkeley-based outdoor brand, The North Face, makes the same claim of doubling billions in five years and publicly states that expanding their brand in China will be a big part of that. For North Face, an authentic outdoor down maker, the doubling down will be in plastic fibers of polyester and nylon, not natural fibers of down and wool.

"Double-faced" About the Environment

At the same time North Face is expanding to China, the company has been named the lead for the Conservation Alliance. Yet there is no plan to get manufacturing in China, or anywhere outside the United States, in line with the sustainable and environmental accomplishments of carpet mills in America and/or with EPA regulations. Both Greenpeace and the head of the United Nations have spoken about the horrific pollution to a famous area of textiles in China called the Pearl River Delta. Meanwhile, brands such as North Face promotes their Conservation Alliance, saying it is saving seventeen thousand miles of rivers, but doing a total double-face about river pollution from textile manufacturing in China.

North Face is not alone. Nike claims a $6 million machine helped them collect 86 million plastic PET bottles from landfills for a recycling program, but doesn't point out that 72 billion are produced in America each year. Furthermore, "not just doing it" says that 50 percent of the bottles were used outside the home (outdoors), meaning 36 billion are unlikely to find their way to a recycling center, such as the one at your curb. Columbia plays with tinfoil insulation as if the Wizard of Oz is going to get a brain and keep you warm, which makes some folks in Oregon wonder if Columbia's reflective tinfoil space-age jackets will act like solar panels to produce energy from the landfills when they get dumped there.

How did the world of outdoor textiles move from true grit to marketing wit? Plastics replaced natural materials, and the supply chain became a mass production using cheap labor and refusing to follow the environmental regulations accepted as the creed of manufacturing in Europe and America. Check out the environmental feature of Patagonia's website, "The Footprint Chronicles," which shows their supply chain and their honest reasons why offshore manufacturing takes precedent over making things in America. Only simple designs can be made in America and be cost effective, according to the website. This ignores the reality of water pollution in that global supply chain, which has spurred the United Nations head and Greenpeace to begin a public and corporate awareness campaign.

It also ignores the truth that in 1985, as published in a Patagonia employee newsletter, the growth of sales was finally going to be held to 35 percent a year.

That growth, all came from buying my Polarfleece and other fabrics made in America. Polarfleece bunting was sewn only in American factories at that time, which begs the question: why is it not profitable today to keep producing in America under EPA regulations?

The outdoor brands today send Internet messages, playing on the innocence of youth. They urge you to get outdoors while there is still one to enjoy, and to experience the thrill of wearing plastic to stay dry while watching your sweat run away from the plastic fiber. Your sweat may be the last drop of clean water on the planet unless something is done now to stop the pollution in textile processing.

Things were not planned this way in America during the 1960s. Polyester and nylon fibers began to blend in with cotton and wool to save water consumption and make more land available to grow food and create homes for the baby boomers that came after forty years of wars. This "stitch in time" is for sure, in my opinion, a time to learn and take immediate action, a call for us all to get our country back to the healthy lifestyle that our parents and grandparents settled here to have and to give to us. Instead we are earmarks stuck in a country of landfills, which define the failure of human ingenuity to recycle and renew our products and manufacturing, instead of turning them into waste.

Polarfleece became a survival fabric for myself and the remaining workers in American textile mills and sewing factories. At its creation, I was assisting in the development of PET bottles and films to be recycled into carpet fibers and then textile fabrics. It took thirteen years to complete the plan (1980–1993) and get Polarfleece respected for its wearing performance and bottle-recycling program. Patagonia pioneered the Polarfleece fabric and recycled fleece, and enjoyed a controlled growth of 35 percent a year doing so. Thirteen years after the first recycling, Patagonia had saved 86 million bottles from landfills, using them in fleece outerwear clothing. Today their Common Threads program details, by design and style, chronicles its manufacturing and ability to use recycled fibers and recycle the garments. Patagonia textile clothing has tried to do what a carpet mill in America did to become sustainable since 1996.

Patagonia states they still offer simple designs in America and Mexico but have opted to go offshore to manufacture the higher-end garments and designs. The big question is: why are the simple designs used for two centuries here in America not good enough for today's clothing? Why force the complicated ones into offshore manufacturing, which fuels the polar pollution? In my opinion, Patagonia still ignores the reality that making their own apparel would allow them to close the loop and become truly sustainable. Yet the simple, American-designed cotton hoodie sweatshirt remains one of the best sellers in retail and is found everywhere. Shirts with buttons and sleeves, and pants with legs and zippers, are all that simple in design. Polyester Polarfleece/Polartec, including Patagonia Synchilla™, which uses the same fabric, have yet to be equaled in a simple vest and full zip jacket.

At the same time, the number of PET bottles onsumed went from 2.5 million an hour in 1993 to 12 million an hour in 2010, with 80 percent going to landfills instead of being recycled into simple-designed clothing made in America. Whatever it costs to recycle 72 billion bottles, to make the footprint fuel efficient and keep water and air pollution at zero emissions, it can only be done here in America where we consume them.

The New "Green": Dollars

Textile pollution far exceeds that of older times, when automobile makers faced the truth and did something about it. Nike opened its first factory in China in 1981. Columbia created its first ski jacket—the Bugaboo—in 1986. Ten year later, in 1996, Nike hit $4.7 billion in sales and ignored the opportunity to get involved in recycling bottles into American-made fleece and other fabrics. They also ignored the open courage of an American carpet mill to disclose the issues of pollution and energy using nylon fibers here or offshore.

As of 2010, neither Nike nor Columbia were in the top one hundred green companies in their home state of Oregon. However, both are hitting record sales and earnings for their investors in Oregon and around the globe. Patagonia has begun a garment recycling program, but the issue of offshore sourcing with polluted manufacturing cancels the benefits to American landfills. North Face and most of the other outdoor makers are not seeing the reality of water pollution in their products vs. the much smaller water pollution issues in America. Acid rain, which was prevalent in America from our own pollution, could be reappearing in the Asian pollution we see every day from across the Pacific. China confirms that 220 of its cities have acid rain.

Many other brands also pollute, but the brands that are public corporations are the most outspoken about their products and superior benefits in performance and design. Timberland, where a third generation of the founding family operates it as a public corporation, talks sustainability yet produces in polluted waters in Asia—and especially China. The company recently told their investors they will soon have 110 retail stores selling the Timberland brand in China.

This race of the top American brands to be the biggest in China is only possible if the Chinese government is being double-faced about their concerns for pollution. A leading official claims the pollution arrived earlier in China's economic growth than was planned for by the industries with manufacturing facilities in China. Does that mean the doubling of billions in sales by American brands is going to slow down and clean up the pollution, or are they just as bad as oil companies about wiggling around the black-magic slippery slopes they profess to explore?

In Oregon my favorite recreation mountain area is Mount Bachelor, part of the Oregon Cascade mountain range that includes Mount Hood and Crater Lake. The weather observation station on Mount Bachelor's summit has captured soot, dust, and chemical pollutants from China. In the photo below, taken on the summit of Mount Bachelor, the Polarfleece jackets shown were produced in America and followed EPA regulations for water and air pollution, thus producing zero emissions and assuring a healthy recreation environment at that time. Today my fleece pollutes pristine lands and waters in America because of the air pollution created in China from making Polarfleece knockoffs.

The photo features myself in the original North Face Polarfleece full zip jacket with piping, and my son wearing the first printed Polarfleece fabric done in a classic buffalo plaid. The North Face jacket was sewn in its Berkeley, California, factory by the authentic North Face company. The buffalo plaid was sewn in Seattle at one of Patagonia's contract sewing shops, which they shared with Union Bay Sportswear.

Chapter Four:

Textile Water Pollution

Developing nations and large corporations have shown that they ravage the environment as they climb to power. Our own country destroyed a good portion of our natural resources during the 1800s. Britain did the same in that century, during the Industrial Revolution. Today the most pervasive contamination of water pollution in the history of the entire world is found in China.

Over-the-top financial success shared with textile clothing, footwear, and gear brands in America has brought with it huge environmental failures. Some 90 percent of the groundwater in China is polluted, and citizens jokingly say they know the new fashion colors of textile products by the color of their rivers. This pollution means that 320 million citizens—equal to the entire population of America—have no clean drinking water. We have learned that Americans throw away 72 billion plastic bottles a year, of which only 20 percent are recycled. The thirst of America, defined in a swoosh of clothing and shoes, overflows landfills in America, and that same swoosh in my opinion is the leading polluter, with many factories in China producing products that knocks out citizens' clean water.

These facts about drinking water and textile pollution are not pretty to read, especially when you want to wear outdoor clothing that helped cause the pollution. However, the Chinese government has now come face to face (pun intended) with the reality of the trail walker setups that have turned Mount Everest into a walk in the park—with a rumored $40,000 trail fee. Big business not real exploring has turned high altitude climbing into supply lines connected to cell phones in a real time Disneyland theme most can see in that famous theme park called the Matterhorn. Linked to adventure channel surfing on cable tv the experience is over as fast as the commercials allow you to delete the weather channel forecasts of what they are doing on the tallest piece of planet Earth.

The cover-ups are more obvious than the denim overalls and ski bibs that started the outdoor industry in America in 1850 and kept it here until 1980.

Preventable Pollution

The year 1981 saw the opening of the first official Nike" factory in China, where textile makers could hide out from EPA regulations that had finally saved the drinking water and air of America. The new air thing burst onto ancient lands of farms and poverty, and never stopped exploiting, even when the exploitation resulted in a hundred thousand deaths a year, according to the World Health Organization. The facts confirming the ugly, horrific truths were published in 2010 by news organizations such as CNN.

This pollution never had to happen. What makes this worse than any other pollution story is that the dues had been paid in America during the early 1970s. Those EPA regulations were known to every business and CEO and others who took their manufacturing offshore and allowed the pollution to be repeated. While waving their corporate logos, they make the Exxon Valdez look like another small mess in a bathtub. Even the initiator of giving 1 percent to the planet of its profits Patagonia, a company borrowng a pristine wilderness country for its logo, has ignored the truth of the EPA regulations in America by going offshore for production after its start-up years in America.

During start-up years, it was fashion designers' greed that got the credit for a fashion of pollution in cotton. Once they realized that their fashion needed synthetic outdoor performance fibers, these designers pushed the same pollution into technical textiles. That was followed by the performance-driven polar pollution of outdoor product makers and retailers. Fearing they would fall into the "Gap" of fashion knockoffs using technical fabrics, each company ran to Asia. Macys on Thirty-fourth Street in New York City found their street curb of granite the new North Face climbing wall. The logo of North Face arches like the shape of a street curb when the retailing focus is mainstream department stores. Begging the question of what happened to that half dome authentic gear made in their own factory in Berkeley California? Directly across the street from Macy's, Old Navy sold a ten-dollar Polarfleece knockoff that pilled and matted like a hound dog's fur in a hunting trip to the Jersey wetlands. Higher-end aisles from Fifth Avenue to Bloomingdales on the east side offered authentic knock-offs in the designer logos of that time, the late 1990s. Polo rode the theme of the outdoors from natural fibers into fossil fuels. The destiny of polar pollution was going full circle, from America to Asia, and whipping up winds to both poles of the world. The result is the worst water pollution in the history of the world, created without a disease or national disaster. Ending with the bundling of authentic brands into high rise corporate offices overlooking a simple three hundred year old park of wilderness left on Manhattan Island known today as the Big Apple's Central Park. It was not the target of terrorists. The target was a real time tallest structure raised with oil and corporate greed exactly like the polyester and nylon fibers used in outdoor gear and clothing.

We spend billions searching for water on other planets, knowing that only with water comes life as we know it. Yet to make clothing, footwear, and gear, we hide our wallets and run to offshore lands of people who are misled and mis-fed by their government and their businesses. China's Development Research Center now admits that water pollution is a drag on their economy. When they try to present a "green trade policy," the so-called green tax is blocked by the green of more profits and leaving things the way they are. This appears to be a replay of America back in the 1960s. Only when a fire appeared on the surface of a Midwest river did those elected to serve finally vote in the EPA.

Rather than spell out the EPA regulations, I want to present facts about China's pollution issue and simply say this cannot happen in America. Nor should it have happened in China. Most of the companies discussed in this book started when following EPA regulations were part of doing business in America. Words cannot express how wrong China's water pollution is and why it should have never happened, given our own triumph with the EPA in 1970. The following facts are true and alarming. After you read them, we will move on to the lifestyles of the outdoor-products pioneers in America and their respect for and commitment to the EPA when they started their businesses.

Asian Pollutants Cross the Pacific

To begin with, the pollution is not just a problem for China and its citizens. A reported 30 percent of the daily pollution on the West Coast of America, especially in California, comes from the pollution practices of China, where the biggest polluter is textiles. From the beaches of Ventura and Patagonia, to the Bay Area of North Face, these companies' marketing hides the truth about the fibers and fabrics they left in America, regulated by the EPA, to source offshore in Asia. The beauty of the Oregon and Washington coast hides even bigger polluters, such as Nike, Columbia, and REI. The wilderness and lakes, rivers, and streams beg for a return to the ways of the indigenous teachings regarding that land and water. As Chief Seattle said when he gave his land to America, "We are webbed in blood to the land and water, whatever we do to the land and water, we do to ourselves."

Portland, Oregon, takes pride in its current environmental footprint. "Emissions have fallen by more than 20 percent per capita since 2000," said Susan Anderson, city sustainability director. Portland is clearly headed in the right direction, and the industrial district employs a hundred thousand blue-collar workers. In the next county and the nearby city of Beaverton, white-collar workers in well-known textile offices, colorfully wearing polluted, tainted dye-house fashions of polyester and nylon, do not check the air quality leaching into Oregon from across the Pacific, where their products are produced.

The only way to end the pollution is to force the offshore manufacturing to apply the U.S. EPA standards to the users of its manufacturing services. If China refuses, then like what happened in America, only those that do comply get to stay in business, even if it means bringing the manufacturing back home.

It was here in Portland that wool and then synthetics were made until a quick thinking running shoe found a cheaper way around the EPA...taking the "sneaky" out of sneakers. These companies here in America have full knowledge of the EPA regulations to stop pollution. They know the pollution involved in offshore manufacturing, and just like the companies whose oil wells leaked, they are responsible for cleaning it up. They sell billions and make tens of millions so they can afford to stay in business and replace the machines, while nature rebuilds the losses and damage to her and to us as her stewards.

History tells us of earlier business greed on the famous Columbia River. Around 1900, salmon canning was a major industry in the Gorge area of the Columbia, just east of Portland. A famous invention called the fishing wheel faced into the river's flow and caught so many salmon, the indigenous people feared its extinction. A reported bounty of four hundred fifty thousand cases of canned salmon a year was finally brought under control. Then a few decades later, in the same areas of the Columbia, powerful dams were built to create energy for the region, and once again water was changed to meet the economic wants of humans.

It is said that water vibrates as it flows and that those vibrations change the patterns of the natural world that lives within the lifecycle of water. Humans have created vibrations of greed that are now a threat to our water supply and the population that needs it to survive. An interesting fact about water is our bodies are made up of 80 percent water, and that water also has vibrations.

Facts about Pollution in China

In addition to these facts the credits listed as sources of the information cover the facts and words as they are repeated in the book to assure the reader the facts are correct and have been reported in public publishing channels.

According to "Water Pollution in China," published on May 18, 2009, on Scipeeps.com:

- 70 percent of Chinese lakes and rivers are polluted.
- 90 percent of their groundwater is polluted.
- 320 million citizens in China have no safe drinking water.
- The WHO estimates that 75 percent of all diseases in China come from water pollution.
- The WHO puts water pollution-related deaths at 100,000 per year.

Aaron Raybin, in "China, pollution, and textiles: a cotton problem?" published on January 25, 2010, at http://blog.airdye.com, repeats the above statistics and adds these facts:

- China produced an average of 36 million bales of cotton per year from 2006 through 2008, making it the world's largest cotton producer.
- China buys 45 percent of U.S. growers' cotton.
- Cotton growers account for 12 percent of all pesticides used in the world.
- Cotton crops require seven times more fertilizer than pesticide.
- Eco Fashion World states that 2,700 liters (700 gallons) of water is used to make a single cotton tee shirt.
- Aral Sea in Uzbekistan is a lake turned into a desert from cotton farming.
- In 2005, China provided 24 percent of the global textiles, according to Danamex China Business Resource. In dollars, this represents $117 billion.
- Processing in the textile industry is among the most environmentally damaging.
- Textile processing uses heavy metals, carcinogens, fabrics, dyes, organic materials, starches, and bleach, as well as a large amount of energy and water.
- According to Bluesign Technologies, growing cotton for textiles requires between 8,000 liters and 40,000 liters of water per kilogram of cotton.

Production creates up to 600 liters of wastewater per kilogram of textiles. This results in chemically saturated and toxic wastewater.

- Only 10 percent of dye wastes are recycled. The rest go back to the water supply via rivers or underground pipes.
- The *Wall Street Journal* has reported that treating contaminated water can cost more than 13 cents per metric ton.
- Former chief economist at Morgan Stanley, Andy Xie, said, "Prices in the U.S. are artificially low. You're not paying the costs of pollution, and that is why China is an environmental catastrophe."

In addition, the polluted waters are being used over and over because there is no clean source of water for dyeing in China. No facts have been found for synthetics, but my own knowledge of textiles and dye houses in America allows me to say the findings are about the same for pollution from polyester and nylon. Synthetic fibers follow the same path as cotton, but use far less water in the oil fields on their way to factories that mix chemical byproducts of oil to make the fibers.

This raises a very alarming issue: how healthy are the fibers and fabrics in clothing and footwear coming from China and other parts of Asia? Changing to offshore production moved the manufacturing beyond the regulations and created very large profits. Now more than ever, these brands of textile products are very important to Wall Street investors. But the growth in China is like putting a giant cap on a leaking offshore oil rig.

My memoirs seem like a wonderful American dream of creating a business in something you love. Let's let our minds rest for a while and enjoy the show-and-tell of life before the suits of Wall Street discovered Nike, Columbia, VF (North Face), and many more.

Chapter Five:

From Home to Factory

Once upon a time, there was a simple way of doing things close to home. Looking back from here to there, from natural fibers to the plastic textile fibers of today, it is difficult to remember that plastic textile fibers are not much more than fifty years old. Natural fibers, on the other hand, have been used for as long as five thousand years.

The natural fibers of wool and cotton were easily the most important fibers in clothing and gear for outerwear until the 1980s. A hand-weaving process was incorporated into many inventions in Europe, starting around the mid-1700s. Textile mill buildings spoke to a new vision and purpose of productivity and mass employment. In the mid-1800s in England, the town of Saltaire was built, centered around a mill and also providing services such as a hospital, churches, and public parks. The town's founder, Sir Titus Salt, became known as a leader in industrialism and paternalism, setting an example for the world to follow. In America, Woolrich is a similar example of town and mill.

Textile production boomed in Britain until 1958, when the British Government, under the Cotton Industry Act, ordered the machinery scrapped. More than one hundred five thousand machines were destroyed.

The beginning of plastic fibers, called synthetics, created the same situation for cotton in the United States in the 1960s. The American style of manufacturing began in the early 1800s, and by the beginning of the 1900s, production was in the hands of very large manufacturers of textile machines. This continued until the 1950s.

One of the largest machines used in the industry is a carding machine. Many textile yarns and processes used this machine with fibers of cotton, wool, and polyester. The machine is made up of a series of large and small cylinders covered with tightly set wire teeth. The cylinders revolve and tease out fibers into a fine web of parallel strands. After carding, the fibers look like a nonwoven blanket. Layers of this product became fiberfill, which provided a big opportunity for polyester to compete with wool and down for insulation. Other cardings are condensed through a funnel into a soft rope of sliver which is then carried to a yarn-spinning operation.

My first job in textiles out of college in 1965 was selling cotton and acrylic yarns to sweater makers and pile-fabric mills. In 1967, I moved on to selling polyester fibers, simply because the cotton mills were being run out of business by cheap imports and synthetic fibers.

Growth from Inventions vs. Marketing

Fibers change, but not the machines that process them. The first practical spinning machine was invented in 1765 by James Hargraves in England. He named the machine after his wife, Jenny, who spun cotton thread in their cottage home. The original "spinning jenny" is in a museum in London.

Weaving looms trace back to the 1400s and 1500s. Inventions from cotton were quickly adopted by woolen manufacturers by the 1850s. Weaving is done by taking a thread (yarn) and going over and under other threads in the opposite direction. James Northdrop, who went to work for the Draper Corporation in Hopesdale, Massachusetts, in 1894, is credited with the innovation that created the automatic transfer system patented by Draper. The system allowed one weaver to tend up to thirty-two looms. The result was a standardized loom that used replacement parts, just like the Model T Ford. These looms served as the key to Draper becoming one of the most important machinery companies for textile weaving, from natural fibers to synthetics.

In 1888, Alice Gabardine invented gabardine fabric. Alice was the owner of Gabardine Mills, which produced the fabric. The tough, tight construction was smooth on one side and diagonally ribbed on the other. Gabardine fabric clothed the twenty-seven men on the Shackleton Trans-Antarctic Expedition (1914-1916); it was believed to be produced by Burberry, which still uses it in their jackets. Edmund Hilary climbed Mount Everest wearing waterproof woven-cotton canvas.

Outdoor clothing and outdoor expeditions, explorations, and adventures can all thank these inventors and their machines for the quality and performance of the fabrics they use to keep people alive. Wool clothing saved the lives of the men on the Shackleton Expedition during the two years they were trapped in the ice of Antarctica. Wool has been the most respected outdoor fiber and fabric on the planet. A process called fulling—also known as felting—became very important in the woolen industry. It uses the felting properties of wool fibers and heat, moisture, friction, and pressure to shrink the wool material in both length and width, thus compacting it in appearance and feel. Many fabrics are fulled to the point where the yarns and weaving are obscured, making the fabric look like felt.

Then high-speed machinery was created to speed up the processing time to finish fabrics in a harmonious flow from fiber to yarn to fabric. These machines gave us today's modern textile mills, dependent on chemicals and dealing with the resulting waste.

Chemicals like those used in plastic fibers are also used as synthetics for our food and medical drugs. Could the plastics in drugs and foods wind up in textile fibers for outdoor fabrics, clothing, and gear in the future? Time will tell. Today, in patented medical fabrics, antimicrobial chemicals are injected during the extrusion process that makes blended nylon and polyester microfibers. This is no small feat considering that the microfiber chamber is smaller than one denier, which is about the size of a hair on your head.

What is missing, as of 2010, is the manufacturing of polyester textiles in America, especially that which uses recycled plastic bottles to produce polyester fibers. We have let go of the lessons learned about labor, engineering, and inventions made by American workers.

Arrival and Departure of Manufacturing in America

Manufacturing textiles made of both natural and plastic fibers in America united the people immigrating from Europe and Asia and other parts of the world to live and work in America. When I worked with textile mills and sewing factories during the years of plastic fibers, from the 1960s through the 1980s, I saw firsthand how they were a melting pot for immigrant workers to begin a new life while they learned to speak English and give their kids an education.

Prior to that, immigrants brought with them training in working with natural fibers, including machinery and engineering from Europe produced during the Industrial Revolution. During the two World Wars, manufacturing in America allowed the United States to beat those ruthless powers that brought pain and suffering to people around the world, including our own citizens at Pearl Harbor. Peacetime prosperity in textiles resulted in clothing, shoes, and gear for work and recreation.

Plastic fibers became welcome partners to natural fibers as America demanded more food and land for workspace and homes for its citizens. During the 1970s and 1980s, the science of plastics created comfort for outdoor activities and the ability to stay outside longer without getting cold or suffering from heat-related stress. Skiwear began to use thin, lightweight polyester fiber-fills, moving away from bulky down and overheating on the slopes.

Then the science of manufacturing plastics expanded globally, to third-world countries and other industrial-minded countries such as India, China, and Japan, all of whom learned to produce nylon and polyester fibers. Since 2000, that outdoor-designed innovation has been all about giving away American manufacturing for good. In only ten years, by 2010, the richest and largest surplus in the history of America has been raped by a two-party system of government that might easily bring the founding fathers out of their graves. Rather than staying in their chambers and doing what is right and required from the taxes of American citizens, they have given away manufacturing jobs, especially in textiles, over the past forty years, while few to no jobs in textiles have been given back to America.

The lack of manufacturing goes hand-in-hand with job losses among the American middle class. Education alone won't change that. Our higher-education system still ranks far ahead of any other country, as proven by the large numbers of students who come from around the world to be taught here in America. American students face tough decisions about which jobs and careers are going to be protected once they get that college education. An estimated 150,000 students leaving high school and college each month face the task of finding a job here in America. Foreign students can return home to a much higher ranking with that sheepskin from an American college. Other social wants of our youth today are fed by electronic toys and Internet communication, short-circuiting the creative thinking encouraged by rambling into the outdoors for knowledge and recreation.

One can only hope that high school history courses will start to teach about John Muir and Aldo Leopold. As John Muir said in 1901, "Thousands of tired, nerve-shaken, over-civilized people are beginning to find out that going to the mountains is going home; that wilderness is a necessity; and that the mountain parks and reservations are useful not only as fountains of lumber and irrigating rivers, but as a fountain of life."

Compare this to the hundred-plus years of American immigrants building businesses and creating manufacturing jobs. It is time to bring things back to America. Our political system is frozen at the switch, unable to turn on the lights that gave us our greatest hundred years in the history of America through manufacturing. Those years, 1900 through 2000, were clearly a legacy of excellence for American manufacturing in terms of creating our jobs and quality of life.

Today we are a society as simple as a "Pod of I's" that cannot see out the "Windows." We are like the sheep we brought to America for textiles.

Time to Bring Textile Manufacturing Home

There are three basics to survive and grow smarter during our lives: a place to be protected and safe in a dwelling we call home, food grown to eat, and clothing and shoes to protect our bodies from heat and cold and anything else in the natural world. I believe we should always have the ability to manufacture what we need—not just want—in these three areas of our lives. Using the principles of sustainability, we must rebuild our infrastructure and bring manufacturing back.

Past examples assures us we can do this. Consider the American-born and -educated bioengineers who built machines capable of looking inside the human body and replacing defective organs with artificial ones. In another case, a chemist from DuPont, tired of corporate life, left after ensuring he was given part of the Teflon patent for himself. The product he made became known in the outdoor textiles industry as Gore-Tex, a micro-technology for creating waterproof, breathable fabrics. The pores of Gore-Tex are twenty-thousand times smaller than a water drop, thus keeping water out, while allowing water vapor from our body to escape.

New instruments and drugs have revolutionized the treatment of diseases and extended the length and quality of life. For outdoor textiles, the equivalent developments are warmth without weight and moisture management using polyester, first in fiberfills and then in the technology of Polarfleece. A further development of using recycled polyester film bottles to produce fibers for Polarfleece started us on the path to a healthy, sustainable, renewable resource. Fleece became the mainstay of every outdoor participant who has found polyester less of a threat to water consumption than cotton, and the water bottle a way to renew more fleece fabrics made of polyester.

These manufacturing accomplishments extended to American labor and our environmental issues, as well. A focus on nature has become the mission of outdoor products, thanks to Patagonia owner, Yvonne Chouinard, or "YC" to his friends. Patagonia's reputation for quality apparel is the result of using fibers, fabrics, and clothing manufactured in America when the company first started. EPA standards had cleaned up pollution enough to allow a focus on recycling and reusing the fibers and fabrics.

At that same time, other textile makers—mostly American fashion designers ignoring pollution issues—began to challenge the cost of manufacturing textiles in America. Without owning any manufacturing equipment, a brand was created with smart marketing and possibly a single patent. In four letters: N-I-K-E. Today that company owns more than four hundred patents to innovate how you tie your shoes and pull your clothes over your arms, head, and legs, but provides no manufacturing jobs in America.

Of course sustainable marketing is very important today. What is missing is the fact that 72 *billion* bottles are produced a year, with 17 *billion* recycled and the rest going to landfills. That's 21 percent being recycled. That 86 million claimed by Nike is not measurable unless you are looking at a photo-finish Nike garment and a hundredth count. Another way of looking at it: Nike states that 2 million bottles are dumped every ten minutes, or 12 million an hour. That gives Nike seven hours of playing time a year on the recycling field. One might say that's just a dribble of bottles saved compared to the number produced and used on their way to landfills.

Prior to the polyester fiber stitch-in-time development and a bottle-recycling program for renewing and reusing fibers, wool was the clear choice for anything worn outdoors for any reason. But wool carried with it the feeling of itch and scratch. Recycled wool, called reprocessed wool, earned the highest marks in itch and scratch. Recently, super-washed merino wool has been introduced to many outdoor clothing products. For a comparison, merino wool requires shearing five sheep to make a garment, while recycling plastic bottles requires ten bottles to make a shirt and twenty-five bottles to make a Polarfleece-type garment. Wool recycling has been around for centuries, from present-day reprocessing, to taking apart items such as blankets and remaking them into clothing. (Reprocessing is explained in detail elsewhere in this book.)

The basic makeup of synthetic fibers (which I call plastics) follows a simple fiber construction. Polyester, nylon, and polypropylene are made from melting, extruding, and setting a petrochemical-based product, similar to plastic. The fiber cannot breathe, absorb, or release moisture. When made into fabric or fiberfill, it is limited to one-way moisture movement and limited breathability, which can create a chill area when moisture sits on the outside of the fabric.

Wool fiber, and especially merino wool, is able to absorb and release moisture, cool or warm the body, and help regulate temperatures. Wool's natural ingredients also keep out bacteria and protect from odor. Merino wool fiber has more than sixty thousand follicles per square inch of skin, producing over 100 million individual fibers in each wool fleece. By joining the fibers from the five merino sheep needed to make a garment, you can tie a bow around the entire world.

Merino is the most hydrophilic of all fibers and can absorb and release ten times more moisture than synthetics. Each fiber can absorb up to a third of its own weight in moisture without feeling clammy or wet to the touch. Merino wool is then capable of releasing this moisture into the atmosphere to keep you warm and dry. Compare this to the previous twentieth-century brands, such as Pendleton, that had their own virgin-wool manufacturing in America, but didn't use merino wool. This is why synthetics became so popular. The wools in America were mostly not merino, and even virgin wools from Pendleton created that itch and scratch, while synthetics used soft, almost silky fibers.

The present economic crisis keeps asking, where are the new jobs? The consequence of textile synthetics being produced offshore seems part of the answer.

The outlook for jobs after "Black Friday" in November 2010, while folks looked at retail sales and especially those from outdoor makers, was not good. Twenty-eight thousand lost their jobs in retailing in November 2010, making that last Friday in November a red day for jobs, not a black day. Perhaps retailing, which was picked to create jobs after manufacturing was sent offshore, is not the economic recovery solution.

Manufacturing in America brought us out of the 1930s depression. The manufacture of outdoor clothing and outerwear played a big part in that recovery. In the 1960s, made-in-America outdoor textiles found the new polyester and nylon fibers a boom greater than the electronic toys of today.

America's lighthouse for our new plastic product economy lofted a "windows on the world" eatery at the highest level of the Twin Towers until that horrible day, September 11, 2001. From that destruction rose smoke and ash—not a determination to give back. A bubble formed over the entire landscape of America as its fortune from innovation gave corporate CEOs manipulated interest rates and created the biggest giveaway of America's home equity since the Great Depression.

By 2008, the giveaway was over. Interest rates had clearly extracted all the equity in citizens' homes, and our country was weeping and asking, who is going to give it back? Since then, we have seen the longest ever time span of a recession without jobs restored and unemployment reduced. Today, this topic covers every political race in America (pun intended). Between the Internet and its Googles, Twitters, and Facebooks, we find a 24-7 mass of cable channels anchored to it.

Much of this book relates to the technology of innovation in plastics, which has swallowed the hearts and minds of America, and especially our youth. Briefly, let's now review the important fibers, comparing plastics to natural fibers, with the natural being wool and down and cotton.

Wool

The development of woolens and wool mills in America began in the late 1800s. Woolens manufacturing is best described as a series of vertical businesses following the concept of harmonious operation. After purchasing raw wool fibers, one mill location handled the processing, spinning, and weaving to prepare the woolen fabric to be made into finished products, such as clothing and blankets, in another on-site mill building.

Jobs in manufacturing textiles accounted for a very large portion of the population of most major cities where mills were located, and many smaller towns were known simply as textile mill towns, providing employment, schools, and housing, and giving residents the foundation for a middle-class life.

I became the owner of the name of one such mill after its demise in the 1960s—Portland Woolen Mills in Portland, Oregon. Back in 1920, the *Portland Commerce* printed a full-page story of the mill and its eighteen buildings of harmonious operations. At that time, the mill used 4.25 million pounds of wool and made 1.5 million yards of fabric. Employees numbered 450 to 500, with a payroll of $500,000. The mill produced woolen cloth for suits and overcoats, blankets, steamer rugs, automobile robes, and fabrics for upholstering closed motor cars. The value of the company in 1920, based on inventory, the plant, equipment, wool, and woolens, was $1.5 million. One third of that value was spent on payroll. The cost of living in 1920 (a woolen suit cost twenty-five dollars), combined with the number of people living in Portland in 1920, clearly shows the economic value of having this woolen mill making products in America, using American grown wool, also from Oregon.

Today, billions in sales from leading Oregon textile brands do not bring to the same city the economic benefits received from this woolen mill and the more than twenty other mills then operating in the area.

The first Portland Woolen Mills was built in 1905 on the same riverfront land where Lewis and Clark camped a hundred years earlier. Within fifteen years, the mill consisted of eighteen buildings and provided a substantial economic impact in terms of products, jobs, and income for the local economy. It is worth noting the famous "striped trading blanket" used by Lewis and Clark was the icon of the mill's blanket, produced on their former campsite.

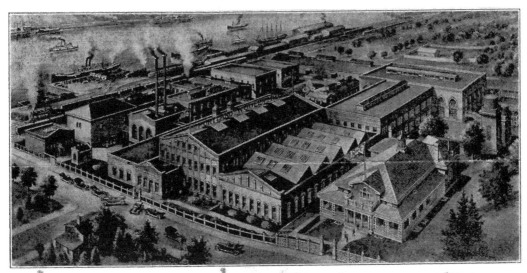

View of the Six-Acre Plant of the Portland Woolen Mills, Showing the Eighteen Buildings that Make up this Establishment

4 250 000 ......

Down

The next fiber to be incorporated into the outdoor textiles marketplace was down, which began to be used for cold weather clothing and sleeping bags in the 1930s.

Eddie Bauer invented and was awarded the patent rights for quilting down for outerwear and sleeping bags in the mid-1930s. According to the company's history, Eddie Bauer almost froze to death during a fishing trip on one of his favorite rivers in the Seattle area. Remembering how his ancestors in Russia had stuffed straw into their clothing's arms to keep out the cold, Eddie Bauer created a quilted-down jacket. Eddie Bauer's inventions for blowing and lofting the down and feathers into the sewn panels of fabric resulted in patents for the quilting process.

By the late 1970s, China had become the major supplier for down, and the price had tripled from ten dollars a pound to thirty dollars a pound. This clearly shows China's intentions when its supply takes control of a marketplace. Back then, the newest synthetics of Gore-Tex and Polarfleece were ready to come out and change outdoor textiles. Thus, China's move to take control was ended at that time. In my opinion, China's message in raising prices that high was to say they wanted to make the down products in China, not just ship the down to America.

Down faded as the synthetics came on strong, until recent years. Now, down outerwear is the latest fashion from outdoor makers claiming authentic roots to their companies. One of the easiest ways to see how down's warmth has been reduced from years ago is to note the smaller channels and extra stitching in today's down outerwear. Every time you punch a hole in a fabric with sewing thread and/or compress the loft of down into smaller spaces, you lessen its warmth and comfort, which are the reasons for wearing down clothing. If he were here today, Eddie Bauer would be in shock to see his patents used to create quilted cold spots in all the knockoffs from leading outdoor brands.

Another key point about sewing down is that the fabric should wrap itself tightly around the sewing thread to keep out moisture, as well as cold air. Moisture quickly reduces the loft of down and its insulation values. The fabrics used today ignore this important part of making down outerwear. Today's down outerwear uses very shiny finishing on the fabrics—both polyester and nylon—partly for fashion and partly to keep the down from leaking. However, the shiny finish creates a very slick surface that can turn a fall on ice or snow into a fast, out-of-control slide downhill. This was known years ago, but the danger it poses on ski slopes and for back-country hiking, climbing, and extreme skiing is ignored.

Polyester

In the 1960s, plastic chips called polyester were melted and extruded through a shower-head machine called a spinneret. Fibers were then crimped and heat-set to make specific sizes of yarns for weaving and knitting. A nonwoven technology called fiberfill created batting without the need for yarn. Both cotton and the synthetic polyester and nylon fabrics were used for cover fabrics that held the quilting and fiberfill.

In the early 1980s, the technology of Polarfleece incorporated the finishes of wool, the warmth of down and fiberfill, and the new feature of absorbing only one percent of its weight in moisture. Using knitting machines and yarn, rather than fiber itself, this fabric technology would become one of the most popular on the planet by the end of the twentieth century and create tens of billions in sales for outerwear and activewear clothing brands.

Polarfleece broke the glass ceiling of natural fibers in more ways than one. In 1993, I created the first-ever polyester outdoor fabric from recycled plastic bottles. Now the worlds of glass bottles and natural fibers are waiting for the real sustainable cleanup of 72 billion bottles a year to be recycled into polyester performance fabrics.

Without Polarfleece, the technology of warmth without weight would most likely still be found only in battings and insulations made of fiberfill, down, and wool. I say this because when the owner of Malden Mills was put into bankruptcy in the early 1980s and did not have the funds to meet his payroll, had he closed the mill, there would be no Polarfleece fabric or technology.

Just when, how, and why polyester would have been reborn from earlier double-knit suits? My thought is, probably not at all. The guts of myself and the owner of Malden Mills to stay in business in America at that time, despite the bankruptcy, ensured the development of polyester used 100 percent in a fabric that did not make you sweat to death.

Cotton

No matter where you look, something made of cotton fibers is always being worn. Outdoor cotton sweatshirts were created in America more than eighty years ago. Cotton jeans go back to the mid-1800s. The 1927 L. L. Bean leatherette, called cotton chamois, became one of the most popular outdoor shirts from 1933 until the present. Gabardine and canvas were the mainstay of expeditions, for clothing, tents, and backpacks. Campers, hunters, and fishermen trusted cotton, especially in changing outdoor recreation weather.

Today, 45 percent of the American cotton crop is exported to China. Pollution caused by processing cotton, especially for making denim jeans, comes from the lack of environmental controls, which threatens the world's supply of clean water. Organic cotton addresses the issues of chemical spraying in the field, but not the consumption of water to grow it and process it into textile products—for example, it takes seven hundred gallons of water to make one cotton shirt.

Nylon

Invented by DuPont and introduced into women's stockings in the mid-1900s, nylon became the most important fabric for outerwear and skiwear. The smooth filament construction of nylon created new carpeting, as well as tightly woven fabrics for skiwear, outdoor clothing, and gear such as backpacks and sleeping bags.

For the weaving mills that changed from wool and cotton to nylon, however, the technology of dyeing nylon became overbearing. The natural fibers of wool and cotton allow dye stuffs to mix into the fiber itself, whereas for nylon, the process coats the fibers between 50 percent and 100 percent with dye stuffs, and the difference washes out into wastewater.

As a result, dye houses were built to do the dyeing, separate from the ownership and location of the weaving mills. Companies called converters bought woven nylon fabrics from the mill and sent them to be commission-dyed at dye houses.

Chapter Six:

Textiles in America

The manufacturing of textiles came to America with those who immigrated here, mostly from the mid-1800s through the early 1900s. Small businesses have fueled the American economy and way of life since the country's founding. Herein, I submit, lays the right use of the word "authentic" when we see a brand like many of those presented in this book and many more that make up outdoor textiles. As manufacturing began to use machines, much more capital was needed to keep a business going, hire workers, and repair and replace machines.

In the early years of the twentieth century, our nation became linked by efficient transportation and readily available electric power. Allowing for new management strategies, businesses grew larger.

Small and mid-sized manufacturers played a very special role in outdoor textiles, especially those in the Northwest. In the spring of 2001, the Wing Luke Asian Museum located in Seattle's chinatown presented a very complete telling of the outdoor textile manufacturers (commonly called the apparel manufacturing industry) that created "authentic" made-in-America outerwear, gloves, sleeping bags, and backpacks. Wool fabrics were sent to Seattle in the early 1900s, mostly from Oregon, spurred on by the supply of gold-rush pioneers and loggers. In the early 1930s, Japanese American women formed the majority of the workforce. This continued for decades. After the Vietnam War, companies added workers from many other Asian countries, including the Philippines.

if tired hands could talk

Apparel manufacturing in America, especially in the Pacific Northwest, reached its peak in the early 1980s, then disappeared to offshore manufacturing. Lower wages and lack of regulation—especially environmental controls—resulted in the resurgence of sweatshop conditions and catastrophic air and water pollution in the same Asian countries from where those citizens immigrated to America.

Today it is somewhat of a riddle to determine what is authentic outdoor clothing and gear. Labor to produce the first decades of clothing and gear came from American Japanese workers; after the Vietnam War, they came from all over Asia, when America opened its door to refugees and immigrants wanting freedom.

Then from the 1980s through the present, companies shifted back to Asia for that labor. This begs the question: to be "authentic," should the product be manufactured where it was first created?

Allow me to submit that authentic should also mean manufacturing that complies with environmental regulations created to make sure healthy products were made in America. For many decades, the importance of a healthy environment has protected our quality of life and life itself. In the last quarter of the twentieth century, American industry (manufacturing done here in America) spent just slightly more than one trillion dollars to renew and replenish the environment. This resulted in the cutting of toxic emissions by almost 45 percent by the end of the century. Other measurable improvements are recorded for waterways and soil and air. At the core of this environmental accomplishment are made-in-America products manufactured by American workers.

As we have seen, during the first decade of this new century, manufacturing of apparel, footwear, and gear has been done offshore in catastrophic environmental conditions. At the Wing Luke Asian Museum's exhibit, If Tired Hands Could Talk, the workers' stories told about making authentic outdoor apparel and gear. They made down clothing and sleeping bags that were the same in design and materials as those being offered by today's outdoor brands. Only today, they are made in catastrophic environmental conditions using sweatshop labor.

Companies such as Black Bear Manufacturing Company, Seattle Quilt, Sportcaster, Skyway Luggage, Sunset Sportswear, Roffe, Eddie Bauer, Far West Garments, REI and Thaw, Down Products, Tempco, Filson, and many others designed authentic products and hired workers to manufacture those products in the historic Pioneer Square District of downtown Seattle.

Large warehouses were easily set up for the assembly-line work of cutting fabrics and sewing apparel. Each and every product—from woolens, to down-insulated and fiberfill-insulated outerwear made with nylon fabrics—records its authentic origins in Seattle and was represented in the museum exhibition.

In northern Seattle, next to the University of Washington, the Seattle Museum of Industry maintains exhibits that include the first authentic recycled Polar-fleece jacket—which I donated—as well as the authentic patents for quilted Eddie Bauer down outerwear and sleeping bags made in Seattle.

"Made in America" stands for who we are and what we are as a country and people, in both past centuries and the present one. Making things in America clearly requires overcoming the disproportionate impact of government regula-tions not required when manufacturing offshore. The once-smaller companies making outdoor products here in America are now owned by large corporations or are themselves public corporations. The designs of the products they all make came from authentic, made-in-America fibers, yarns, fabrics, machines, and management processes that created an assembly line of workers and safe, healthy environmental conditions inside and outside the factory.

Let's use The North Face as an example. This authentic company was started by folks in retailing in the Bay Area around San Francisco to manufac-ture their own products, just as Eddie Bauer did in Seattle. The authentic North Face was best known for its dome tents and sleeping bags. They mixed down-quilted jackets and vests with a popular nylon cotton fabric called 60/40 cloth to make mountain parkas. According to the locals around the North Face factory in Berkeley in the 1970s, a company named Class Five was the first to use the 60/40 cloth in a mountain parka. This was the first "we have to do it, too," which was a way of life as I traveled around Berkeley, selling nylon fabrics and fiberfill in the 1970s.

Those domed tents were constantly in design at North Face and Sierra Designs. Polarguard fiberfill was shingled into the warmest synthetic sleeping bag by Snow Lion and North Face. Apparel design was easy, as the almost forty-year-old Eddie Bauer quilts were never improved upon during those years.

Trying to show these outdoor icons synthetic pile fabrics and cotton-blended sweatshirts got a laugh and suggestion to go over to San Francisco and find a sportswear company. Today these fabrics are hot sellers in the North Face outdoor world, inked into the black by corporate minds from Vanity Fair, a sportswear and intimate-apparel icon that let go of those nylon panties for a more exciting culture of outdoor brands such as North Face, Jan Sport, andTimberland. When these well-known brands bring out products they call authentic outdoor gear and apparel, consider that the indigenous folks who created them are best known in a museum.

As the Wing Luke Asian Museum illustrates, the changeover from sweatshop labor to fair wages and piece-rate work, which could double minimum wage, is credited with building a middle class of workers in outdoor textiles and especially apparel manufacturing.

By the time I was born in 1944, child labor and sweatshop abuses were removed from America by citizens coming together to form unions and to develop a pride of workmanship. Without that workmanship, America would not have survived World War II with Germany and Japan.

End of an Era in Textile Manufacturing

Today most of the textiles made in America are required by law to be made here for the U.S. Department of Defense. Our troops proudly wear shoes, uniforms, outerwear, and socks all made in America. The same is true of all their gear, including sleeping bags, water bottles, and combat equipment.

On the other hand, while most everything in retail stores across America has a label of an American-based and American-owned company, the sewing and manufacturing of those items and the textile fibers, yarns, and fabrics are produced offshore, mainly in China. During the 2010 holiday season, several stores seemed to be offering everything made in China.

What was once the famous garment district of New York City has given way to only designer showrooms of finished products made offshore. Growing up in the 1960s, I would visit the loft of my Uncle Henry's office and warehouse in that garment district. His factory in Tennessee made a line of then-popular raincoats with cotton-shell fabrics and zip-in and -out pile-fabric liners made of synthetic fiber (plastic), commonly called private-label Burberry knockoffs. Back then, it was common for a high-rise building like 1407 Broadway in New York City to have more than thirty floors of textile clothing showrooms and a design studio. Blocks away, on West Thirty-seventh, Thirty-eighth, and Thirty-ninth streets, other buildings had floor after floor of sewing and/or warehousing of textile clothing. Fabric cutting was done there or in larger lofts across the rivers in New Jersey or Long Island. The miracle on Thirty-fourth Street, Macy's, easily found the textiles it wanted without having to wait a month or more for the container vessel to bring them from offshore; instead, carts full of clothing traveled two blocks from their warehouse to the Macy's receiving dock.

From Maine to the deep South, textile manufacturing played a major role in employment and innovation in America. Going across America, well-known brands were based in cities and towns all the way to the West Coast. Each had a manufacturing factory, including sewing workers, cutting-table workers, designers, and office staff. Their sales showrooms were found in those high-rise buildings, such as 1407 Broadway and Apparel Marts, in the bigger cities across America.

A challenge to these natural fiber companies was beginning as I began my job as a sales account manager in New York City in 1966. I was responsible for selling, developing, and marketing polyester fibers (plastic). These fibers were quickly produced from oil byproducts commonly called chemical chips of plastic. They were then the equal in value to today's computer chips. They converted most everything that used natural materials to these synthetics, or plastics. The corporations that developed these man-made materials became known as chemical giants. DuPont and Celanese traded like big-board winners, adding their names to the "blue chips" of Wall Street. Their challenges to natural fibers, and especially cotton, soon found the world's largest cotton growers and brokers investing in designer-brand clothing to simply, in my opinion, protect their investments in cotton. There were no activists counting the gallons of water used to grow cotton or the amount of fertilizers, or preaching about going organic.

Designers began to have their clothing made in Asia, and soon enough America was falling in love with them and their clothing. They used their names as the brand, rather than a catchy name from Madison Avenue or decades of family names. In addition to expensive high-end fashions, these designer brands featured clothing for work and play and lounging around the house. Cheap offshore manufacturing labor was then a perk, enabling the consumer to buy top designer clothes at moderate prices. This was first seen in sportswear and especially denim jeans.

My career in textiles focused on outerwear and a new polyester fiber for insulation and batting: fiberfill, or nonwoven blankets from carding. Offshore outerwear was to become skiwear made in Asia, but it was not a fashion thing for the sportswear designers in the 1970s. Outerwear became the intellectual property of textile suppliers of fibers, yarns, fabrics, and processing for many years, from the mid-1960s until 2000. Fiber crimping and texturing, special dyeing, and finishing were all required for outerwear made of nylon and polyester fibers. These technologies were created in America, with a few from Europe. Much of the manufacturing equipment still came from Europe, which continued to lead the world in manufacturing machinery for textiles. Each of these technologies became part of today's biggest brands of outdoor clothing and sportswear, including footwear and gear.

Currently, textile profits are supporting grants for programs that get kids outdoors and that protect American public lands and help with environmental stewardship of our waterways, lands, and habitats. Best awards go to Patagonia and REI for these programs. American citizens seem to be spending more on recreation and on the brands that are trying to give back, rather than give away. Make no mistake: job losses and family lifestyle changes were horrific when textiles went offshore by the 1980s. There was no "crying couch" on the Internet, no 24-7 cable news media to cover it. Political offices did not hang on the where-is-it-made labels of clothing and textiles. And what remains is the unknown environmental pollution in Asia, which counters the goodwill of getting kids outdoors here in America.

Personally, I know how the pain of losing to offshore manufacturing knocks you down, and it is very hard to get up again. The combination of creating products for the outdoors and getting outside to enjoy them gives a meaning to "recreation" that turns it into "re-creation." How do you apply this to plastic vs. natural materials? Looking into nature, we see things constantly evolving from one form of life to another. Outdoor textiles is the closest material to bond with nature. For centuries, they were made of natural fibers; only during the past sixty years have they been using plastics.

Offshore Environmental Nightmare

Wake up call: the environment where the manufacturing takes place for products shipped to America is now an environmental nightmare. The National Resource Defense Council (NRDC) has committed their efforts to water, which includes water-supply issues and the pollution of water from textiles. A program called Clean by Design focuses entirely on the textile industry. A study of more than a dozen Chinese textile dyeing and finishing mills, including studying five mills in-depth, concluded that as much as two hundred tons of water are polluted with every ton of fabric produced. A best-practices program found that dyeing it right the first time is the best way to save water and reduce pollution. This was the only way American textile dye houses did things and was a big part of building the quality reputations of the companies that are the leading outdoor brands in America.

There is a reasonable explanation for why this repeated dyeing of fabrics is a problem that pollutes waters to the point of being unsafe. The textile users (American brands) of these Chinese suppliers had very qualified people working in their factories in America, when they purchased American textiles. As a sales rep selling fabrics, I daily received lab dips and requested approvals from my customers. As computers got involved, color matches became almost perfect in American dye houses. Groups like NRDC are important and work with the best of intentions, but between the Chinese government and the profits of the businesses operating there, trying to shake out the pollution is a game we cannot win.

Political discussions always turn to money and who is going to pay for it. As the book *River Keepers* points out, citizens netted fish and put them in tanks to watch the mutations and deformity in an effort to prove that our government needed to stop it. Fines were issued, but companies found it cheaper to pay the fines than clean up the pollution. Folks kept after it, and finally the courts ordered fines big enough to get the changes done. The foundation of our EPA has never lost a challenge in forty years. Since Chinese citizens do not have the same rights as citizens in America, who, if anyone, will stand up to the pollution and create change?

I wrote this book about outdoor recreation textiles made in America from my experiences and career in supplying outdoor recreation makers with fibers and fabrics—mostly polyester, which is commonly known as plastics. Mostly notably, I co-created and marketed Polarfleece during my forty-plus years in polyester fibers.

Polarfleece, which started as a brand of fabric, is today a word meaning higher fabric technology. The technology created in outdoor recreation fibers and fabrics (synthetic fibers/plastics) has opened a global marketplace that rivals any other consumer marketplace. Companies create Wall Street-size profits, and the big board stock index can actually be moved by running shoes, Polarfleece garments, and moisture-management underwear.

A mere forty years ago, the plastic chips of chemicals used to make synthetic fibers fueled the same kind of growth and profits, with all the textile manufacturing being done here in America. Furthermore, compare today's global textile business to a hundred years ago, when wool and woolen mills in America were second only to steel in revenues for the American economy. Yes, right behind brands of automobiles stood brands like Pendleton Woolens and Jantzen. Two hundred and 75 million pounds of wool a year was produced in America a hundred years ago, compared with 10 percent of that in 2000 –2010. The 1913 poundage of wool ranks just under the wool produced today in Australia and New Zealand.

Between 1900 and 1950, while America was digging coal for power and energy and drilling oil for transportation and machines, sheep were grazing the lands of America to keep her citizens clothed. Clothing was simple and functional. Blankets were used to keep warm and hats to cover the head.

Today, fashion races off runways, while outdoor recreation clothing glides down snow-covered mountains and into bubbles of whitewater, searching for smoother spaces. Some even dangle in mid-air, grasping tiny bits of rock ledges, with a single rope for safety. REI, a co-op founded by climbers in Seattle, proudly placed the first American flag atop Mount Everest in 1963, with its president, Jim Whitaker, wearing Eddie Bauer down clothing made of the then-new synthetic nylon fabric filled with the best goose down in the world.

Plastics: "A Stitch in Time"

The phrase simply equates to forty years of plastic fibers vs the hundreds of years of natural fibers being processed into machines to make textile fabrics and products. In the beginning of that stitch in time, I was getting my business degree at the University of Montana in Missoula, Montana literally lured to Montana to catch the famous rainbow trout and get an education so I could afford to come back to Montana for a fishing vacation with my family after graduation. After seeing the movie *A River Runs Through It* and reading the book, I wondered if I could write a story about outdoor recreation textiles and Montana, about my flying (not taking the train) from New York to Montana to go to college, and about being offered, after graduation, a real *Graduate*-sized opportunity to get into "polyester." Just like the movie said, plastic was the future.

Did that Montana gift horse come to me as easily when I returned to New York City and took a job at Celanese Fibers Marketing Company? Well, the first thing I learned after taking that job to sell polyester fibers for outerwear and sleeping bags was that folks really did not want to change from cotton, wool, and down—all natural fibers. Thus began the challenge and adventures of "plastic vs. natural," in what I believe today is nothing more than "a stitch in time."

During the late 1960s, the chemical chips used to make polyester fibers were also made by the same companies selling the polyester fiber. I was competing with big public companies such as DuPont, Monsanto, and Eastman Kodak. DuPont was also the largest producer of nylon fibers, and its big competitor, Allied Chemical, was a lifetime warrior for nylon fiber rights and profits.

Marketing was the key, and advertising was done to the tune of millions of dollars through consumer promotions, which used mostly print media. Along with consumer magazines, catalogs from Sears and J. C. Penney were read with as much attention as we pay to the Internet today. IBM business machines and Xerox copiers promised the office wardrobe needed to keep up with this rapidly growing textiles-by-plastic marketplace.

When you left your office, there was no way to call you, no way to connect except through a pay-phone booth, until you got to your customer or back to the office. The same was true when you left home. And the same was true when you went outdoors to recreate and be in nature or just walk in a local park, to play a sport or just watch one.

Kids had school clothes and shoes, and playclothes and shoes. Adults had the same—work clothes and shoes, and home/playclothes and shoes. Work and school clothes were dress-up, and play and home were dress-down. Jeans were for workers, not fashion. Golf shirts were a status of doing well, and tee shirts a signature of the blue-collar worker proudly displaying the union label that supported his work, pension, and benefits. Raincoats covered the trenches of city workers, while wool coats warmed those in the working fields of the countryside. Quilting was a fashion design for bath robes and outerwear inspired by Eddie Bauer down clothing. Plush pile coats were giving way to quilts, using a new washable polyester fiberfill. Pile liners in outerwear and fake-fur coats marked a new way of fashion. Wool was the sign of a century of made-in-America, from the sheep to the machines that scoured it and created yarns and fabrics. Factories full of union-made sewn garments told the story of sweatshops becoming workplaces with fair wages, pensions, and health-care benefits.

Since my job was to sell polyester fibers to makers of what was called outerwear clothing, where did I draw the line between dress-up and dress-down, work and play? I soon found the answer at two very big trade shows for outdoor clothing.

One was a ski show in a hotel in New York City, where skiwear makers from all over the country came to show the newest fashions for skiing. Brands like White Stag from Portland, Oregon, and Gerry Outdoor and Aspen Skiwear from Denver, Colorado, mixed with New England brands such as Sun Valley, Slalom and Baltimore's Head Skiwear, New York state's Grandoe glove-maker, and Europe's top brand, Bogner. Three dozen or more makers were there, all featuring wool sweaters and nylon fabrics filled with down. Duofold underwear, made of wool, cotton, and a small mix of nylon fibers, traveled from a rural area of New York State more famous for two-hundred-year-old settlements that were part of the birthing of our country.

These fashions were not sold to department stores or chain stores or local clothing shops. They were sold only to specialty ski shops and high-end fashion clothing retailers. Skiwear, primarily made and sold near the ski areas, became the next hot fashion for outdoor clothing. "Hot" was in, with names like Hot Gear for kids, and Globe, a New Hampshire fire clothing maker that took shiny nylon fabrics to a luster of fashion brighter than the red fire trucks that wore their fire-protection suits. Sport Obermeyer, showing the famous skiwear brands, and designers from Europe that made USA skiwear from Aspen, Colorado, added the slope and natural feeling to what was hot in ski designs. Alpine Designs properly focused on the higher-altitude slopes of powder and fun, especially in the western states. A sister company, Camp Seven, featured down sleeping bags and tempting visions for my polyester fiberfills. A young skier going by the name of CB sped downhill to record speeds and returned home to Vermont to create the first polyester fiberfill insulated ski pant, sending chills into the established brands of stretch wool pants in Europe and America.

Held on the floors of an Eighth Avenue, New York City hotel at the time, this ski show headed out west to Las Vegas in the early 1970s, when the makers and buyers from all across America found their slots on the slopes and in those famous fashion-inspired ski specialty retail shops. One of the first to Vegas with a new brand was Swing West, created out of Raven Industries in South Dakota. Also known for making hot-air balloons using the lightest nylon fabric in the world from a U.S. textile mill, Raven went on to become one of the first to create nylon fabric, fiberfill-insulated snowmobile suits.

The other big trade show was a sporting goods show in Chicago, featuring everything from fishing and hunting gear to boots and clothing for the serious outdoor recreationist. Camping was included, and Coleman made life in the outdoors almost as comfortable as being at home. Tents, cooking gear, sleeping bags—you name it, it was ready for the retailer to buy.

National Geographic, in its July 1966 issue, featured the camper lifestyle as it followed the Mission 66 rollout of rebuilding public lands. Roads, lodging, campgrounds, and safe access to the wild were added to national parks and forests, as well as access to scenic adventures in the lands and waters, flora and fauna of America. A real wilderness was just beyond the safety of the public designs of national parks and forests. That 1966 *National Geographic* Mission 66 story told us that by the year 2000, we would have six months off from working full-time, as the innovations and technologies of the 1960s assured each citizen the health and security of a life only available from American technology and science.

Today, some forty-five years later, just eight miles outside Portland, Oregon, I look at the forty miles of the Cascade Mountain range and its signature summit, Mount Hood. The Willamette Valley is filled with farms of strawberries, blueberries, marionberries, and blackberries. The foothills of the Cascades are lined with the famous Hood River fruits of cherries, apples, peaches, and pears. Many mornings find me above the valley, seventy miles away from the coastal fog that engulfs the valley floor. The sun rises early in the east, somewhere between the north or south side of Mount Hood, depending on the time of year. Oregon's urban-growth boundary, a national model of how to preserve farming lands from development, assures the farms and fresh produce, at least for the rest of my lifetime. Local supermarket chain New Seasons gets the fresh produce as it ripens at the farms and orchards. Fresh air and star-filled nights make this part of my life peaceful for sleeping.

Yet, my days are filled with the constant churning of knowledge and experiences that have left the landscape and lifestyle of America in its deepest recession and with its greatest economic challenges ever. Is it really that different from the previous challenges to "change" that we have faced before as a free nation, a country that is committed to allowing anyone the opportunity to have a rich, healthy life, both personally and professionally, while also preserving and protecting nature and especially our public lands and waterways?

We are less than 300 years old, holding on to being number one, while the countries of our ancestors in Europe—three and four times our age—seem idle and unwilling to stick their head up again after hundreds of years of their own wars and powers of rule and religion.. Water pollution is not found in these same rivers that flowed for textiles more than a hundred years ago and that powered machines until newer engines were created.

Currently, we are moving away from sustainability. We should stop doing that. Comparing America and China shows what we have accomplished to be sustainable. Europe demonstrates the reality of accepting a sustainable lifestyle. Balancing nature with the wants of humans, there are still many challenges ahead globally, with Oregon as a think tank for topics from local food and water, to textiles and energy. As we begin the second decade of the twenty-first century, Oregon and especially the Portland area, is the search engine of creating outdoor and active sportswear textiles for clothing, footwear, and gear.

Why isn't there a fast-growing workforce being assembled to manufacture textiles in Oregon for the large number of brands already here and the many more moving to Oregon? Skimmed off the top, the cream of textiles is a farce smothered in the catastrophic pollution of water and energy as a result of sending the production of clothing, footwear, and gear to China and other areas throughout Asia. Yet, the history of textiles coming to Oregon paints a perfect Norman Rockwell picture of the twentieth century.

Chapter Seven:

Textiles in Oregon

Today, I find myself rooted to Oregon. Seattle and Portland in the Northwest have been my hometowns since 1973. I enjoy seeing outdoor clothing worn daily, no matter what the place or occasion. Polarfleece is everywhere, as are nylon jackets and polyester tee shirts and running clothes.

Here in Oregon in the early years of the twenty-first century—just as it was a hundred years ago—there are a few very big makers of clothing and footwear. Two of these clothing makers, including their footwear, are now standout public corporations: Columbia Sportswear and Nike. They are doing what those before them did: finding ways to put clothing on a body through two arms and two legs, and cover two feet and one head. Outdoor clothing has become a mixture of work clothes and playclothes, home clothes and travel clothes. The catchword for outdoor clothing today is performance, which is known as layering in base, middle, and outer garments.

A near-obsession with sweat means that synthetic clothing fibers and fabrics manufacturers put every possible chemical into the fabrics to control odor and keep you comfortable. Sweating, as most people know or should know, is a healthy thing to do. It pushes moisture out of our bodies through our skin's pores and tiny holes when our body heats up and the water inside us rises to the surface of our skin. We are actually doing this all the time to keep our skin from drying out. Yet in what has become a catch-22, we want to be active outdoors while not wanting our clothes to be wet with sweat or any other kind of moisture, be it rain, snow, or even mist.

Adding to the catch-22: wool performed this function for centuries, so why the changeover to plastics? The marketing minds of polyester and nylon, mine included, discovered that natural fibers such as down, wool, and cotton get wet and hold moisture. Polyester fibers do not absorb moisture above 1 percent of the fiber weight. In order to gain the competitive edge in switching outdoor clothing from natural fibers to man-made synthetic fibers of nylon and polyester, we attacked the moisture issue—especially sweat.

Active Sportswear

The stampede into jogging and walking, and sneakers becoming running shoes, put this type of activewear at the top of the list for solving sweat issues. It highlighted the fact that natural-fiber clothing gets wet and taught Nike that clothing was as important as their famous waffle-sole running shoes.

Watching the muscle-framed bodies of athletes—especially males—slip into synthetic fibers and fabrics that were used for women's loungewear and casual clothing was really a funny sight. Smart minds saw the advantage of lightweight clothing helping performance and stretch fabrics staying closer to the body. Seeing is believing, and as this unfolded and the eighty-year-old Champion cotton gym sweats gave way to the soft, silklike fabrications of nylon and polyester from women's apparel, the minds and bodies of athletes went for it hook, line, and sinker. Cotton sweat suits were replaced with nylon track suits, and the fashion got so hot that even Bloomingdale's and Nordstrom had to put it on their racks. Fashion designers raced after the Nike and Adidas designs, assuring the Nike camp a big payout and changeover to their kind of sweat dressing.

Nike quickly gobbled up some key talent in Portland from companies such as White Stag that were losing ground in skiwear and all but out of sportswear. Today the famous White Stag brand belongs to Walmart. Jantzen, now a licensed brand of Perry Ellis, also felt the Nike crunch for talent, and Speedo sought the safety of warmer weather in California. Could anyone really believe the famous Jantzen diving suit was made out of wool?

The nylon ripstop fabric that climbed to the top of Mount Everest in 1963 now races on ski slopes around Oregon, puffed up with goose down, and on the Willamette Valley floor, it found a waiting partner for running wear at Nike. Today's ultralight 1.1-ounce nylon ripstop wind shells proudly say Patagonia and mark a place in Oregon or anywhere else that outdoor clothing is worn. The fabric was created in the United States for hot-air balloons and military jacket liners. It found its way into sails, replacing cotton.

This combination of oil-based synthetics, polyester, and nylon that make you sweat was destined to cure its own odor issues through more chemical additives than a race car trying to win the more-famous track events (pit-changes pun intended). Soon polyester was easier to work with than nylon, and price plus softness allowed polyester to get on its own track and leave nylon fibers in the dust forever.

The minds and hearts of former White Stag and Jantzen employees sparked the Nike engine as the clothing maker moved from an old elementary school building on Powell and Thirty-sixth Street in southeast Portland to a bigger complex in Beaverton, a suburb west of Portland. Soon Nike would have a college-sized campus and many employees designing and marketing the fast-selling apparel and running shoes.

Often, success in business is measured by the longevity of employment, and for Oregon, and Portland in particular, where Nike started, those former White Stag and Jantzen workers kept their dreams of Oregon beaches and mountains in their lifestyles. Others who were the bread-and-butter factory workers did not fare as well. When the Jantzen minds overlooked how the "sweat dressing" was turning to Polarfleece, their factory workers became prime targets for sewing Patagonia clothing in order to turn that brand into one known for quality of sewing that assured the best fitting and wearing garments. Jantzen survived as a sewing factory for many years. An ex-White Stag production manager, Jim, joined Patagonia and watched over its production in that Jantzen sewing location along the Columbia River in Oregon. When Jantzen dropped out of the sweatshirt market, I watched the last days of Jantzen products made in Oregon slowly come to an end. My days ahead were to become a legacy of polyester fibers in Polarfleece technology. It was unsettling to see Jantzen close up their manufacturing because they thought Polarfleece and sweatshirts, part outerwear and part sportswear, could not keep them going.

Jantzen had started in 1910, knitting wool for women in their own factory upstairs and selling the products as Portland Knitting Mills sweaters and hosiery in a street-level store. The founders were John Zehnbauer and Carl Jantzen, both members of the Portland Rowing Club. In 1913 they made rowing suits for their rowing club. The rowing trunks stayed up like the cuff of a sweater without a drawstring. Today that waist feature is used instead of a belt in every activewear garment. In 1915, they branded a one-piece designed bathing suit as Jantzen. It was created on their needle bed in a rib-stitch, lightweight fabric, also made out of wool. In 1921, Jantzen changed the name from bathing suit to swimming suit, and in 1923, their famous red diving-girl logo was featured in Vogue and Life magazines. Today Jantzen is among the seven best-known brands in the world. Their American innovation and knitting are still sold under the Jantzen brand, but it is owned by Perry Ellis and produced offshore. It is a licensed brand that surely inspired folks like those who started Nike to believe in the good fortunes of working in textiles in Portland, Oregon.

To this day, the influence of American textile-mill loungewear fibers and fabrics inspire activewear and outerwear. Vanity Fair (known as VF) was a very successful intimate-apparel and loungewear company that followed the use of those fabrics into activewear and outerwear, as we will see when we get to North Face. From Jantzen on, the marketing of sportswear was divided between activewear and sportswear, and Nike quickly swooshed it all up.

Outerwear

In another part of Portland, along the banks of the famous Willamette River where Lewis and Clark had camped and where the one-time largest woolen mill west of Cleveland, Portland Woolen Mills, survived for sixty years, a family-run hat company was transforming from makers of hats to hunting and fishing clothing with signature styles that appeared in the famous Eddie Bauer catalogs. Columbia Sportswear was staking out its own made-in-Oregon homestead. This "little engine that could" was run by a family team of mother and son after the father/husband died suddenly of a heart attack. Columbia scoured its way past the old woolen mill next door and made fishing along its banks pay off into a public offering that was too good to turn down on Wall Street. They followed the Nike jet trail to Asia, where they began sourcing outdoor clothing made of Gore-Tex, Thinsulate, and fleece. Most of it was manufactured in Korea, which had been a prime source for making Pacific Trail outerwear since that famous consumer brand added Korea to its American sewing factories during the late 1960s and early '70s.

A family called the Moungers punched and educated their way from sidewalk vending in Seattle to starting Pacific Trail, the country's top department-store outerwear brand. Larry Sr., a boxer, began it, and his sons Larry Jr., a lawyer, and Glenn, the astute businessman, soon hired sales reps across America and employed hundreds of workers each in sewing factories in Manti, Utah, and in Spokane, Wenatchee, and Seattle, Washington. The famous Eddie Bauer down outerwear was out of patents and soon became the number-one selling outdoor jacket and vest in America under the Pacific Trail brand. Ultimately, Columbia bought the Pacific Trail brand for not much more than a keepsake. Credit goes to the Gore-Tex and Thinsulate technology, which Columbia birthed into hunting and fishing clothing in their Oregon riverbank factory.

Family death takes its toll, and while Columbia was past the sudden death of Mr. Boyle Sr., the Moungers now faced the sudden passing of their dad, Larry Sr., who was unable to prevent the breakdown of his domestic factories and the workers he employed and respected so much. The torch passed from Pacific Trail to Columbia, but it was not a fast-track one like Nike's race to jogging and running shoes and apparel, which obliterated the almost-century-old southern textile mills and cotton athletic sweatshirts. I had a ringside seat for it all. Pacific Trail bought millions of yards and dollars of fabrics from me as I worked for Blank Textiles, family-owned by Adolph, his wife, Janet, and son, Mitch. Columbia figured out the technology leap to Gore-Tex and Thinsulate, which made them very good profits in their hook-and-bullet outdoor clothing before the next phase of skiwear and sportswear.

In the early 1980s, after gas lines evaporated and an era of "how much can you have" took over the minds and pockets of America, offshore manufacturing of textiles took on a very fast pace. The bumper sticker "Whoever dies with the most toys wins" said it all, adding the implication "not required to be made in America." Built on designer brands that owned no manufacturing, the so-called rag trade became a business of marketing brands, not fixing sewing machines and dealing with union stewards.

But the bigger they were, the longer and harder they fell. Eddie Bauer, whose domestic factories puffed out the most down clothing and sleeping bags in Seattle and Alabama, went into a crash that never ended. The icons of out-door clothing of the Northwest changed, and only the 1980's Olympics that saw Levi take control of active sportswear stood in the way of the Nike, Adidas express to textile manufacturing in Asia. Levi was to far removed from activewear and the winter Olympics held in America lacked authentic outdoor leadership in apparel.

Had Pacific Trail or anyone else been aware of the amount of branding and licensing you can do to textiles when you do not have to do the manufacturing, the Mounger sons might well be the billionaires of the sportswear, active and outdoor owners today. I remember seeing a tennis shoe at Pacific Trail. Larry Jr. was a top tennis player and one of his best friends was tennis pro Tom Gorman. The tennis shoe was much like a Nike shoe, and at that time, had Larry seen the future, he too could have built a company of athletes. The cost landed in the USA of under $4 was a shock to us all, to be told.

It was at this time that I took serious the sweat-dressing fashion thing and pushed hard to sell Malden Mills knitted sweatshirt fabrics and let go of the nylon fabric empire in outerwear. Skiwear was clearly moving offshore, and it was time to pay attention to sweat-dressing. It became a theme song for Nike to get light and do it right, using nylon and polyester fabrics and taking the cotton out of sweat-dressing. "In and out" was Nike's way to learn from the U.S. mills and then take that knowledge to Asia, where they built their clothing empire to match the running-shoe bonanza.

It was a race that never had another Olympics for American textile mills. It sealed Oregon's woolen-mill legacy into a century-old trading-blanket and ceremonial-robe business for Pendleton, while all the others were lost. Today Pendleton is weaving a special blanket to celebrate the White Buffalo Sanctuary near Bend, Oregon. The blanket features Oregon wool blended with hair from the white buffaloes. There is no need to recycle anything, since the sheep breed mostly twins at a time and the buffalo gladly give up some hair, which of course grows right back.

Today the air hangs heavy in people and profits as these public corporations, Nike and Columbia, outscore the Ducks and Beavers of college sports fame in Oregon. Uniforms show the Nike swish, and fans stay warm and dry in mighty Columbia outerwear. Weather in the Oregon Willamette Valley richly allows the best fruits and wines for a world-class marketing theme of GROWN IN OREGON, while MADE IN OREGON textiles are simply a memoir for those of us who lived it and worked it. Microbrews are made in Oregon, while microfibers for Nike and Columbia are made thousands of miles away.

Looking back over the last hundred years of Oregon textiles, the landscape was created by settlers carrying hand-weaving looms across the famous Oregon Trail in the mid-1800s. This was followed by the machinery boom in the early 1900s, when mills sprung up to make wool and woolens. Wool gave way to synthetics and goose down in outdoor clothing by the middle of the twentieth century. Sewing also went from a machine at home to a factory. Designs moved from heavy woolens—even swimsuits of wool—to lightweight nylon and polyester. Jantzen and White Stag employed and deployed their workers over to the Nike track fields and Columbia slopes, trails, and waterways.

The best-memoirs award goes to the Oregon-bred and family-owned Pendleton Woolen Mills. No company has ever been more important to or successful in outdoor clothing in Oregon and probably all of America. Like the classic picture of a cowboy in a saddle after the wars of democracy and slavery ended, nothing is more American than Pendleton. The company started out as a scouring mill for raw Oregon-grown wool. Facing a bankruptcy, the Bishop family and the city of Pendleton joined dollars and saved the Pendleton mill. Family blood came on strong, from the industrial-woolen inventor Thomas Kay side, to the Bishops and sons, who were educated at top textile schools in the east. Family bank money ensured that investing in raw wool kept the Oregon wool in Oregon, assuring the best-quality woolens for clothing and blankets. Native American art and culture were used in blanket and outerwear designs, giving those tribes income and bringing federal dollars to Pendleton during the Great Depression. The scouring of washing brushes and humming of yarn shuttles placed fabric for sewing into American workers' hands.

Oregon is known for its rain and storms and the legacy of Pendleton, which was still working when the Nike/Columbia bubble created a perfect storm that changed the fabric of textiles from woolens to plastic balloons. Down was blown out and polyester in fiberfill and fleece resisted the moisture, enabling the technology of Polarfleece to rise. Dynamic changes in manufacturing allowed outdoor companies worldwide, not just in Oregon, to gain richly from those with higher education and other workers who toiled in labor-intensive American textiles jobs.

Clothing and shoes are the most basic coverings we humans want, and we need to be comfortable once we push off the wool blanket to get out of bed and begin our daily life. The technology to have these simple coverings made of plastics has gone too far and still needs to get more focused as we grow in population, while the resources available are being counted and stacked into less than fifty years of available consumption. Synthetics commonly called plastics are not renewable resources as they come from oil by products.

That said, the difference in today's clothing and shoes using resources that are not renewable, compared with resources used for thousands of years prior, begs the question: just how long are these brands going to survive? Even more important, how long will they last compared with other clothing and footwear brands that came a century before them—the fibers and fabrics from the lands of our ancestors and from indigenous natives here in America.

Textile Pollution Exposed

Again a reminder about today's textile pollution, especially the water pollution in the rivers and lands of Asia where activewear brands purchase their manufacturing and materials: the environment is in ruin. Reports state that 600 of 2,000 dye houses have been closed in China. Committed to water protection and based here in America with a strong team of leadership that includes Bobby Kennedy Jr. co founder of Riverkeepers now Waterkeepers, the Natural Resources Defense Council (NRDC) under Linda Greer developed ten practical, low-cost, best-practice opportunities that would quickly reduce water usage by 25 percent and fuel by 30 percent in less than one year. This plan could create drinking water for 12.4 million people per year. The reduction of carbon dioxide emissions would be equal to taking 174,000 cars off the road. Cooperation from leading textile brands and the retailers that purchase the fabric based apparel and shoes has yet to report on the progress of this program as this book went to publication in September, 2011.

Why are the outdoor makers not convinced? Some 30 percent of the air pollution in California comes from across the Pacific; North Face breathes it every day. Yet we only hear how important it is for the youth and citizens of China to have the American-dream outdoor experience. Polluted rivers don't allow that to happen. Rivers in America do, because before North Face and so many more became players, the American-made textile folks cleaned up the rivers by accepting EPA regulations as the right way to manufacture here in America.

One of the famous icons from Pendleton's dyed woven plaids is the famous board shirt for the rock-and-roll surfing culture during my youth in the 1960s. Today that board shirt seeks a seat at the table in the outdoor activewear corporate boardroom. The Bishop family, now in its third generation of owning Pendleton, will, in my opinion, within a few moves, call a checkmate (plaid board shirt), with the winner taking all, as real sustainable clothing follows from the roots created by Oregon wool and Pendleton. It will leave the public outdoor brands red-faced for being among the worst polluters ever in American textiles. For me there is a new vision of another polyester playing, as I move my first pawn into a strong position for sustainable synthetic waterless dyed fabrics and apparel. Once again I have looked to Pendleton as I did when I created polarfleece to show me what is coming back into fashion and function in outdoor textiles. Knowing the third time is always a charm the romantic part of outdoor clothing found me warm and comfortable in my Pendleton loggers coat while attending college in Montana, in the early 1960s, winning the surviving of making textiles here in America with polarfleece copied from their woolens with polyester right to the famous buffalo check designs in the early 1980's, and now as fashion repeats and returns to the 60's the famous board shirt from Pendleton tells me to go waterless to keep the textile fabric clean and sustaining our ways of living.

Chapter Eight:

Fiberfill to Fleece

Entering the 1970s, the EPA was coming after textiles, and I was trying to place polyester fibers in fiberfill. Because polyester fiberfill fibers were not dyed, I had an easier time meeting the new EPA regulations. Nylon fibers in outdoor nylon fabrics used chemical processing, especially dyeing, which polluted water and air, and that had to change. In 1970, I was trying to convince folks covered in down at factories such as REI's THAW factory in Seattle to use a polyester fiber for insulation (fiberfill) that would not float through their down-blowing machine into a sleeping bag or outerwear jacket or vest. Jokes about polyester double-knit suits from REI's founders assured me they knew where polyester stood at that time. It was EPA approved to be free of toxic chemicals but not technically understood for outdoor apparel and sleeping bags.

The A in THAW stood for Lloyd Anderson (REI founder) and the W for Jim Whittaker (REI president); T and H were for very smart manufacturing guys who put the assembly line in place. The University of Washington-owned building that housed THAW overlooked the Puget Sound's pristine "Emerald City" landscape spotted with green/white ferry boats, making sure high-rise bridges did not turn that landscape into a San Francisco–Berkeley look-alike.

You might say I was a duck out of water trying to make polyester work like down. The best-quality products used goose down, not duck down, because it was warmer. Furthermore, for my fiberfill, I had to make a polyester fiber that was better than the staple fiber used with wool and cotton fabrics.

Performance, not fashion, is the key to a satisfied customer who wants to keep warm while outdoors. A famous Eddie Bauer/REI battle in Seattle came about after Jim Whittaker returned from climbing to the summit of Mount Everest in special Eddie Bauer-designed down gear. Bauer began plans to get into retailing, but since REI was their best retail customer in Seattle, that was seen as a conflict. REI, then a members-only co-op, feared losing its members to the Eddie Bauer retail store. As a result, REI built THAW and began a mail-order catalog business, while Bauer added retailing to their mail-order business.

Warmth without Weight

I was treated to my education in warmth-without-weight from both companies' engineers in their own factory that sorted goose down from the feathers. Their blowing process filled panels of sewn nylon fabrics with down, to be used for garments and sleeping bags. The least amount of expensive down, then costing $10 a pound in the 1960s–70s, was used to create the required warmth for what was called fill power—600 fill being acceptable and 650 to 700 the very best. That number was calculated by putting the down in a glass beaker and letting it settle without any pressure. Down being lighter than feathers, the plume of the best down won the filling ratings. Given that today's down fill-power numbers go above 800, I suspect a new system of fill power is being used. That kind of loft was never accomplished by anyone when down was processed in America. Feathers were kept in the mixture to support the down that rolled over them as air kept lofting the down over the feathers. Boeing airplane engineers had nothing over the REI and Eddie Bauer guys, who could make feathers float better than air over the wings of those famous jet airliners built across town. Patents were created for down-blowing machines and processing. After visits to the enclosed down rooms of REI and Eddie Bauer, down was vacuumed off my clothes as soon as I walked out. At $10 a pound, every feather counted.

Workers in the factory, including sewing operators, were paid piece-rate wages so that production was increased and hourly wages brought them enough money to set aside funds to send their kids to college. These were fair-wage jobs of a hardworking middle class not to be discarded for third-world cheap-sweatshop child labor. Today, retail workers in REI and Eddie Bauer stores don't earn much more than those factory workers did in the '70s and '80s.

The science of separating raw down from feathers and waste (such as feet) was married to the art of engineering machines that measured its loft and floated it through a machine to create a final product for the factory where the garments and sleeping bags were made. The engineering required to regulate the air flow carrying the down, as well as the tubes with controlled openings, was designed and kept secret in the factories of each outdoor clothing company that made down outerwear and skiwear. The science became an art, and the technology was better kept private than shared through patents.

How this technology went offshore involved a series of moves based on companies' owners aging and their kids not wanting to work as hard as their parents did when it came to labor relations and responsibility for workers. While this is true of the many outdoor companies that made knockoffs of original Eddie Bauer and REI products, the reality is that after Eddie Bauer and REI shifted to offshore, an REI mega outdoor store chained up across America, with retail stores and a burst of branded Eddie Bauer sportswear appeared in Eddie Bauer retail stores. The easy offshore way to outerwear and sportswear, using both synthetic and natural fibers, has became wildly profitable and requires a different level of workforce and pay than does producing products here in America.

Outdoor Pioneers

The technology created by the minds and hands of American explorers such as Jim Whittaker and outdoorsman Eddie Bauer, using college-educated engineers and "tiresome" factory workers is now simply called offshore production by the corporate suits that make today's brands of down clothing and sleeping bags—North Face and Sierra Designs, for example. And yet, both those brands were not created in offshore factories at all. Both came out of a retail environment in Berkeley, California, where college-educated folks could enter the world of business and aspire to owning and running their own company, just as Eddie Bauer did. Berkeley was, of course, the home of the University of California hippies and flower generation, and its crosstown rival, Stanford, was inking higher marks for those who wanted a degree suited up in bachelor's of science and master's of business degrees.

Being allowed to visit both North Face and Sierra Designs in the mid-1970s and talk with the company founders, Happ and George, was a very important part of building my own confidence in the idea that you can make something here in America, get it to market, and make very good money doing it. The Berkeley crowd was not a generations-old family like Pendleton, nor was it part of the "patented quilts" life of Eddie Bauer. The faster-paced department store and chain store retailing of the bigger brands such as Pacific Trail, Far West, Black, and Sunset gave the Northwest a nationwide reputation for producing the best-quality general down and polyester outerwear in America. Before North Face could afford the marketing funds to say how good they are and to "never stop exploring," their authentic tents, down sleeping bags, and down outerwear were used worldwide by serious outdoor climbers and hikers. Sierra Designs, credited with starting it all from a retail store, took the "hook and bullets" out of Eddie Bauer down and followed its namesake Sierra mountains for serious outdoor recreationists committed to protecting nature, while being outdoors long enough to enjoy it and return safely. Tent designs became more scientific than cabin designs to allow their users to survive in the woods in extreme weather and winds. George, Paul, and Mark led the way in Berkeley, while up north in Seattle, the Jan Sport minds created equally designed wonders that would not blow off a mountain.

With this design mentality for tents and the science for blowing down, just how did I ever get polyester fibers into sleeping bags and quilted jackets? The magic of polyester is that the fiber itself does not absorb moisture; thus, it never gets wet and does not collapse and lose its warmth and loft to moisture.

Polyester Fiberfill

Fibers made of polyester followed wool and cotton fibers into layers called batting, and then more directly, into fiberfill. Here is an overview of the manufacturing process that uses polyester fiberfill: In the process called carding and garneting, The design of crimps in polyester fibers tried to copy the shapes of down, and finishes were added to increase softness. Hollow polyester fiber technology modeled the hollow fur of the caribou to provide more warmth with less weight. Down-blowing engineering gave way to the mechanical wonders of polyester fiberfill, which was added to a multineedle quilting machine used to make anything from a quilt design on a bathrobe to the famous quilt-channeled down outerwear and sleeping bags. Fabrics were fed into the quilting bar and covered both sides of the fiberfill, making a sandwich with the fiberfill as the meat in the middle. Once removed from the quilting machine, the fabric, now with fiberfill in the middle, was spread out on a cutting table, where designed pieces were cut, bundled, and carried to the sewing floor—usually in large carts with canvas sides. There they were assembled and given the signature made-in-America union label, as well as the company brand itself.

Every outerwear maker, whether they used wool or down, found a reason to add polyester fiberfill to their outerwear and sleeping bags—except Eddie Bauer, REI, and Pendleton. For me at age twenty-nine, my destiny was to move from New York City to Seattle and become part of the pioneering of polyester fiberfill in the land where it mattered most: a land connected to the outdoors, not just a place to stay warm in the winter like the East Coast and Midwest. But before that move, I spent years building polyester fiberfill into skiwear before the hard-core down-fabric makers in Berkeley, Colorado, and Seattle were ready to switch authentic outdoor clothing and sleeping bags away from down.

Skiwear and quilting became the target of choice for my polyester fiber-fill from the mid-'60s until I moved to Seattle in 1973. Skiwear was pushing technology ever faster as metal skis and quick-release bindings entered the market. The ski slopes added high-speed chair lifts, and steeper terrains made skiing more exciting and challenging. A boom followed in the early 1970s. Down was simply too expensive and quite honestly too warm to be used now that you could ski faster and do more runs using chair lifts. Fiberfill required less and less quilting and became increasingly thinner to meet the needs of skiers who wanted more freedom and less sweat. Sewing holes in fabrics creates cold spots; thus the less sewing (quilting), the more warmth and comfort.

I saw the opportunity to sell fiberfill directly to skiwear makers rather than to a processor who made the fiberfill. But selling the finished fiberfill product while working for the second-largest polyester fiber manufacturer in the world was not a practical thing to do. I was viewed as a mill, rather than as a fiber maker. Simply put, fiber makers sell fiber to mills or yarn spinners but not directly to finished-product makers such as those that make apparel and bedding. Thus I was expected to sell fibers to mills that made fiberfill and not to their customers. I quickly learned that I did not have a fiber of the same quality as DuPont or Eastman Chemical (Kodak). What I did have was a patent on a fiber technology that used long fibers, called filaments, rather than short fibers, called staple fibers. The challenge was this: would my boss be able to get the research-and-development money to develop an improved staple fiber for fiberfill, or would he decide that we should work on the filament-fiber patent and bring out a new fiberfill technology?

A decision was made that the only way to get into the polyester fiberfill products for bedding, pillows, and mattress pads was to use the patented filament fibers and technology. We simply did not have the fiber machines available to match the DuPont fiberfill fibers, which were a special coil crimp called Dacron 88. Thus polyester was, for the first time, going to create a fabric called fiberfill using only filament fiber. No carding fibers, no sliver, no spinning. The long length called filament was the finished fiber. It was miles long and hundreds of thousands of fibers across what was called a tow band—uncut fiber until you reach the last inch in the bale ready for shipping and processing.

Instead of keeping the patented filament-fiberfill machines in our fiber factory at Celanese in North Carolina, my boss put deals together with pillow makers around the country to install the patented machines and pay them to process the filament fibers into pillows. Then the decision was made that we would sell the pillows to retailers ourselves as Celanese pillows and keep the pillow makers as processors, not finished-product makers. This decision troubled the rest of the fiber business in Celanese and its loyal mill customers. Those customers worried that the long-range plans would result in more direct making and selling to retailers of the new patented filament polyester fibers. Pressure mounted yearly until finally the pillow business was turned over to the pillow makers. They were given a license to use the required Celanese brand of Serene™ for the pillows. When the Celanese fiberfill pillow (Serene) division sell-off came in the early 1970s my boss, Claude, bought out the Northwest's facility and moved to Seattle. I followed him to run the sales of fiberfill and quilting, while he did the pillows himself. At that time, Polarguard patented fiberfill was widely respected and was used exclusively by the military for sleeping bags. Polarguard would go on to be the first fiberfill made of polyester to be used by the "no, we do not want polyester" makers, such as North Face and Sierra Designs. The prefix "Polar" would find a second coming among these authentic outdoor makers when I cocreated Polarfleece in the early 1980s.

The years from 1973, when I moved to Seattle, until the early 1980s saw the boom and bust of made-in-America outerwear, skiwear, and sleeping bags. In 1973 when I was twenty-nine, the world was my oyster in polyester fibers; ten years later I was fighting for my life to keep making polyester in outerwear in America. But in 1973, the no-quilting thing found more to get involved in than Polarguard filament fiberfill and quilted polyester fiberfill.

J. P. Stevens, also a big manufacturer of fiberfill, among their many other knit and woven fabrics, created a fiberfill that was punched into Remay™ nonwoven scrim in yet another attempt to get out of quilting down for skiwear. Known as Polyslim™, it was so popular that every skiwear maker in America and Europe used it. When DuPont released Mylar from its military-use-only restriction, J.P. Stevens added this reflective material layer to the needle punching and a space-age vision for the future. It gave us in Seattle a golden opportunity to make this kind of fiberfill to assure us lots of business as soon as we had the technology working in Seattle. We found an old woolen needle loom and after many trials believed the mylar space thing was really only meaningful where there is no atmosphere. However, the polyester fiber including the hollow core construction once needle punched into the non woven substrate remay soon brought in millions of yards of fiberfill sales for myself and JenCelLite.

The most respected skiwear maker at that time was White Stag, based in Portland, Oregon. White Stag was one of the first companies to make skiwear in America. In 1913, while Jantzen was creating bathing suits and rowing trunks, Harold Hirsch started a canvas-clothing company for loggers and mill workers, along with his partner Harry Weis. Hirsch means stag mule deer in German, and Weis means white. By 1929, White Stag was making skiwear in Portland. In the 1930s, it was one of the three skiwear makers in America, the other two being Slalom in New Hampshire and Sun Valley in Massachusetts. In 1941, the White Stag button-front ski suit was used as a workers' suit by Rosie the Riveter and the rest of the workers in the World War II shipyards and aircraft plants.

White Stag made gabardine ski suits and sweaters from Oregon wool using the gabardine fabric patent from Europe. Gabardine was respected for its warmth and durability, which was well proven after the Shackleton Expeditions of 1914–1916. In 1966, White Stag began using nylon fabric and polyester fiberfill for insulated skiwear. Shortly after Jim Whittaker reached the top of Mount Everest and down outerwear was sought worldwide for skiing, I began a longtime business with White Stag skiwear president, Peter. White Stag was a loyal and important customer even when its skiwear production was moved offshore. We exported the needle-punch fiberfill to Asia during the '70s for White Stag.

Time marched on and a new fiberfill Thinsulate™ was created by the giant 3M company. In the late 70's ' rolling out from 3M, the tape maker of America how fiberfill would move offshore to Asia. Thinsulate, heavily armed with millions of marketing dollars, anchored its technology to outdoor footwear and boots, and soon added that factory in Asia to support the business. Skiwear makers, already turning to Asian labor and fabrics, embraced the Thinsulate with open arms, and my needle-punched fiberfill was soon to be an ancient woolen mill board, no longer needed. I pushed on, trying to make fiberfill into a fabric and insulation, all in one material.

Fiberfill Turns to Fabric

Research into creating a fabric like fiberfill on the needle loom soon proved that polyester fibers, unlike wool used on the needle boards, did not lock tight enough to become a fabric like wool. I turned to the Malden Mills sweatshirt and baby bunting fabrics made of polyester and asked: why not have the fleece finish on both sides, like wool fabrics? It worked, but the needle board broke the knit stitches and the fabric fell apart. I was now ready to begin the original double-faced synthetic textile humor of being a "double-faced guy out to get you."

Malden was a powerful mill for product development and a leader in high-pile fabrics. But my lifeline of selling sweatshirt fabrics for Malden was being trashed by Nike setting up shop in Asia and skiwear going hot on the trail of Thinsulate. Was Asia going to win, or was I going to get Malden to finish the race to produce the first-ever double-faced polyester fabric that could be both insulation for a jacket lining and a warm, comfortable, washable sweater? Nobody gave me a chance to win, and the ski industry politely told me to get a job selling fiberfill or fabrics made in Asia; ski sweaters are made out of wool, period.

Today, writing this book of course gives me the chance to explain how I accomplished this feat and to reflect on the importance of Polarfleece being created against the will of the skiwear and outerwear makers in America. They had resolved their future to making their clothing offshore in Asia. This book gives readers the opportunity to learn about that change, and especially see how change that goes against the will of corporate business plans is not easy to do, but can be done successfully once you figure out how to make that change happen. In this case, the change involved developing a polyester fabric that would be a finished material, not an inner liner like fiberfill or Thinsulate insulation.

Bonding fabrics was a big deal at that time, so it was tempting to go that way and simply glue two fleece fabrics together. But I knew everyone could do that, and for sure, the movement to offshore would make it an easy one to knock off. Besides, if Polarfleece was going to be a fabric and an insulation in one, the technology required a double-faced fleece with natural loft and lots of breathing to prevent overheating. The marketplace was still loyal to down, and bonding was simply a method to stabilize thin sportswear fabrics to drape like wool.

The courage to take on the ski industry and my former customers—all powerful brands like Head, White Stag, and Roffe—was not an easy thing to do. Nor would it be easy to unseat 3M, one of the largest and most powerful marketing companies in America and the world. But I knew that the owner of Malden had the courage to do it, and he soon found a way to double-face the fleece being made on his bunting and sweatshirt machines. The fabric was soft and light in feel and looked very good dyed a gray heather like a sweatshirt.

This is where the perfect storm began for polyester in activewear. Nike rubber soles with waffle cleats. Now what to wear on top? Turn that wool sweater into a gray-heather fleece sweatshirt that looked woven but felt like a knit. Then double-face the fabric construction without quilting or needle punching. Take the warmth-without-weight of down and fiberfill and the fleece of sheep to a technology of its own. You get Polarfleece. It started in gray heather, then expanded to charcoal heather when that color became fashionable, and finally, as any classic fashion does, wound up in black. Printed in a buffalo plaid, too, it was simply called Polarfleece.

Polypro & Fiber Pile

Performance was the key to outerwear and the silver lining (pun intended) came from a Norway outdoor-clothing maker by the name of Helly Hansen. Polarfleece required no technical testing. It just one-bettered the legend from Norway in look, feel, and comfort. Moving production to America, into a commercial building in Redmond, Washington, before Microsoft was founded,

Helly Hansen began knitting their famous Lifa™ polypro underwear for sales to skiwear and outdoor retailers in America. The fibers for polypro were dyed in Norway, so there was no need to build a dye house at the Redmond factory. This was a big plus at the time, given the demands from the EPA to reduce waste and eliminate pollution in water and air emissions.

Added to that product line was the fisherman's pile-knit sweaters called Fiber Pile™, also fiber-dyed in Norway. While Lifa underwear impressed skiwear retailers, the fisherman's pile better suited Eddie Bauer and REI. I quickly connected the Fiber Pile sweaters to my polyester double-faced Polarfleece, and REI agreed to try it out. Malden was in full compliance with EPA regulations, especially in the dye house that added color to Polarfleece fabrics. Skiwear folks politely told me no skier would ever wear a sweater made of fiber pile or polyester fleece instead of a high-fashion, color-coordinated wool sweater. Wool, too, was fiber-dyed, and the EPA regulations that encouraged waste reduction resulted in wool saving the costs of energy and water associated with fabric-dyeing synthetics like the polyester in Polarfleece.

At that time, the environmental issues were not part of marketing; only performance was brought to the consumer's attention. Helly Hansen and I indirectly teamed up. Gordon, the Helly Hansen president, kept a close eye on my Polarfleece as it helped his Lifa underwear sales in what was being called a layering system to keep you dry and warm with very little weight. I set my sights on trying to win Helly over to my double-sided fleece. But Helly made the Fiber Pile fabric and sweaters in their own mill in Norway and did not want to add an outsider's fabric to the mix. Because Malden was afraid to enter the business as a garment maker and wanted to stay focused on making fabrics, my only hope was to sell the double-sided polyester as a Polarfleece fabric.

Looking back, this decision was clearly a mistake. Since the fabric Polarfleece was the entire garment, Malden should have followed the Helly Hansen example and made and sold Polarfleece garments. Today Helly Hansen has retail stores across America in malls, proving that Polarfleece should have moved into garment-making to keep out the knockoffs from offshore, including the brands we sold fabric to.

The Consumer is the Real Employer of Labor

Reviewing a hundred-year-old story about wool in Oregon clarifies this point. In the minutes of the March 1913 annual meeting of the Manufacturing Association of Portland, Oregon, we find the following words:

"Mr. and Mrs. Consumer did you ever stop to think that you have it in your power to change any conditions that you do not agree with? Did it ever run through your mind that the consumer is the real employer of labor? And whatever kind of goods you demand, whether it be Oregon made goods, made in clean, healthy workrooms, or goods made in sweatshops of the thickly populated East? I say again that whatever kind of goods you demand the storekeeper will very soon supply you with. If he finds that you are leaving his store because he has not the goods you need, he will soon find out and get what you demand, so it is up to you. Don't blame anyone else because possibly yourself or some of your friends are out of employment, on account of most of the goods on the shelves in our stores being manufactured thousands of miles away and leaving our own factory with little or nothing to do. You must remember that we consumers buy these sweatshop goods because we think they are cheaper. The store keeper sells them because we demand them, and he also makes more profit. What is hidden as greed is really success because we get dollars for it".

Simply making a chart today, with one side for "made in America" and the other side for "made in China," as was done at that 1913 meeting, when the two sides were "Oregon" and the "East Coast," the list goes like this: Money for raw materials goes where the fibers are. Money stays here in America, or it goes to China. The same is true for making the yarn and fabric, as well as the item of apparel or gear; the money for power and lights, mills' profits, retailers' profits, and so on, all remains the USA, or all stays in China except for the retailer. Following the 1913 example, look at one outerwear jacket with a revenue of well over $100 (vs. $25 in 1913). Pick a total amount, say a million jackets. Add the revenue amounts from the "made in America" side vs. "made in China." Look at the figures really hard. See that only one company in America is making the money if the product gets made in China, only one company is employing workers in America, and there are no monies coming in for raw materials—fiber, yarns, and fabric—for power, and for profits from items not made here.

The apparel was all made here for more than one hundred years, and everyone from owners and executives to laborers made a good wage with benefits. They bought homes and sent their kids to school and on to higher educations and training. Simply called the middle class, it is exactly what a country like China once hated and now flirts with to take away the jobs and homes of American citizens. Ask yourself what you can do to change these conditions and return to home-made goods, to stand up and begin manufacturing in America, using the EPA as the foundation of health and wealth for us and the planet.

If manufacturing is not brought back to America, the only money not sent to China will be the profits of the brands and the retailers. Retail jobs are not growing, and the offshore brands are not hiring more people to offset the high unemployment. Manufacturing was the foundation of the health and wealth of America and those missing businesses reflect exactly what has happened to the middle class of America: our unemployment stays at 9 percent for several years, while China's economic growth stays at 9 percent a year. Do you get it? It's not the banks, it is us who are doing ourselves in. As of 2010, the value of China's textile exports totaled $200 billion a year—that's $200,000,000,000. Look at the zeros in this number. Inside each one is a textile business, from chemicals, to fiber and yarn, to weaving and knitting, dyeing and finishing, and finally to cutting and sewing.

Today as I write this book, the jobs, products, and processes to make fiber and yarns and fabric are all gone. The need to move them offshore did not result from shoddy materials or poor quality workmanship by American labor. It came from the greed that we now call profits in a new form of capitalism, which, in the reverse of the Robin Hood story, takes from the people and gives only to the rich. Explaining who created the materials and technology for outerwear and activewear shows that those controlling it today never did the development or manufacturing or inventing of the fibers, yarns, and fabrics.

One focus of this book is to teach and predict the future of textiles, especially for new technology to be started with fibers and sold by the fiber maker and/or yarn maker as a finished product to the retailer and consumer. Wool was obviously handled that way, with mills such as Pendleton buying wool fibers, processing them into yarns for woolens, and making clothing and blankets. The business was so big in America a mere hundred years ago that wool was second only to steel in revenues for the entire U.S. economy.

Today, countries such as Australia and New Zealand rely on wool fibers and wool products to keep their economies profitable. At this time, we are seeing a return to wool outerwear, especially in base layers and underwear, with fine micron merino wool, super-washed to control shrinkage and give it a soft, comfortable skin appeal. This technology was not there to help the wool clothing and outerwear makers when synthetics got started in the 1960s. Their wool growers are partnered with the finished product, as shown by the successful products made under the Ice Breaker™ and Smartwool™ brands.

REI Chains up to Synthetics

REI in the late '70s brought in a former chain store Sears vice president to be REI's new president. His knowledge from being at Sears taught him to build REI into a much bigger retail and mail-order business. Savvy about what plastics and synthetic fibers had done for Sears and their outerwear and camping products, he opened the door to plastics at REI. In came my locally made fiberfill from JenCelLite in hollow-fiber polyester and patented Polarguard. The Berkeley outdoor gang got the word, as did folks like Jan Sport. From the Helly Hansen "layers," more pile was requested and Patagonia brought it to them. REI put in my new Polarfleece and then wanted a brand to sell alongside it, just as they did the Helly Hansen pile. Patagonia had the inside track to the brand to sell REI Polarfleece. Their baby bunting fleece fabric, called Patagonia bunting outerwear, became impossible to keep in stock. It was the same as my Polarfleece, just a different brand name. Three years later, in 1985, Patagonia, my best customer, was trying to slow its growth to 35 percent a year and not lose retailers like REI.

Polarfleece Saves Malden Mills

Malden was then in its first bankruptcy (1980s), and only Polarfleece, mainly sold as bunting by Patagonia, saved the apparel machines from being forever shut down at the mill. Pile machines were scrapped to Asia. A simple meeting with myself and Malden's owner, Aaron, nicknamed the Silver Fox by his mill workers, saved the apparel division. Safe workers' jobs allowed Polarfleece to become one of the most respected fabrics in the world. This was the first of two efforts to save the mill and its workers. The second came after a devastating fire in 1995.

Today and for the past ten years, the guts to keep making a new fabric like Polarfleece against the tsunami of offshore textiles now begs a simple question: why are we trusting all our textile manufacturing to foreign mills and governments? Some $200 billion comes from China alone. Sold at retail to you and I, it totals close to $1 trillion that America gave up to China with its slave labor and outrageous pollution of their water and our air.

It wasn't easy for brands wanting Polarfleece to get started and find the funds to build the fleece clothing. When Patagonia lacked the money to buy all the fabric demanded for their bunting (Polarfleece), the REI sewing factory THAW agreed to buy my Polarfleece and sew up all the Patagonia orders, including for some of REI's biggest retail competitors such as L. L. Bean and EMS. Yes, it's true, the REI-branded Polarfleece and Patagonia bunting fleece were both made in the same factory. In fact, they were exactly the same fabric, all bought from myself and Malden. Back then that seemed strange, but as the

Asian outerwear/activewear industry grew, the brands all began to share factories—and do to this day. So here we have an example of a retailer, REI, owning its own factory to make its brand of clothing and making another company's brands, as well. That factory was built to make only down sleeping bags and outerwear. It added the Gore-Tex seam-sealed machines once Gores waterproof membrane was established, and the history of Gore-Tex began a ride alongside Polarfleece.

Back in Portland, the Pendleton folks looked on but did not stray from wool. Polarfleece, while created from my knowledge of fiberfill and the warmth technology of down, was really a man-made copy of the famous woolens of Europe (fulled fabrics) and Pendleton woolens in America. As skiwear manufacturing ran away to Asia and Nike demanded to make activewear offshore, my Polarfleece was staying in America.

Offshoring vs Old Growth

Today, textile clothing and footwear companies such as Nike, Columbia, North Face, and Patagonia keep profits up by manufacturing offshore. Nike does $19 billion, or 10 percent of China's total exports of textiles, using, but not owning, a reported 330 factories in China. Loyal employees in America are facing tough times, losing so much equity in their homes that they're faced with deciding on short sales before the more difficult evil of foreclosure. More to the point, their neighbors are losing the jobs that used to make things in America, adding to the foreclosures; they are caught in the same trap of no more equity in their house while being forced to pay the mortgage that's higher than the value of the home. So how do they, as the 1913 speaker said in Portland, demand from their retailers that items be made here in America? Is that what really needs to be done?

Credit for keeping jobs in America in the late 1970s goes to REI and the stable of brands they ran through the aisles of their co-op retailing store, made of thick old timbers and with the smell of workers' hands. Climbing the wide, planked wooden stairs of that REI store reminded me of the stairs and walls of the textile mills back East that supported the brands and products we have reviewed in this chapter. Outdoor photos taken by co-op members lined the walls as I climbed from one level to another in the three-story building. The building sat among many old buildings across the top of Capitol Hill, one of Seattle's oldest neighborhoods. The hill itself was logged by early settlers who got their money for the trees and left stumps that had to be blasted by hand, rather than dug out. Decades later, those timbers built the buildings like the one REI settled in; a block away, our JenCelLite factory made fiberfill and quilting.

Change happens when growth occurs, and REI left that heritage of old-growth framework and co op members-only for a glass-inspired climbing window along the downtown Seattle I-5 interstate at the bottom of Capitol Hill. Pollution and noise cut deep into the quiet of Capitol Hill when the interstate was built around the time of the 1960's Worlds Fair in Seattle. REI being engulfed in constant freeway pollution seems to reflect the pollution from the factories that supply them from across the Pacific Ocean. Will the emissions from interstate traffic and the water pollution from made in China textiles that cover the REI store in layers of clothing turn out to be a "polar pollution" alert to the health of their customers?

Shortly after REI's most famous founder and president Jim Whittaker resigned, Big Jim, as he is called, started a business called Because It's There, in a six-story walk-up to the factory; the elevator was only for freight, shipments out, and materials in. When his products were knocked off by offshore textiles, Jim got out before the venture took too much from him; he began a life of devotion to the environment and wrote a great book about it. His second summit climb to Everest, in 1990, was the Peace Climb, but for Jim it was also a chance to clean up the garbage left from all the climbing being done on his favorite mountain.

Now in 2011, from those highest ice packs on earth, water flowing through Asia's rivers seems destined to become dyed in the fashion colors of those running the aisles of REI retail stores. The young offshore laborers that make

REI's private-label goods are no longer protected in REI's own factory or those of its suppliers. While the males in China, born one to a family, are allowed to advance, get educated, and breed, many of the females are sent off until they are old enough to sew for REI, at disputed ages and origins that include slavery from birth. REI is not alone. REI simply fell into the "GAP" trying to get off the mountain, and now uses the same sources for its manufacturing. Nike operates hundreds of such factories, while a nearby "mother" (Columbia) spreads it out over many countries, trying to be all things to all arms, legs, feet, and hands. Meanwhile, retail seems to be in complete denial about things such as best practices being offered to dye houses around their locations. GPS may not show the color of polluted rivers, but a satellite photo from space clearly shows very dark water next to the dye houses of China hiding "bugaboos" in the water.

Meanwhile the air atop Mount Bachelor, Oregon's weather station, captures soot, dust, and chemicals swooshed across its face; its timberlands plead for less carbon. The acid rain searches for shields of healthy breathable air and water. The tiny Wall Street of nearby Bend, Oregon, twenty miles away, promises that the Sunriver Resort community where I tested the first recycled polyester outdoor fabric I created in 1993-94, has found a new way of blocking out the pollution from China. Kids wonder if the adults will hear the words "only you," as they get off the ski chair a top Mt. Bachelor next to the weather station.

Chapter Nine:

Outdoor Brands Change to Outdoor Suits

Polyester is the foundation of the present outdoor apparel and gear technology, followed closely by nylon fiber for the more rugged outer shells of travel bags and stormproof jackets, coats, and parkas. Let's inject a brand that really started it off.

Backpacking

Once again returning to Seattle and the land not far from Boeing, the brand Jan Sport conjures up my kids' school packs, my travel bag, and the durable framed pack for hiking and travel. Although this memoir goes further back to the Hirsch-Weis Manufacturing Company of Portland and its famous cotton canvas day packs for hiking, for now let's focus on Jan Sport.

Jan Sport was a new brand, not a carryover from older products of wool, cotton, or down. Murray and his wife, Jan, created the company when Murray, in his father's garage, took some Boeing metal framing and bent it into a frame for a backpack. Because the metal came from Boeing, it was super light. Jan Sport, more than any other brand, is the cornerstone of the movement of youth and hippies into the outdoors in a generation when nobody had to tell you to get off the couch and get outside. Before the word backpacking caught on, these people were called "pine-cone eaters." Getting stoned was not about ducking falling rocks on a climb, and Bro was a word of real friendship, as shown in photos of Jan Sport products. Today, Murray and Jan are not faced with wondering what to do with their fortune—it was taken long ago when others knocked off their famous backpacks in Asia.

Something also happened to the Berkeley gang of today's hottest brands. While the hippies protested the government, it was our government that allowed the offshore textile movement that shut down and forced out made-in-America products. Jan Sport was one of the first brands to be sold to a bigger corporation (K2) that moved production offshore. In small buildings at Payne Field, just north of Seattle, former military barracks and warehouses contained the Jan Sport factory, while across the runways, the mega buildings created 747s for Boeing. Without government protection to keep manufacturing here in America, corporations finally got them all. Missing is any accounting of why the fabrics produced offshore in Asia were done without the EPA regulations that were required and obeyed in America when the companies manufactured here. The Berkeley/Seattle college crowd stationed at REI inspired the movement of youth into outdoor-recreation products. It's ironic that the marketing minds in outdoor gear and clothing today are almost obsessed with trying to reach kids about getting outdoors, while hiding the horrific issues of pollution, including hundreds of thousands of premature deaths from pollution in China.

Jan Sport became America's book bag, from their college bookstore roots to every grade and high school in America. Both Jan Sport and North Face are now owned by VF Corporation, which trades publicly on Wall Street. Recently a very funny parody of North Face came out when a college student threw his hands up at the price of North Face clothing. His real godfather printed up sweatshirts and tee shirts with an upside-down knockoff of the North Face vertical climbing logo. Called South Butt, once the brand was listed to be registered, the suited-up corporate lawyers of VF filed a lawsuit against the student. Well the kid lives in Missouri, so the "show me" I'm wrong attitude might be more culture than youth. Now if this kind of thing had happened back in the '70s with a college kid attending a school near EMS or REI, what kind of person from Boston University or Harvard School of Law or at the University of Washington law school would have filed a lawsuit?

Let's bring this into today's world. Burn your backpack or tee shirt to protest the corporate suits that own Berkeley-founded North Face and Jan Sport.

Come on man, the stuff is made of oil-based fossil fuels, and it melts and burns enough to give you second- or third-degree burns. The EPA clearly points out that the words "environmentally friendly" do not match up to any products made from oil. So how smart is the present world of polyester compared to the '70s version of down and wool? Truth is, almost everything burns except wool. So take off those polyester running clothes and be sure to wear wool when flying. Wear anything but a polyester garment while sitting three-across in a packed 737 for six hours. The odor of polyester moisture management in outdoor tee shirts is still not ready for those kinds of close quarters.

Where am I going with this? I mean, really, I was the guy who told them to use polyester in outdoor fleece and fiberfill, right? Yes, I was, and at that time nobody was planting roadside bombs or hijacking planes to be used as fuel bombs for crashing into high-rise buildings. We were celebrating our freedom: come out from under the desk in school, no more siren drills; get outside; be happy and enjoy the freedom of our public lands, which our parents rationed over while the textile products of folks like Eddie Bauer comforted our dads and granddads in combat during World War II. The most alarming fact about youth today was reported on 60 Minutes. There are now 16 million homeless children in America. They line up at school-bus stops in front of motels, not their former homes. This is by far the most disgusting result of not making things here in America. Those kids shoulder the backpacks of the earlier times of hippies, like those who created Jan Sport and many other businesses in America using American workers and products.

Since 1975, I have carried my books, sample fabrics, and travel gear in two Cordura-nylon soft-shell bags made in Berkeley at North Face. Those bags carried the first yard of Polarfleece and every new fabric I sold after that, up to this day in 2011. Doug's bringing the blue bag was a sign it contained something to want.

The 1970's

The era of the '70s was founded on small outdoor makers such as Sierra Designs, North Face, Jan Sport, Gerry Outdoor, and hundreds more, all of which had a factory close by and a desk to sit at and write orders. Simply by getting up and walking fifty feet to the factory, you could check production, meet with quality control, review the shipping area, and meet with folks like me in R&D and purchasing meetings. Oh, did I say "small" outdoor makers? Yes the outdoor makers were just that: small, privately owned, and living their dream of having an education and a business of their own that allowed them to do what they loved the most—get outdoors and have fun. There was Richard, whose dad created Kelty packs, sharing an ocean-view factory with his partner, Rick, who made Sierra West tents, Gore-Tex jackets, and Polarfleece pullovers. The Pacific breezes in that famous Santa Barbara town inspired a big baggy short called Big Dogs. Muscle-sized thighs between Big Dogs designer Gibb and Patagonia baggie-shorts guys finally proved length and width does matter.

Years earlier, in 1975, I began driving a Volkswagen camper. With sandwiches and water loaded in my small on-board fridge, I was off to Berkeley to meet with North Face and Sierra Designs. Exhausted as I got off Interstate 80 after fifteen hours of driving, mostly on I-5 from Seattle, I crashed in the public area of the Berkeley Marina about two in the morning and slept in the van. That was 1975, and my own fiberfill and nylon-fabric era was just starting. A few years later, with a solid bank account from selling nylon fabrics and polyester fiberfill, my rented car was parked in the same marina, but this time I stayed at the waterfront Marriott with my own shower and warm bed. The debates over textile pollution were also settled at this time. EPA regulations were in full force to stop water and air pollution, especially in textile dye houses in America, coloring those baggies, tents, fleece, and Gore-Tex.

In 2009, I visited the North Face outlet store still in Berkeley. The factory is gone, and the newer office building is starting to age into the culture of Berkeley, with old and new small business and residential buildings mixed among the many blocks. A fresh breeze brings the saltwater bay air that still looks west into a foggy downtown San Francisco and the arches of the Golden Gate bridge. Berkeley is timeless, yet lonely without those companies and their factories making their outdoor gear and clothing. It's hard to imagine that in just thirty years, it's all different and North Face has reached almost $1 billion in sales. None of their products are made here in America in their own factory to ensure the quality and create jobs to invent better products. Catastrophic environmental issues caused by their offshore fabric suppliers' dye houses polluting the water is covered up by marketing chimes calling out for exploration. Imagine kayaking outside one of their suppliers' dye houses in colored water to match your soft shells and waterproof pants and jackets.

Sierra Designs, headquartered in Boulder, Colorado, and others from that Berkeley gang of the '70s are not to be found. The list of who is missing might make a good memorial wall never to be climbed. Names like Class 5, Trailwise, and Donner Mountain did not make the cut as the corporate suits bought up the Berkeley gang one brand at a time; the owners only dreamed a short sale would be an honorable ending. Boulder, Colorado, brands such as Gerry Outdoor, Alpine Designs, Aspen Skiwear, Camp Seven, Frostline Kits, and many others all built quality outdoor products using American-made, EPA-regulated materials, and called it quits rather than be a polluter and labor looter in Asia. Their only mistake was owning manufacturing that required adhering to America's labor and environmental laws. Yes, fair wages and medical benefits cost more than cheap labor in Asia. Obeying environmental laws for clean air and water also requires higher costs, compared with running textile factories in the don't-ask-don't-tell pollution world of Asia.

The Microsoft era changed the college minds shopping at EMS and REI, and the result was a new culture shopping those stores for more digital experiences, unaware that the water pollution in Asia was anchored in the electronic toys, as well as the clothing. Toxic chemicals are used to wipe the Apple screens in offshore production, giving a wake-up call to the old polishing-your-apple thinking.

One outdoor maker rooted to the environment never had a price on his head—YC at Patagonia. Openly revealing his footprint of corporate responsibility, he matched his dedication to building safe climbing gear to his clothing. At the time when Helly Hansen first shared polypro and Fiber Pile sweaters in

REI, this legend of Yosemite rock climbing, YC, was listening to two of his buddies' stories about outdoor clothing. One of the original North Face folks, Doug was a close climbing friend and mentor. The other buddy, Royal, was from up closer to Yosemite. He had found the designing talents of his wife to be enough to give her a place to work and make money and not be too far from Yosemite itself. Maybe we should call Royal Robbins and Patagonia the outer banks of the Berkeley Gang. Let's give in-town San Fran credits to Doug and his wife, Suzie, for building a business based on organic cotton and a real vision for sustainable business before it became a fashion tool for synthetics and fossil-fuel fibers. Called Esprit, it gave the Levi folks something to think about as they went through the Olympics and an outdoor-sports exploration of their own. After Doug sold his share of Esprit, in the early 1990s he moved to Chile. Instead of retiring, he followed the true grit of an entrepreneur and took his $125 million and bought his way into building the largest privately owned outdoor preserve in the world. Remaining ancient forests are almost three thousand years old. His goal of preserving 700,000 acres was completed and could be more by now. His Deep Ecology Foundation proves by his example that a private person can spend his wealth preserving nature where governments cannot or will not, and hopefully others will follow. His once-famous lime-colored organic tee shirts shimmer in the forest colors of a nonhuman area, which, he asserts, is equal to human area for mankind to preserve and protect.

The 1980's

The rest of the San Francisco bay area belonged to Levi Strauss. Teaching Levi about nylon fabrics and fiberfills and why Polarfleece was important found me doing an exchange thing from San Francisco across the bay to Berkeley with folks from North Face: sharing the testing and R&D at North Face with inventory management and other building skills from Levi. This ensured the right tech stuff for the Levi winter Olympics clothing from North Face minds, and North Face began to see a future beyond climbing walls.

For me, I saw the ten years of the 1980s as a stay-at-home, make-it-in-the-USA way of living. Oregon became my place to play outdoors, in the quiet recreation village of Sunriver, biking, hiking, golfing, fishing, and skiing, while Polarfleece became the best top to ever be worn over a pair of jeans. Then Nike went totally offshore and Columbia was following, so my time in Oregon was play, not business. Seattle broke down to the waves of Asia and imports, too.

Sometimes it is a small world after all, and while Patagonia began to contract-sew its Esprit-fashion-inspired colors of fleece around the Seattle area, one of the contractors showed the Patagonia baggy shorts to Union Bay Sportswear, thinking it was a cool idea for the famous Union Bay jeans designers to try and do. Turned out, the Patagonia fashion colors in bunting Polarfleece had more appeal, and before Levi could jean up the skiers' retail shops after the Olympics, Union Bay was selling Polarfleece in winter white and fashion colors to every department store in America. This move doubled all my fabric orders from the Berkeley gang and the outer banks of Patagonia on Ventura, California's, surfside. It took a few weeks before I could sleep without asking, why did this importer of jeans do it and Levi just thought about it? Getting to know the folks at Union Bay, especially the president, Steve, I saw firsthand the fashion challenge from the big-name designers they competed with. Seattle had founded a denim fashion movement on the waves of Brittania and Union Bay, and others jumped ship to create a town full of hot fashion jeans and brands. The bright red Union Bay still hangs out over its waterfront, named Lake Union, in downtown Seattle, along with its hard-working, very smart owners and employees.

Not far from where I picked up Pacific Trail's weekly orders of nylon fabrics, I enjoyed several aftershocks from the Union Bay Polarfleece run. That run also built the lifeline of the Polarfleece brand itself in more ways than one.

Polarfleece Goes to Court

When it became a household word from the racks of REI to the shelves of Macy's and sportswear retailers across America, a few famous importers tried to steal the brand identity with knockoff fleeces. These guys were also hard-nosed competitors of Union Bay jeans. Since they were all based in Seattle, the venue for the lawsuit was easy to work out with just one law firm in Seattle. Word of the pending lawsuit scattered the troops, but one remained strong and ready to fight: a jeans-maker named Normandy Rose. As the name implies, I was on my beach at Normandy in a battle that would etch Polarfleece into the brand-name hall of fame. It was business as usual at REI and with my Berkeley gang and Patagonia, making Polarfleece skiwear, outdoor wear, and whatever else America walked themselves and their favorite pets in. Polarfleece was everywhere.

For the first time in my life, my deposition was taken and I would be a key witness at the federal court trial for trademark infringement against Normandy Rose. Their books were full of Polarfleece invoices to retailers all across America, and local Seattle department stores were also guilty of putting up the signs saying Polarfleece on the imported racks of garments. Of course Normandy had no invoices from any sales from myself and Malden for Polarfleece fabrics. The trial was over as fast as it started, with the judge calling both sides into his chambers and telling Normandy lawyers it was going to get worse for them and asking both parties to try to find an agreeable settlement. Roughly $450,000 was agreed upon, and the issue of Polarfleece knockoffs, especially using cheaper fabrics and labor in Asia, was not going to rise up at that time or for many years to come.

I viewed the victory as a very big win for making things in America, and soon, unless it was real Polarfleece, the retailer and consumer did not want to buy it or wear it. The sales plan and marketing of the brand name were now on solid ground, and Malden quickly saw an end to the bankruptcy from the inventory of sweatshirt and pile fabrics. In less than four years, we began the climb that assured that making textiles in America was not over in 1984.

Retailers always have a way of getting back at you, and the fashion retailing of Polarfleece was just too risky for us and finally not worth doing anymore. Union Bay had sold close to $20 million in Polarfleece each year, and that was almost impossible to see ending as quickly as it started. As the saying goes, that's fashion folks, and my big "f" is function, more commonly called performance. For myself and Malden, we now had a good, strong brand name known to the consumer and respected by retailers as the only quality of double-faced polyester fleece that the public would buy. Printing was established for the fabric, copying classic wool plaids such as the buffalo check design; that technology was going to be the icon for sales in Europe and a big part of making the fabric stay important in America.

Pilling

Another issue surfaced, which turning out to be a blessing for moving forward. The softness of the polyester spun fibers began to break down into tiny pills of fiber after a year's wearing and repeated washings. This turned off the sportswear brands' fashion minds and most of the skiwear makers, as well. For the REI/Patagonia crowd that showed up on ski slopes with fleece tops and jeans, the function of the fabric—not getting wet and keeping them warm— did not lose out to the pilling. Levi Strauss created a Polarfleece-lined jean for the Olympics, and the high-end wool stretch ski pant now had a moment of fear to deal with during the Olympics. Patagonia saw sales leap by 1,000 percent (yes, one thousand percent), and the outdoor clothing fashion of Polarfleece ended the 3M Thinsulate insulation for outdoor apparel. Yet another confirmation that you could still win at making fabrics and clothing here in America.

At this time, the mid-1980s, the sales of most of the now-famous outdoor brands were in the millions, not hundreds of millions. The private folks who owned the companies were enjoying working at what they loved and getting outdoors, rather than sitting and sweating over quarterly profits and public reactions from Wall Street. Patagonia became a business-magazine role-model "anti-marketer," and retailers such as REI, L. L. Bean, and Lands End could not keep the Patagonia fleece on the racks long enough to get to an inventory. Every million in fabric sales I did grew four-fold into sales for brands like Patagonia and then another four-fold at retail in sales to the consumer. My $5 fabric sold to the consumer for $50, plus a jacket. Coming out of a recession in the '80s, the fleece was a winner for all involved.

Locking in Outdoor Retailers

The Berkeley gang was then a nationwide outdoor club, and I refused to allow Polarfleece into retail stores or apparel makers that would try to knock it off again in Asia. I drew a big line in the sand for REI, EMS, L. L. Bean, and thousands of specialty retailers, to protect America and thousands of workers in our mills, as well as retailers and our customers. At that time and even today, thirty years later, no fabric except denim had become so popular as the source of a piece of clothing by itself. Between 1980 and 1985, Polarfleece danced with denim in fashion with Union Bay, under the denim in Levi ski pants, and as the best comfort-and-warmth jacket for wearing outdoors, brand by brand, period.

By 1985, with sales secure and the marketplace happy with made-in-America fabric and sewing, it was time to build a new fabric, address the pilling, and find a lighter weight for skiwear. Malden had, for sure, become satisfied that money spent in development would keep the profits coming, and the fears of offshore knockoffs were not going to be realized. Just how was the middle class of America going to keep working, buying homes, raising their kids, funding college, and having enough for old age? Asking this in 1985 seemed foolish, but today the reality is more than upsetting. Staying focused on change back in 1985 is exactly what we did with Polarfleece.

Pilling was a definite issue to get rid of, as the offshore fabrics got closer and closer to a true double-faced finish. The issue of too much warmth for skiing and many other outdoor activities soon found us working hard to get out a new fabric and finally to the decision to make a system of fabrics.

The system of layering first appeared in that Helly Hansen plastic-fiber, seam-sealed sailing jacket and Fiber Pile sweater. Plastic was here to stay.

Polyester Tees up to Underwear

Polyester got a further credit, replacing most of the Lifa polypro-fiber thermal moisture-management underwear, also from the Helly Hansen playbook. The first-ever plastic-fiber-to-fabric-to-finished-garment marketing by Helly Hansen failed for them only because the technology of Gore-Tex and Polarfleece proved to be superior in performance, especially in washing. Polypro simply hates water, leaving it with body odors, and melts at very low temperatures. Polyester washes better and can survive home-dryer temperatures. Polypro's best use in this area was ropes for boating lines, and that hung (pun intended) the polypro fabrics and products.

Patagonia found a polyester fabric made in America that they called Capilene™, and the race to get retailers out of polypro was yet another checkered flag for Patagonia. My former Malden associate, Tony Mazzenga, started his Wickers™ company first competing with Lifa and then switched over to polyester and a fabric close to Capilene. Retailing being what it is, the big companies, such as REI and L. L. Bean, decided they wanted their own brand of polyester moisture-management underwear, and Wickers accepted what is called private-label business with both of them, which put up a red flag for Patagonia that they don't get it all. This polyester moisture-management trend easily found offshore sourcing, and Nike and the running guys were finally ready to win it all.

The field was pretty level in those days. Nike was more interested in the shoe business and running clothes, while Patagonia grew as big as most skiwear makers. Only YC's mind-set of not wanting Patagonia to bury the world in oil-based fibers until recycling and renewing was established kept the finish line in view for Nike to run ahead without a sustainable outcome assured. The Berkeley gang was still trying to be a serious group of authentic outdoor companies not interested in being too big, nor wanting to be taken over by outside investors. Levi's, after the Olympics and time on Wall Street, bought back their stock and returned to a very happy private life along their wharf by the Bay. They let go of skiwear, athletic sportswear, and just about everything but those jeans, which still could be counted at two-plus pair in most people's closets. Columbia seemed settled with Gore-Tex and Thinsulate camouflage clothing for hunting and fishing and finally had a bottom line that was solid black ink.

Nobody could see the changes coming from the Regan era, but for sure today, most folks have to ask: was it really worth it to get all that freedom of movement of manufacturing out of America? A handful of brands that closed domestic manufacturing to stay in business will for sure say yes. Why is it better to manufacture in China and other Asian countries when the economy of China is about to overtake America as number one?

The Emperor's Clothes

Maybe it is about the emperor's new clothes after all. There is an organization called the U.S. China Business Council (USCBC). In 2010, the top concern of this council was the availability of labor in China. They defined labor in terms of recruitment and retention. Businesses were reported to be watching two emerging issues: collective bargaining and government-set wages. China's government had clarified that collective bargaining for their workers was a key component of its plan to redistribute income and boost domestic consumption, and cities, including Shanghai, were releasing specific regulations to promote collective bargaining. While this is going on, the central government is considering a plan that would set guidelines for future wage increases. The provincial government announced double-digit increases to local minimum wages during the same time.

While commercial success remains very high for American textile companies sourcing from China, the growing trends of protectionism and policies that could curtail market access and fair competition are of major concern. A further breakout from the USCBC shows a model that is far above the simple make-it-in-China-because-it-is-cheaper. After labor, other concerns are administrative licensing and business approval, competition with state-owned enterprises, intellectual property rights, cost increases, transparency, protectionism risks in China, and standards and conformity assessment.

Just who is the emperor of the clothes and shoes? Is it the Nike-led setups that line China like a happy-hour bar crowd, or is it the China that controls corporations for the sake of its people? The $200 billion in exports of textiles seems to say that China is in control of textiles being offered in America. The American brands are just facebooks waiting to be owned by the Chinese social network. Those playing the game of monopoly-not-money of insider trading might want to check the board of chutes and ladders to see what is coming next. The Chinese government steps in and orders things for the people of China. That includes telling American corporations what the rules are and how they are to be obeyed, not getting tangled up in lobbying panic attacks on the Congress and president of the U.S. government.

If we remember what we learned in school about labor and government controls until the age of plastic, we seem to be seeing a repeat in China of the building of the middle class. At this time, China's middle class is bigger than the entire population of America. Thus, for the first time since the Industrial Revolution, China will soon have a larger stake in the world economy than America.. Before we throw in the towel and admit that the emperor (China) is going to take over the status lost by natural fibers to plastic, let's relive more of the lore of the outdoor. In so doing, hopefully the memories will sink in and bring about the courage to change what's happening and stop this horrific pollution and abuses of youth in China that is bringing about the collapse of manufacturing in textiles.

The 1990's

Back in the 1990s, the vision of doing things offshore was not supported by the economy that was created by dot-com and Microsoft technology. Wall Street counted that technology, not sweatshirts, tee shirt moisture-management clothing, and footwear. These years are best called outdoor suits as corporations started buying the popular outdoor brands to borrow a line from Woody, the former owner of the real SNEWS, the outdoor bible of product testing and reporting on what's hot and what's not for outdoor retailers and product makers. It took me awhile to get on Woody's good side as he watched how Polarfleece went from little authentic outdoor makers in the '80s to the expansion and investors in the '90s. Patagonia was too small to be in the big-time Vegas ski trade show in the early 1980s, and I was almost thrown out of the show for having Patagonia and North Face garments at my booth. Needless to say, I left the show a day early, which caused quite a stir, until a fashion show a year later in New York City found myself and Polarfleece invited to the upcoming shows no matter where they were hosted. The layering of Polarfleece and Gore-Tex was here to stay on ski slopes slowly and then a total white out on the North Face side of ski runs woke up everyone to "never stop exploring" the outdoors rain, snow or shine, winter or summer.

Sounds simple and "okay, what's next?" But before we do the corporate takeover results, the actual takeovers were more like selling stock short on Wall Street. Lined up in the best retail stores in America were very big designer-clothing brands featuring shops-within-a-shop retailing. Freeways began to generate outlet store malls with some of these brands, and a never-ending line of credit from your bank fueled the shop-till-you-drop world of consumer spending never seen anywhere in the world. Labor was cheap and easy to find in Asia and other third-world countries, and textiles supported more jobs for sewing than any other industry. This really brought about the downfall, sell-off, and trade-out of American made textile fibers, yarns, and fabrics to Asia, and an endless supply of shoes and clothing.

Polartec

One yarn/fiber was saved, and that yarn went into a new nonpilling Polarfleece fabric, which became the cornerstone of the next step: the Polartec system of fabrics. Exclusive to only Malden worldwide until the big fire of 1995, the dynasty of Polarfleece was etched into the rocks of outdoor trails, mountains, riverbeds, and climbing walls. The fabric, designed from a former Malden fabric called pile chinchilla, became known as Synchilla™ in Patagonia fleece and then Polartec™ in Malden Mills. Both brands were really the same Polarfleece fabrics.

When I found out the new nonpilling fabric was decided using the chinchilla pile finish, I was overjoyed. Years prior, in 1968, I had met for the first time my hero in outdoor clothing, Dick Bell, owner of Mighty-Mac. Malden shared with me that Dick had talked them into the chinchilla pile finish for his famous out-erwear. Plush pile was shiny and often looked like plastic because acrylic and polyester fibers shined with the heat finishing the pile face. The slight curl of chinchilla required a dull-finish fiber and that, according to Mr. Bell, made it took like a real chinchilla. Dick's advice to me was: make a fabric look and feel as close as possible to a natural fiber fabric, and it will last a very long time.

Dick Bell's famous outerwear company was based in Gloucester, Massachusetts. His family was among the first settlers in that area in the 1600s and had been making sailing clothing and outerwear for three hundred years. The white-bearded guy in the yellow sailing slicker with his white wool sweater showing is the Dick Bell icon. When I visited Dick and showed him my Polar-guard fiberfill around 1970, he gave me a coat with a pile lining that, he told me, was a chinchilla-looking fabric. He realized that the fiberfill quilting was new and lighter in weight, but, as he also showed me, he used cheaper fiberfill quilted in the sleeves to make it more comfortable to wear. At that time, Dick got into the skiwear business and used my Polarguard fiberfill for his jackets. The signature of Mighty-Mac was a T-bar on the zipper pull, which fit perfectly with the T-bar used on ski lifts.

My goal to take fiberfill and make a fabric, which started in JenCelLite on our woolen needle loom where we made our famous needle-punched fiberfill in the '70s, was now finally coming true with Dick's thinking in the late 1960s about the future of fiberfill. I had nothing to do with Malden's decision to use the chinchilla finish on the nonpilling fabric. I had everything to do with creating

Polarfleece and then there it was: Dick's vision still alive over three hundred years, from his family to his sharing with me.

Dick was a very loyal customer of Malden's and laughed out loud thinking about what I was going to do to their pile fabric business with my fiberfills back in the late '60s. When I was trying to get onboard with Malden during my move to Seattle in 1973, I used Dick as a reference to help get the job. They were not thinking of hiring in Seattle, but Dick told the Malden owner to hire me, simply because I was the guy who brought in the quilted fiberfill that killed pile liners at Malden and elsewhere. Laughing when he told me, Dick said, "I told him you owed him, Doug, and he should hire you and make you get it all back for him."

And so it was: a soft, lofty double-faced chinchilla-finished Polarfleece that did not pill. Nobody but Patagonia really cared about the double-faced fleece because of the pilling that made the fabric look like a wet, unhappy dog. Even North Face was afraid to risk another round of the fabric pilling because they were trying to get higher prices for their outerwear and the fleece was just too funky for them. Marmot, Moonstone, Sierra Designs, and all the others—skiwear makers included—were moving on, probably back to down, Thinsulate, and wool. If the new finish didn't work, I would literally miss the boat away from offshore mills, and nobody was going to throw me a lifeline.

Bitter about seeing everything move offshore, I approached Patagonia with caution and hope, showing them the new fabric. Kate and Cyndi, the real talent team at Patagonia, told me over lunch, with smiles like high-school giggles, that there was good news and bad news. Taking the bad news first, they told me they were canceling all their existing Polarfleece bunting fabric orders—200,000 yards valued at $1 million in sales. Laughing as I turned red with fear, they shared the good news: they wanted to replace it all with the new chinchilla-finished Polartec fleece we got from the mill. "It works, it doesn't pill and we love it," they said. The torch of outerwear was passed from Mighty-Mac and Dick Bell to YC and Patagonia. Dick was right: what I owed Malden was given back, and the events to come are what happens in your life when you simply let the universe guide you and follow the spirit that finds you.

Trying to keep my New York City roots out of sight on the beaches of California and Patagonia, 1985 through 1990 became the best time of my career. Patagonia feared me giving the new nonpilling fleece to Union Bay or others and was afraid Malden would give in to the Seventh Avenue designers now that the pilling problem had been solved. Knowing that the actual production could not get into the millions of yards for more than a year, I simply suggested that Patagonia write a letter asking for an exclusive. The letter worked for a worldwide exclusive, the sales doubled to about 500,000 yards, and Patagonia and Malden and myself were on the ride of our lives. As soon as the nonpilling Polartec™ fleece appeared in retail stores, it sold out; nobody wanted anything else. Yes there was still other business and other jackets and brands using Gore-Tex, Thinsulate, and whatever, but everyone knew the nonpilling fleece was going to become a denim-jean icon fabric and garment.

At that time, I really didn't pay attention to the offshore stuff or how good or bad others were doing. I, too, was an exclusive with just my one customer, Patagonia. Never again has a fabric become a true partner to a brand of clothing, simply because production moved offshore and the four-letter-word company from Oregon said they were going to get it all.

Buy Outs

The reality soon took its toll on the small outdoor companies; one after the other lost money to the point where they went out of business or were taken over by investor companies. From memory, I would say Sierra Designs and Kelty went first, then Jan Sport to K2 and finally VF Corporation. Sierra West became Big Dogs (not the same as Sierra Designs), and it too went to an investor. Wilderness Experience, owned by twins Greg and Jim, tried going public, but the stock never got above a dollar. Their timing was ten years too soon:

Gore-Tex, Polarfleece, and Cordura weren't important on Wall Street at that time.

Our "most interesting personality" award for being ahead of the curve goes by the name of Simon. Losing it all in his first round in Berkeley under the name Snow Lion, Simon returned to Berkeley a hungry tiger and bought up North Face from bankruptcy, added Marmot, which was also failing, and Moonstone. The outdoor brands became known as Simon and the Suits. Somebody should have made up a song, a movie should have followed, and I'm glad nobody wrote the book. REI became the modern Hudson Bay Trading Company, building brands of outdoor this-and-that into a Sharper Image for climbers and hikers and white-water rafters. While Simon and the Suits played with company brands, YC and Patagonia made a precisely engineered outfit for each outdoor recreation adventure. Nike turned pro, giving out millions to the best athletes in professional sports, and Columbia stood on the shores of the Willamette River in their hometown of Portland, Oregon, and never lost their favorite spot for shooting and fishing.

Patagonia catalogs were more widely read and followed than National Geographic, Field & Stream, and Ski Magazine. Today a coffee-table Patagonia photo book sells for $50. Photography came from the best in the world, and amateurs in faraway places showed villages where YC went to explore and find peace. Story has it that YC and his wife used the new Synchilla for a pillow while on some faraway adventure and washed it in unmentionable water before giving the final okay to put it into production. The story became a big success in a follow-up catalog.

Many Patagonia catalogs still fill my special files on developing the fleece. One of my favorites shows a riverbank with YC and several friends, including Doug from Esprit, when Patagonia was first getting into stand-up shorts and fleece was still to come. At that time, surfing and fishing were YC's real loves, and his passion to save the planet and protect nature soon turned his catalogs into masterpieces of wisdom and experience. His profits went to his passion, and even today Patagonia remains private.

Simon crashed under the pressure of trying to play one inventory and brand against the other. However, the brands went on, as did the key employees. North Face was picked up in its second bankruptcy by VF, which now has a stable full of outdoor-brand derby winners, including Jan Sport and Eagle Creek. VF ran away from its old-time competitor Warnaco as both of these icons of loungewear/intimate-apparel raced onto ski slopes. White Stag, owned by Warnaco, which was first on the slopes, gave way to VF and the North Face extreme way of skiing. White Stag now is a brand in name only, owned by Walmart.

Private investors' tens of millions and Nike/Columbia's billions set against a backdrop of REI's and L. L. Bean's billions in retailing all show that what was once a simple little industry of outdoor makers and climbers' co-ops has certainly reached a level valued second only to the dot-com economy for the most popular consumer spending. Remembering that only a hundred years earlier, the number two spot in our economy belonged to wool, what will the next hundred years look like? Especially when we now know the fossil fuels used to make the billions of outdoor recreation products will be exhausted. Is plastic going to run out after all?

Global Polarfleece

The global marketing of Polarfleece and the system of Polartec fabrics stands out as a milestone in textiles in modern history. The combination of Synchilla fleece, which began the next generation of Polarfleece as Polartec, allowed many companies—especially Patagonia and North Face—to become more profitable than any other outdoor brand in our history, both in America and around the globe.

Patagonia's exclusive rights to the nonpilling double-faced fleece lasted about eighteen months. It was REI that demanded and broke up the exclusive, wanting to have their own REI brand on the new nonpilling fleece. Hot on their heels were L. L. Bean and Lands End wanting the same thing.

Once the exclusive ended for Patagonia, Sue Chernak's printing designs on the new Polartec system of fabrics got a big push from a skiwear maker named Serac. Skiwear was ready to get back into fleece, but the weight had to become lighter, and fashion was demanding prints. Serac, a very high end skiwear maker, had started in Seattle in the '70s and moved to Sand Point, Idaho, for a better quality of life. That move helped a good friend and old Pacific Trail employee, Jim, work closely with me when he joined Serac after their move to Idaho. Jim knew the value of Polarfleece and how wrong Pacific Trail was to never get into that fabric.

To meet the demand for lighter weight, a special yarn was used to make the fabric one-third lighter than the Synchilla fleece, made during the exclusive with Patagonia. The yarn was then exclusive to Malden, which lasted until the fire ten years later in 1995.

Serac rocked the ski industry with the new Polartec prints, but the other skiwear brands watched instead of jumping in. Many of them were trying to sort out thirty years of making skiwear in their own factories and being faced with sending it offshore now. Offshore was a big fear, and the skiwear owners had aged to the point where it was better to retire, sell the buildings for a profit, and just let go. Seattle saw entire square blocks in the famous Pioneer Square do just that.

Legacies in Seattle

Today some of those brands' names can still be seen painted over the red bricks in the historic Seattle Pioneer Square landmark buildings. The most famous were companies such as Sportscaster, Tempco, Comfy, and Black. Sportscaster was started by Marvin Burke, a young man who was selling fruit and impressed Larry Mounger Sr. of Pacific Trail so much he offered Marvin a job. Marvin took the job, but quickly left and went out on his own. Marrying into a wealthy family, he turned to making skiwear fashions and was among the first to style nylon fabrics into down-insulated skiwear. He had bought up an entire square block in Pioneer Square by the time I met him in the late 1960s. That block today houses many retail stores on the main floor, and dot-com and other professionals on the upper floors. The basement, once home to his outlet store, is a secret passageway to the popular Seattle underground tour. Pioneer Square was the old part of Seattle that burned to the ground in the big fire of 1898. After the gold-rush years, companies that had supplied goods for miners traveling to the Yukon and Alaska stayed and started making and selling clothing, travel bags/packs tents, and sleeping bags. After the fire, Seattle rebuilt on top of the streets and buildings, and this underground is a movie set of real props that have been preserved for over a hundred years and is still open daily for tours to the public.

Marvin quietly kept the Sportscaster brand away from importers and suits. He didn't need the money and was too respectful of his workers and his own love of making his world-famous skiwear in Seattle and Wenatchee, Washington, to see it go offshore. Marvin was in many ways like Dick Bell, but he lacked the three-hundred-year heritage of making clothing in America that made Dick and Mighty-Mac so impressive.

Watching these brands not stay around when Polartec was taking off in the late 1980s was bittersweet and taught me a new kind of retailing known as private label.

Private Label Polarfleece

A few of the old companies followed into private label, keeping factories going in Seattle to make fleece for L. L. Bean, Lands End, and Eddie Bauer. One company that had been only a sewing contractor for many of the famous skiwear brands in Seattle and Colorado became bigger than ever: Cascade West Sportswear was known throughout the skiwear world as one of the best sewing shops in the world to have make your skiwear. From Roffe in Seattle to Sports Obermeyer in Aspen to custom one-piece ski suits for the best designers in the world, the family-owned Cascade West had a mom and two sons doing it all. Alma, Eric, and Charlie, who had had key jobs in Pacific Trail, were building fleece as fast as the fabric was made and shipped to Seattle from Malden's New England mill in Lawrence, Massachusetts.

This put Polarfleece into the very best hands for sewing, and Patagonia and L. L. Bean fought for the production time and sewers' hands. As the 1980s ended, with L. L. Bean, Lands End, Eddie Bauer, and REI all dealing directly with me, I was very secure with the fleece and the private-label and skiwear business. Patagonia was taking their clothing to the entire globe and building respect for nature through conservation and environmental stewardship that would change the mission of outdoor recreation products.

The Boom that Built Polar Pollution

As we hit 1990, the Berkeley gang of "Simon and the East Coast Investor Suits" in both backpacking and skiwear were still trying to get settled. Malden, on its own, took the new Polartec prints to Europe and created a made-in-the-USA footprint in European outdoor brands never seen by any American textile-fabric mill. They matched up the ageless tartan to a polyester print that washed and kept you warm and comfortable. I made a trip to the European Sports Expo in Munich and saw firsthand how big that market was and how determined the European brands were to not let Patagonia take over the marketplace. North Face did not have the funds to even try, as Simon was heading into North Face's second bankruptcy.

The lessons from the brands being lost and private-label growth in fleece were telling me it was time to move further into the market and start selling garments, not just fabric. However, Malden was doing too well and growing as fast as it could make a yard of fabric to think about this kind of movement into the marketplace. The company simply needed to go public with its brand strength and move into making garments both branded as Polarfleece and private label for the big retailers, but that was not going to happen. The industry was still small, nowhere near what it is today. The doors were wide open to stay, go out on my own and make fleece garments, or work for one of the companies I had helped for so many years.

As I counted the few textile mills left in America, the reality of all that off-shore production creating pollution that America declared unsafe and unhealthy drove me to want to put an end to the offshore polar pollution. At that time, in 1990, the outdoor textile business was a marketplace I believed would get behind a real environmental push to manufacture in America. Patagonia, REI, and North Face had created a Conservation Alliance to get things started for helping lands, water, and habitats. I pledged $10,000 to become its second member, not knowing if it was going to come out of my earnings or be a donation from Malden. Appointed to the board of directors, I saw the alliance mission statement entirely focused on raising enough money to create a helping grassroots nonprofit to protect waterways, lands, and habitats in America. It was not what we see today, which is an alliance of who can give the most money to protect our natural playground. This big-money thing was tried at a board meeting back in the beginning years, and my vote was the only one to not accept the big donation of at least $50,000. Finally this move was seen as a corporate marketing ploy using the alliance, and the board reversed its vote of eleven-to-one in favor of the ploy, to eleven-to-one against the member trying to use the alliance for publicity for his products.

The ongoing takeovers of outdoor brands continued to knock out the small-business legacy of people and their product ideas in favor of what, in my school days, was called a monopoly. I had no idea at that early alliance meeting that the companies creating and selling outdoor products would become large holding companies, possibly best described as distributors. I use the word distributors because these holding companies do not own or manufacture the processing to make their products. This was true of the skiwear industry that came before the gathering of outdoor companies.

For example, today the Jarden Corporation calls its ownership of outdoor brands and their products "outdoor solutions." Embedded in Jarden's holdings is Coleman. While I was growing up and for many years after that, Coleman was a product brand that clearly gave its customers the ability to be outside camping or just having fun with comfort and food storage. Fifty years ago, the popular Coleman gear and a Jeep were constant magazine promotions, showing Americans how to enjoy being outdoors. Jarden has acquired many more outdoor brands, including fishing-product brands Garcia, Berkeley, Penn, Fenwick, Mitchell, and Shakespeare; outdoor brands K2, Marker, Marmot, and Ex Officio roll out ski products and important outdoor apparel and gear; Stearns life vests; and such other brands as Stren, Trilene, Volki, Zoot, Rawlings, and

Aero. These are not Heinz foods or Proctor and Gamble personal items. These are products created by inventors who wanted to own a small business. Today, this holding company's profits and sales grow quickly as the global supply chain feeds outdoor solutions from the Asian factories that pollute, rather than obey the EPA regulations that the original owners and their products followed.

The more public the facts about production ignoring environmental concerns, the faster the supply chain rushes out products to the outdoor brands within this think-tank of a distributor. This, of course, challenges the other big corporations to build more and collect more brands as they fight over access to the supply chain in China, which, since 2006, keeps covering up the catastrophic results of building their economy as fast as possible.

Weeding out a few examples of when these brands used the EPA-controlled supply chain of textile materials, we find Coleman once buying tens of millions of yards of American-made fabrics, which were sewn in their factories into tents and sleeping bags. With high-technology nylon fabrics from Blank Textiles made in America, Stearns created one-of-a-kind flotation products in their own sewing factories and at contractors in America. Marmot was a small inventor of unique outdoor sleeping bags, tents, and the classic made-in-America-in-Colorado style of outdoor legends such as Gerry Outdoor and Alpine Designs. Marker and K2 moved from leather bindings and wooden skis to modern fiberglass and plastics, all made in ski-inspired areas of the Pacific Northwest and Utah. Rawlings was part of the great American pastime, baseball. Mitchell, Berkeley, and Garcia made the fishing rods and reels stuffed next to Coleman camping gear in that made-in-America Jeep.

Today Jarden might better explore and invent a way to end the catastrophic pollution used to produce their assortment of "outdoor solutions."

Chapter Ten:

Recycling

In 1990, I had just completed a very comfortable vacation home in Sunriver, Oregon, a private community of three thousand acres surrounded by national forests, rivers, and the famous Mount Bachelor ski area. The town of Bend was just ten miles away. Forty miles of paved bike trails and two great golf courses assured that I would stay healthy and outdoors while I sorted out what to do next to keep making textiles in America.

Keeping in mind the size of the industry then, with most companies in the tens of millions, and the tough financial challenges forcing all the brands to find investor money to keep going, I was not swayed into a fear of losing out (losing my seat at the table). I enjoyed the time off and began planning what to do next. It was time to bring in the recycled soda-bottle fiber, and I needed a mill that made its own yarn to do it. I knew that the volume of Polarfleece could now support a production line to make the finer denier fibers needed for fleece yarns and knitted fabrics. That is a critical part of creating anything totally new: the fiber production must be big enough to stay on the production line making the actual fiber needed.

I moved on to a mill that would make the double-faced fleece yarn and fabric in their own manufacturing mill. I did not disclose to them my plan for a new fleece fabric using recycled bottles for the fiber. My timing was good; a few close friends said that this Southern textile mill was trying to find a way into double-faced polyester fleece. Polarfleece was strong and for sure not going away. What troubled me was that most of my former customers were not doing well, and even North Face was rumored to be in trouble again. The best and safest business was still with L. L. Bean, REI, Patagonia, and Columbia. I knew if I did not get an exclusive on my new recycled-fabric plan, my old customers would have too much of a head start for me to compete against them. Of course at that time, in 1992, the bundling of brands by outside investors did not yet have the dot-com empire supplying the money. Travel was a big issue for me as I was tired of it.

My decision took me to Dyersburg Mills, the company that had made the first baby bunting and a mill that spun its own yarn. They had a good investment backer acquiring mills to get ready to go public. I knew if I could get Polarfleece going, those sales would be at a very good profit and would give me a shot at stock when the company went public—and finally a way out of Malden and what I had built there.

I set up the meeting at their New York City offices, and on the way took advantage of going to Portland to see my old associate, Don, then an owner in Columbia Sportswear. I knew I could sell him fleece for his sewing factory in Missouri because it was very close to Dyersburg's mill in Tennessee. Columbia had a big business going in fleece-lined zip-out jackets called bugaboos. The shells were made offshore and sent to the USA as rainwear; by adding the fleece liners in an American factory, Columbia avoided the 30 percent duty for outerwear, which was only half that for rainwear. My knowledge of fleece offered Columbia a good opportunity for better quality and a big savings in freight costs. I worked out a price bid from Don to bring to the Dyersburg meeting for $500,000 of fleece to start ordering as soon as Dyersburg got the fabric into production.

I felt really good getting on that flight and going to a job interview with a $500,000 order in my pocket to start things off. The interview went very well; the potential order shocked the vice president of Dyersburg—that I was that good at this fleece thing. Job in hand, salary plus expenses for a year, and a call to Don assured everyone the order would follow a sample that was okay. The feeling of selling was back in my body, and once again a true loyal friend from the days when we all enjoyed building the outdoor industry had made the deal work out. Decision time to get to the new recycled fleece required me getting the vice president of development at Dyersburg to respect me enough to tell him the development plan. Once the fabric finishing was set, I knew he could take the recycled fibers for my new fleece and make it work.

The new fleece technology involved using recycled plastic bottles—mostly soda bottles at that time. Polyester was the source of the bottles and films. Back in the early 1980s, I had done a consulting project with a waste company in New Jersey, Midland Processing, which was washing silver off x-ray films and found out that film was made from polyester. The company had a huge warehouse full of the films and no market for it. A process to shred the film and get it shaped into pellets was created, and then the pellets were melted and extruded into a new polyester fiber. Soda bottles were processed the same way and of course were a much bigger source of raw material.

A waste fiber company named Wellman Industries had begun making the recycled fibers for carpeting back in the 1980s. As things changed and more offshore textiles were produced, my old company, Celanese, had sold out to Wellman, and many of my former associates stayed on at Wellman. Wellman was a big supplier of polyester fibers to Dyersburg, so everything was easy to access to get a recycled fiber for the double-faced fleece yarn and fabric. It turned out that a former boss of mine at Celanese was now the president of Wellman, and he assured the development of the right-sized fiber to make the fleece yarn that would be spun at Dyersburg.

Fabric in hand, I had a small sewing shop in Sisters, Oregon, make up forty recycled fleece jackets and began testing them around Bend with skiers, bikers, and hikers. Later trade news stories talked about those testers in Bend working at local ski and camera shops wearing the recycled fleece until I was sure it was ready to present to the market. That turned out just fine, although folks were still trying to figure out what happened to the soda-bottle labels, and a few were concerned that the fabric would fizz if it got shook up. These jokes kept me going and were part of my show-and-tell at Patagonia when I presented them with an exclusive opportunity to bring out recycled fleece clothing and outerwear.

Patagonia declined the exclusive because they wanted every user of fleece to get into the recycled fabric and begin to move hundreds of millions of bottles out of the landfills. My goal of using the recycled technology to make my own fleece garments was lost. I had to begin to rebuild myself, selling only fabric, which was not going to be easy given the mess I had made bringing the recycled fiber yarn into what was at that time an exclusive yarn from DuPont for the Malden-made Polarfleece. I knew it was better to get out and make my own garments or work for one of my customers, but who to go to was difficult because very few in the early 1990s were making money.

Deciding to stay with Malden while things settled down and the survivors of outdoor clothing and gear made it to safety, I saw the real outsider-investing in these brands in the mid- to late-1990s. Malden was not happy with the recycled challenge, as most of the yarns for their fabrics could not at that time be made with recycled fibers; my passion to keep the recycling going was not appropriate. I was starting to feel many of my customers' owners did like the owner at North Face. Bill Simon saw his company go to VF for good. Others were bought out, and new management found folks making less income than me. Did I have to use only Malden fleece to stay in the industry?

The choice between selling fleece fabric and making and selling fleece garments that did not use Malden fabric was decided in early December 1995. That day started out with a big storm in Bend, and I drove over the Mount Hood pass in a near-whiteout to get to Portland for a meeting to begin working with yet another former Malden associate, David. He wanted me to market his micro-fiber pile fabrics by creating a marketing plan for the fabric and the microfibers it was made out of. David showed me a brochure from the Glenoit pile-fabric mill, which showed how pile fabric, including microfiber pile fabric, was made from acrylic fiber. In reviewing it, I quickly saw the difference between pile fabric and fleece fabric. Pile was made from fiber, not yarn, and fleece was made from brushing fibers out of yarn. That was enough to assure me I would not have any issues with my noncompete agreement regarding Polarfleece polyester fiber technology. The meeting ended with a warm hug and handshake about 5 p.m.

West Coast time. I finished the trip by driving up to Seattle to stay with my folks for a few weeks, including the holidays. After the New Year, I would take a trip back East to begin working with the microfiber pile.

Waking the next morning at my parents' house, I saw on the TV news that a mill in New England had burned to the ground the night before, at around 8 p.m. East Coast time. The name Malden Mills flashed across the screen, and the film showed the ice and frozen buildings—or, I should say, what was left of them.

The mill had been an accident waiting to happen, with decades of oil and chemicals soaked into the wooden floors and the brick-faced building covered in wood on the inside, with a century-old frame. Offices were in the middle of much of the manufacturing, including R&D, which was smack next to the dye machines and other dangerous equipment. I remembered being in the mill in 1994 and seeing the equipment a wall away from the executive offices and accounting and many other mill employees. Even the mill cafeteria had a wall adjoining the factory full of chemicals and machines.

Finally, by nightfall it was clear the mill had been wiped out and might not be working again for a very long time, if ever. (A photo and the AP story of the fire appear earlier in this book.) There it was a few weeks before Christmas, and Polarfleece and Polartec were out of business until further notice. The list of brands that had started to place orders for the next fall season was just coming in when fire destroyed the mill. Stores were full of hang-tagged Polarfleece and Polartec with brands from North Face to Polo and designers and outdoor icons in-between. The timing of the fire did not hurt retailing at that time, but it did throw the next season's orders into a tailspin that seemed to never end.

This proved to be the final blow to the saga of myself and Malden and the fleece that I had created. From 1996 to 2000, a new outdoor industry was born when all products were moved offshore: production of fibers, yarns, fabrics, and finished goods. Sewing machines were finally shut down in American factories. The legacy of those tired hands that worked piece-rate hours to save money for their kids to get a higher education was now putting that generation into a new employment marketplace. Even REI, a co-op answering only to its members, closed its THAW factory and shifted to offshore production for REI-brand products.

The THAW factory had been relocated a few years earlier to make way for the new Mariners baseball stadium. I joked about the move with my close friend, Jim, president of THAW, pointing out that the baseball field's home plate was right where the first Patagonia bunting fleece sewing was done years earlier. Bunting is, of course, part of playing baseball: when the hitter squares away facing the pitcher and puts his bat out across the plate to just drop a slow roll-ing ball, giving the runners on base a sure chance to advance to the next base. Jim and I together had bunted ourselves and REI and Patagonia away from off-shore production when Jim accepted production of Polarfleece for the bunting jackets that made Patagonia the money to build their dream of business for conservation and the planet. Chief Seattle stood not far from that THAW factory land when he gave up his land to America, saying we are webbed to the land in blood, and whatever we do to the land, we do to ourselves.

Nike's swooshing swing-away style, rather than bunt and respect manufac-turing in America, was the road that was followed. Nobody really missed the end of made-in-America textiles, as the Internet and computers and dot-coms would leave the government with the biggest surplus in the history of our coun-try. By the time we celebrated the start of a new century in 2000, the outdoor marketplace was establishing itself with wise investors and public stock offer-ings of Columbia bugaboos and Nike microfibers. Even more important, access to public lands for recreation was now being counted as an untapped source of money for the government. Outdoor recreation fought for access and did not confess to the pollution it was creating with offshore production—denying polar pollution one more time.

Would our public lands become the country's next theme park? Could the investors really hold together these brands that do not own any machines or the knowledge to run them? Is the fossil-fuel world of polyester really the doc-tor of marketing, as we were told in The Graduate movie? Or is it the wolf in sheep's clothing that will usher in global warming trying to keep itself dry and warm from a cold age that is melting?

Text Book Case of Polar Pollution

For sure, the brands of Nike, Patagonia, North Face, Columbia, and REI would become the next Harvard Business School textbook cases. Reaching into the billions of dollars, these brands defied any normal business growth curves in modern times. They have also covered up their part in creating global warming using the pollution and energy of Asia and the "we don't care attitude" of China, which is now telling them, to a brand, to borrow more, make more, and sell the brand to citizens of China. Just when will the limited natural resources of water, air, and fossil fuel find China saying, no more—we need it for our own one-billion-plus citizens? Instead of our government facing this reality in the new century, it gave up to corporations, while the outdoor corporations played a game of Marco Polo for more access to public lands for recreation and adventure.

Once again the present-day marketplace finds the head of the Chinese government playing ping-pong with America and our economy. Only this time, the tabletop is folded up so everything returns to China: we, China, make whatever you want; we, China, do not spend money for pollution control; we, China, do not obey or acknowledge EPA regulations to make textiles for American companies. After warming up, the volley gets faster. American brands are allowed to sell in China and build stores to offer their American-branded products. Timberland has 110 stores; North Face makes over $1 billion in sales to stay in China. Nike has been quiet after publicly sharing that its sales in China reached $2 billion. Then the head of China changes the color of his paddle and ball to the colors of China. He visits America, leaving his paddle covering the ball on the half-open table, assuring he is the only player in the game when he returns. He wants access to more Chinese-branded products in America's retail stores. His secret developers tucked away in Portland's Chinatown test from a storefront window and shop.

Here's a bit of irony to spice up this repeated allowing of China to take us over. Years ago, almost a hundred to be exact, Eddie Bauer was fascinated with feathers. He was also one of the best in America at stringing tennis and badminton rackets by hand. Trying to make the birdie fall faster and fly better, he put shotgun pellets in the tip and applied for an invention patent. That was the first of many that led him into patents for down outwear. He purchased down from Northern Europe, where the best quality was raised. In the 1970s, China drove him out with triple-cost down pricing and cheap knockoffs. Now with $200 billion in textile exports, the first China-made retailer of Nike shoes to open up in America offers the official badminton shoes, birdies, and rackets invented in America during the Eddie Bauer era, long before Nike. Is this just progress, or is it simply stealing, using female, mostly child, labor and allowing catastrophic pollution of water and air?

What appears to be the only recycling at this time is the grit of America following like sheep down the path of China to replace us and push us into a servant's quarters of investors. The outdoor-textile industry is organized under a trade association, Outdoor Industry Association (OIA), which counts recreation product dollars into over $700 billion and more than 6 million jobs. Putting a Wall Street-sized face on the average citizen's simple rights and pleasures to get outdoors in what is commonly called recreation. The uniform offered like a private school dress code.

Public Lands and Fees

Rights to freely access our public lands for over a century today are tangled into a fee demo program that is widely supported by the recreation product makers. The fee program was presented as a years test in 1997 to get funding for repairs and improvements on recreation lands managed by the U.S. Forest Service and Bureau of Land Management (BLM) during the biggest surplus our government has seen in our history. Lurking behind that public trust of operating these lands based on the publics taxes, corporations especially Disney began a marketing outline for recreation and access to the public lands.

Chapter Eleven:

Outdoor Conservation

The year 2000 marked a starting point for the outdoors, much like a hundred years before, in 1900, with that century's establishment of a foundation to preserve and protect the public lands of America as part of our natural heritage. The designation of public lands as wilderness, national parks, national forests, and blm lands took decades and the strong will of U.S. presidents to approve as law.

Maintaining the lands was the focus as we entered the 1950s. The July 1966 National Geographic featured almost the entire issue on Mission 66, a federal plan to preserve public lands. Reading the magazine while vacationing in Montana and visiting Yellowstone National Park in 1966, I was able to see the work and wonders created by Mission 66. President Eisenhower began the plan in 1956, and it was completed in 1966, surviving ten years of Congress and three presidents. Today it would be an impossible thing to do, given the two-party logger-heads that are causing far more pain and suffering than the real loggers who honored the Mission 66 plan after cries from the public to do so.

Paid for with citizens' taxes, without corporate interests and lobbying, the rebuilding of the public lands—especially national parks and forests—under Mission 66 created paved roads, comfortable modern hotels and cabins, and safe access to the scenic and natural wonders of the lands held in total protection from development for profit and consumption. The flora and fauna remained in their natural protected habitats during and after the construction was completed. Services were bid by private citizens, and facilities were owned and controlled by the federal government through leases, with specific ordinances for signage and number of locations. No McDonalds, Subways, and the like.

National parks featured lodging with old and new hotel-type lodges and also separate areas for camping and backpacking. Travel and camping by trailer or tent was encouraged and supported with clean, safe toilets and running water. Sites of interest had trails and man-made walkways to keep folks safe and protect the sites being visited. Improvements were made to areas like hot springs, paths along waterfalls, and more generous seating at Old Faithful. Roads were simple and two-lane. Some were cut through a giant tree, like the tunnel through a redwood tree. Fishing was allowed and controlled by permits, and regulations for catching and keeping had specific limits and times of months when fishing was allowed.

For me, a favorite activity was wading into Yellowstone Lake in my sneakers and jeans and casting a Mepps spinning lure to catch native cutthroat trout. The nearby Lake Lodge cooked my catch for our family dinner and was a hit among the many things we did during our visits to Yellowstone. In Yellowstone in early July, the weather was hot but could easily change to a thunderstorm or even a surprise day or two of freezing temperatures and snow. Of course this being 1966, my assortment of clothing and gear was limited to what I had with me and thought was important when I packed in New York before flying out to Montana. My college years in Montana had taught me to bring something warm for that summer vacation, and I was happy to have learned that lesson among my classes. My favorite was a cotton flannel, brushed-chamois shirt from L. L. Bean.

Years later, I got into that wonderful company with Polarfleece and recycled fleece, all made at my favorite sewing contractor's factory in Seattle after he moved on from offshore skiwear deserters. Before the mill fire, he made more than a million jackets a year in Polarfleece for L. L. Bean in just two styles, a shelled fleece and a snap tee. During REI founder Jim Whittaker's second summit climb of Mount Everest in 1990, it was L. L. Bean and its owner who supported the climb—not the co-op Jim founded.

The Mission 66 plan did not ask recreation corporations and their coalitions or entertainment corporations like Disney to get involved in trying to tell the federal land-management agencies what was right and wrong or, more importantly, what would be the recreations available on the public lands. The brands of outdoor recreation products in 1966, such as Coleman, were only concerned with proving their products were superior in comfort for camping, as the public accepted the new fibers of nylon and polyester. That was followed by backpacking gear from North Face and by Sierra Designs creating tents, sleeping bags, and backpacks using the new nylon fibers and down, while older companies such as Hirsch-Weis stayed with cotton canvas and wool.

Between the late '60s and 2000, these brands changed hands, and by 2000 they were owned by investors and/or public corporations. Their mind-set, following the corporate model of today's politics, was about how the federal government could assist in providing awareness and more access for their recreation products. They ignored waste in our landfills and pollution in offshore factories. The jumping-off point for the public in terms of meeting the corporation issue on public-land access got started when Congress passed a bill in 1996 allowing the USDA Forest Service and BLM to charge daily access fees to enter just about all public lands and doubling the fees to access national parks.

This issue was brought to an annual outdoor-industry event in Colorado Springs in the spring of 1997. I was there while I was building the marketing for microfiber pile fabrics to become the next thing in outdoor clothing; I had a strong desire to see the pile-fabric technology replace Polarfleece, which was no longer a part of my life. Not too much attention was paid to the presentation that explained how every citizen would be required to pay a daily fee of $5 to access what was, and had always been, free to access in national forests and BLM lands. Before the meetings ended, a key person in the Department of the Interior asked me to help get support for the fee-demo program from my customers and associates in the outdoor industry. It was a compliment to be asked to do that. I saw it as a great way to get myself back into a position of leadership, as I had done creating and selling Polarfleece. The challenge was to use the fee demo program as a tool to get the outdoor companies to support through some kind of tax the funding that was needed to complete the improvements and over due maintenance from the surges of visitors walking, hiking and camping and boating, especially rafting and kyaks with the modern day recreation products. One look into a Patagonia catalog was a testimony to the surge of users into public lands and the calling for protection to preserve the natural habitats, waters and lands themselves.

This opportunity became a very important step back into the heart of the out-door recreation marketplace. It was also really important for both the BLM and the USDA Forest Service to have support from the outdoor-recreation industry if the fee-demo plan was to work. I knew that by the year 2000, the fee plan would be a big part of whoever became the next president. That could eas-ily open doors for me in business and even a political appointment, I figured. I was given the chance of a lifetime when the BLM offered me a trip through their lands in Montana as part of a team of people chosen to help create the marketing of fees to improve citizens' experiences when visiting public lands. Traveling to Missoula, where I had gone to college, the trip began with a visit to an old ranch and a short horseback ride about eighty miles outside Missoula while on our way to the state capitol at Helena for a meeting with the governor of Montana. More traveling across the big-sky lands of Montana put me in Bill-ings for more meetings with the head of the BLM in Montana.

By the end of the four days, I knew I was a key part of a team that would plan the marketing of the fee-demo program over the next few years. That trip was followed by a conference in Sunriver, Oregon, where I lived, at which all the managers of BLM lands came to get further issues set up for fee demo and other important aspects of the lands they managed. The selection of Sunriver was pure luck for me, and I took advantage of it and invited the nearly twenty managers to dinner in my home in Sunriver. From that evening on, I realized I was the key person they were talking to and working with about outdoor products and outdoor recreation interests involving BLM lands.

Next came an invitation to the swearing-in of the next head of the BLM in D.C. During that visit, I was introduced to another leader of outdoor recreation, Derrick, who had organized a coalition of many big companies that produced outdoor products, including the Coleman Company. A dinner followed, at which an award in Sheldon Coleman's name was given to honor a member of Congress who had done something of great importance for outdoor recreation on public lands. I quickly put the pieces together. Derrick's coalition—the American Recreation Coalition (ARC)—was responsible for the fee-demo plan, and I was going to be asked to help carry it into the outdoor recreation group I was working in, which became known as the human-powered recreation group. Derrick's group consisted of old-time folks like Coleman and mostly motorized recreation, from ATVs to RVs and anything with a motor. Before I could decide what to do, there were two camps the BLM and U.S. Forest Service were trying to bring together: the motorized-recreation group and the human-powered group.

Being independent, I could get into this with Derrick as I read his letter asking me to join his coalition and offering me a chance to make money helping to sell fee-demo passes to key outdoor retailers such as REI and L. L. Bean. What had seemed easy was now going to take much searching for me to decide where I wanted to be in this fee-demo plan. Usually at ease doing difficult things from my years of selling polyester to folks who did not want to change to it from wool and down, now I was really being tested to rebuild and replace fleece after the big fire at Malden with a microfiber pile fabric. What troubled me most was learning more about grassroots conservation. I had been a founding member/director of the Conservation Alliance started by REI, Patagonia, and North Face to raise money to protect natural places. I saw the Coleman-inspired coalition run by Derrick as the old school, while the REI/Patagonia team was the new school and strongly aligned with folks like the Sierra Club.

Yet it seemed possible to be on both sides and do as I did with fleece, when I brought skiwear and backpacking into a single marketing plan. That old double-faced thing seemed a shoe I never lost and was always my rabbit's foot. Thinking I still had the floor of the outdoor industry as I did with double-faced Polarfleece, I began to present the fee-demo plan to my customers and associates. Immediately it was clear nobody wanted to take it seriously. They were more interested in funding public lands and recreation from the Clean Land and Water Conservation Fund. Millions of dollars from that fund had not been given by Congress for the recreation uses that would help create better access to recreation on public lands, from local to state and federal lands. The source of those funds was, and is, offshore drilling, and that trail of money was more black magic coming out of the bottle.

Derrick wanted an answer from me about what I was going to do to be part of fee-demo and I just did not think it through at that time. I should have given more thought to getting involved with him to be effective in the decisions. After all, I was a key person to the BLM and they wanted me to help on both sides, motorized and human-powered recreation. My mind raced on to the new microfiber pile and how that would fit into anything I did with these funding issues, which were a serious challenge to keeping public lands open and safe for recreation. Putting the decision off, I pondered the reasons to move back East to be hands-on with the microfiber pile marketing. Glenoit micropile and Concept III's sales office were based in New York City and close to Red Bank, New Jersey.

Living next to the Deschutes National Forest, a five-minute walk from my home in Sunriver, Oregon, and with easy access to the BLM lands in Bend ten miles away, I was able to see firsthand what was going on with visitors and recreation in both areas. During those walks, I thought about the future of these lands. I also thought about how was I going to complete the marketing of the new made-in-America microfiber pile fabrics and step back into the marketplace that I had lost to offshore and that Malden was losing to their horrible fire. I pictured the lands and the Deschutes River near my home as it was then, free of fee booths and collection sites. The Nature Center and underground lava tunnel were free to enter and learn from and enjoy. I understood the development of the ski lifts on Mount Bachelor, and even those now-private areas full of skiers did not always result in profits to keep going. Did it make sense that walking and biking and driving my Jeep on those dirt roads left over from logging were the same as paying for the ski runs? Would that $5 fee really stay at $5, and would the BLM and Forest Service always control the access and collection of the fees? The answer came with a very important message.

At home, I found a letter from Disney. As a Disney stockholder, I was impressed with their profits and growth during the dot-com market boom. The letter was an invitation to a conference at Disney World, not to the annual stockholders meeting. The roundtable conference hosted by Disney was to help federal land management agencies such as the BLM and Forest Service plan the fee-demo program. This really upset me, to say the least. I remembered the Disney vice president on the Montana BLM trip and his sharing that he was trying to see firsthand how Disney could create a wilderness-type attraction at their theme parks. Now it appeared Disney might be trying to become a gatekeeper at public lands for recreation and sightseeing.

Checking further, I found that Disney was at the top of the Sierra Club's list of most-watched corporations that were trying to privatize the country's public lands and develop a theme-park plan for those lands. Why Disney was doing this was not a question that needed an answer. Profits from public-land management were like finding gold under your Christmas tree. Activists were causing logging and grazing to be shut down, and now the tables were being turned to recreational uses to rebuild the lost revenues. The question that had been asked over and over by BLM folks was: what is your group willing to pay to support recreation on public lands?

The decision to try to move East now offered a big second window. The trips I was making to D.C. could easily be done from New Jersey, and this would then be a win-win of being close to the microfiber pile plan in New York and to the BLM and Forest Service in D.C., without being tied to either outdoor coalition, human-powered or motorized. I remember so well the trip that made up my mind. It was a direct evening flight from Newark to Portland. It was still daylight when we arrived in Portland. The quick commuter flight to Redmond near Sunriver landed me just as the sun was setting over the mountains, and the vast open BLM lands stretched empty and peaceful as I walked through the terminal and out to my van, parked and waiting for me. The sky was bright orange and the shapes of hills and the bigger mountains were dark against the sky. It was weird to think that only hours earlier I had been walking on blocks of concrete full of people, taxis, and buildings, without a tree or natural site in view. Settling into bed that night, I became really aware of the opportunity and challenges that were ahead in both plans: access to public lands and once more creating a made-in-America textile fabric while everyone else was doing it offshore. I was alone in them both, not sure where they were going or how to overcome the competition. Once again I remembered my thoughts of making outdoor clothing—not selling just fabrics anymore—and how just like Patagonia, I could create the messages in catalogs that would bring together the citizens of America.

As the summer of 1998 ended, I was getting ready for the move back East, having decided the only way to complete my plans was to be hands-on, and not be self-employed, living in one of the best resorts in Sunriver. I moved to Red Bank, New Jersey, which is about twenty-eight miles from New York City as the crow flies over the saltwater bays that go out into the Atlantic Ocean and the entrances to rivers such as the Hudson. Between working in the office and driving several times a week into NYC, the time passed quickly and was full of challenges with both plans, especially the microfiber fabric plan.

I don't think all the boxes had been unpacked when I was told the financial future of Glenoit was in serious trouble. Their popular Berber microfiber pile fabric was being knocked off in Asia, and the large investment in machines from Europe to retain control somehow did not stop those knockoffs. The development of a true double-sided pile using a needle-loom back-finishing method to compete with double-sided fleece was getting very close to the final approvals, but the financial ability to stay in business was not certain.

At that point, I think it finally sank in that the competition from Asia was too strong and that if you did not make the garment and build a strong brand, the retailer and consumer would never know you were in the game. Malden was flooded in red ink, not red flames, trying to rebuild the mill with a massive loan from GE Capital that was not getting repaid. It was clear to everyone that putting your eggs in one basket, such as a textile mill in America, was too risky, as the Malden fire had proved. In fact, mills were too risky and needed to sell finished products like garments or become a thing of the past. But no mill had the guts to go against their customers, and the power of their brands was well established. What I saw in 1993 and even before that, as early as 1990, was now reality. If you make the fabric in the USA, you make the garment or you will be out of business with or without a fire or contract with a textile-machinery maker.

As for Glenoit Mills, they are credited as one of the original pile fabric mills, and their factory in Tarboro, North Carolina, now employee-owned, continues doing some production, while the cotton fields around it offer a full-photo heritage to tourists who want to see what it was like fifty years ago when the South was a textile world in its own right. The Thomas Kay Woolen mill in Salem, Oregon, sits with its wool-processing machines intact and hosts banquets in the empty sewing rooms, while tourists can see what was the second-largest revenue source in America a mere one hundred years ago. Malden has survived for now as a textile mill supplying the military, since we decided there was a war to fight against terrorists. The clock hands of Malden's famous old tower really move by year instead of hours, from one to twelve, counting when we will finally be free of terrorists, and then that mill, too, will find its peaceful end—probably in real-estate ventures when the economy turns around.

Whatever was written in those beautiful pages of words and photos in early Patagonia catalogs, especially 1980 through 1990, has turned full circle, probably because sometimes too much knowledge is more trouble than leaving it alone. I say this out of a deep respect for YC and his wife and every employee who ever worked at Patagonia. The messages in their catalogs simply became the words and targets of investors and Wall Street guys, who saw how to build with its message, but not make the changes required to preserve and protect nature. Patagonia catalogs showed us the reality of the salmon and its path to being cloned or vanished from the face of the earth. They hit us hard about altering food seeds, and Monsanto made reality of those messages with patents that force farmers to buy Monsanto seed or face lawsuits for using their own seeds. Winds blow and those altered seeds travel everywhere. Now in 2011, somebody is asking the FDA to approve their new salmon, which grows faster and weighs more, using the claims by Doctor Oz that fish oils and omega-3 are simply not available in enough pounds of existing salmon to improve the health of our population.

Did I ever think that the only outdoor clothing company in America to believe in my fleece was so far ahead of everyone? That his profits from fleece would give him the means to show and tell us what we were doing and allowing to happen a decade or more before it turned out to be true? Can any of this be tied to a simple fee plan to repair public lands? The answer is yes when you look at what happened after fee-demo became a way of life on America's public lands. The so-called corporate takeover of nature, by changing free public access to pay-as-you-go public access, became the corporate takeover of everything.

The weapon of mass destruction I submit into evidence is the word fear. Fear is a very powerful emotion that every human being has faced during his or her lifetime on this earth. Back in 1995, I had discovered just how far fear can take you. Fear becomes a deeper emotion when it turns into anxiety, and the treatment decision becomes clouded and very difficult to determine whether it is anxiety or depression that needs to be treated.

My fear developed when I lost my seat at the table in fleece for the second time, with recycling. Having created the recycled fleece as my way back and then locking me out of fleece to offshore makers really sent me to the hideaway home I had built in Sunriver, Oregon. It was impossible to face all my customers again, especially Patagonia, REI, and L. L. Bean and try to explain it. I had no idea what to do to stay in the outdoor business, and anyone I talked to knew that making textiles in America was over. It left me a total outsider to the industry I loved and had worked in for over thirty years. As I woke up in a sweat-filled bed night after night, my fears got worse and so-called panic attacks soon found me not wanting to go out at all; I was afraid to be around people and be in public places, even a grocery store. My counselor found me to be suffering from a deep anxiety, not depression, and told me to use my mind to fight it and to get lots of exercise. Rather than use drugs, which would only numb the fears, I had to work through them. I was suffering from mild agoraphobia and trying to keep myself from slipping further into that illness.

My dear friends Ron (president of Conservation Alliance), Woody (owner of SNEWS), Gordon (president of Helly Hansen and Nike ACG), and Peter (president of White Stag), all still leaders in outdoor clothing and gear, saw me walking at an outdoor show and came up and hugged me, knowing I was in terrible shape. Ron and I had really bonded while serving on the board of directors for the Conservation Alliance started by REI, Patagonia, and North Face. Struggling back to my motel room while a panic attack soaked my clothing in sweat, I knew I simply had to let go and stay away from the outdoor business until I got control of the anxiety issue.

Months passed, and my walking and biking around Sunriver got me physically strong, but I still feared being around people. I remember twice trying to play golf and leaving the course after walking just the first hole both times. I would go to church, and when the choir got up to sing, I would leave because they were all facing out toward me. I returned for the sermon and then walked out again before the service was over. I always sat in the last row, and many times my mom and dad sat with me to make sure I was able to stay. The little grocery store in Sunriver was as far as I could go for shopping, and I only went to Bend to see Woody and my counselor, Thom. I traveled with my folks to and from their home outside Seattle, and my dog Ollie was always by my side. His almost-white tan fur and distinct cocker spaniel body were the safest things in my life next to my folks. Yes, fear is a very powerful emotion that can control our minds and freeze our thinking.

Mine ended a year after it started, in 1996. Then in 1997, fear was used to scare folks into believing that years of disrepair were going to shut down public lands and close roads and campgrounds and even national parks. Quickly the recreation interests of expensive products like boats, RVs, and ATVs wanted the access and roads protected, so they favored fees, while hikers and bird watchers got upset about paying to simply walk on public lands they were already paying for and owning with their taxes. The fear didn't stop there. It went even farther, to the rural communities, now called gateway communities, that had seen their towns almost lost when logging and mining were stopped by the conservation-minded folks and organizations such as the Sierra Club. If recreation was lost because the forests and parks were closed, then the towns again would face harsh economic times.

It was 1997 and the dot-com boom was bringing lots of money to the outdoors and nobody wanted it to stop. Visitors to national parks and forests had set records for the previous ten years in a row, and now the disrepair of roads and facilities like toilets was seen as a major safety and health issue by the federal land managers.

Putting a Face on it with Ears

A recreation roundtable was organized at Disney World, and the marketing of public lands was set in motion. Outdoor recreation businesses feared losing sales, and the users of public lands feared being locked out.

From 1997 until 2001, this issue strangled clear minds, preventing them from thinking it through and seeing that the government was simply trying to pass the public lands off to private ownerships. Ten years later in 2010, citizens are turning their backyards into outdoor living and asking: why did it happen? Who can we trust while listening to foul and abusive language from our government's leaders? Outdoor recreation is now profiled through lobbying and coalitions and branded products' marketing to get youth into the outdoors. Now RV producers and outdoor conservation donations from shoe and clothing sales simply refer to public lands set aside for nature and its habitats as "our natural playground." Public agencies are asked to make recreation more important than any other use of public lands. Federal managers reply with, yes, you are important, but what are you willing to do to support the maintenance and services the public has been receiving while using and visiting public lands? The federal managers were asking this in 1997, when fee demo was started as a test for a year or two, and they are still asking it in 2011 of the same recreation coalitions and product makers.

The conservation movement in America was started by John Muir when he walked the country for over a decade to gain the respect of the president so that public lands could be established. His Sierra Club spends money on lawyers and now markets outdoor products, while trying to uphold the real mission statement for its members to follow. The word wilderness is now a boundary where untrammeled public lands are seen as the next adventure-seekers' ultimate high to enter. Woodsy the Owl's "give a hoot don't pollute" seems to be turned into "don't give a hoot…just take the loot." Smokey the Bear is hiding, trying to believe his fears of being shipped off to Disney World are over.

My efforts to keep making fabrics in America were thin-to-not-at-all with the Asian pile up of my microfiber pile fabrics putting Glenoit out of business. The risk of leaving Oregon and trying to make it in the Big Apple simply was the wrong time in the right place. I knew during 2000 I would keep some consulting going and pick the best time to sell the house in beautiful Red Bank, New Jersey, and move back to Oregon. I was happy to have tried to make it work again. Very happy to have overcome the fears that almost locked me in my house. I understood the reality of textiles being lost in America and nobody caring that it happened.

In February 1999, about three weeks after my birthday, a feature story in the New York Times announced that Levi was closing eleven plants and letting go 5,900 workers. Closing out the twentieth century, that closure seemed to be the final icing for American textile manufacturing. Levi, I believe, was still reporting close to $6 billion in sales at that time. But the soles of rubber shoes and bugaboo jackets faced directly into the lands of America knowing that the classic jeans and tee shirt and sweatshirt of American clothing were now for sure going to be made under those brands in Asia.

Vintage will make a comeback; it always does, as we know from those who started collecting the '50s and '60s cars, sports cards, and comic books. While America lets go of real things for a google of screens and images, the foundation of recreation birthed by settlers and conservation-minded workers seems socially earmarked to believe that jobs in America are not for "tired hands" anymore. Talks about rebuilding America ignore the real world of making things in America. The ethics and morals of preserving the natural heritage of America were challenged in the early years of 2000 by corporations trying to run our government through lobbying, and putting public lands into a pay-for-play arena like a professional sports stadium. Now after a decade, we see the bigger picture of recreation products being produced in catastrophic pollution in Asia and sold to citizens of America.

Chapter Twelve:

Rebuilding Wool

When I returned to Oregon in 2001, my next venture was going to be the rebirthing of Portland Woolen Mills, a brand I had acquired during my fiberfill association with my friend and employer Claude from Celanese days and our fiberfills at JenCelLite. The retailing of Polarfleece was everywhere, and the authentic outdoor brands were kicking out the designer brands who tried their stitch at fleece. I was on the outside with no mill to sell from, and the sales of fleece were going higher than we ever imagined before the fire, which in 2001, was just a memory of ashes falling down.

A Day at the Museum

My trip through the Oregon History Museum was my official start to discovering how to bring woolens back to Oregon. Old merchant newsletters about wool in Oregon provided the title to a book called Later Woolen Mills in Oregon written by Professor Alfred L. Lomax at the University of Oregon. I had pictures of the Portland Woolen Mills from the early 1900s, including one that had written on the top of the photo, "Lewis and Clark camped here in 1805." Said to be the largest woolen mill west of Cleveland, Ohio, the Portland Woolen Mills, under the retail brand "woolothewest," made one of the best-selling wool blankets for homes and bedding in America for decades.

The frosting on the cake was what happened that evening when I returned home. My next-door neighbor and I met outside. I told him about my day looking up the woolen mills and about me owning Portland Woolen Mills. An hour later, he knocked on my door and handed me a copy of Later Woolen Mill in Oregons. He smiled and told me Mr. Lomax was his uncle and that for years he,

Bill, had driven around with his uncle while they collected information about the more-than-twenty woolen mills included in his book. I stayed up all night thinking about how a neighbor had started me in textiles in the first place, in 1965.

Reading the book from cover to cover, I found the history of the Oregon woolen mills fascinating. It described how the local merchants in the Portland area, supported by the banks, decided to create woolens and wool clothing and blankets, rather than see the prized Oregon wool bought by brokers on the East Coast of America. Thus during the early 1900s, while places like Seattle were coming down from the gold rush, Oregon was creating a sustainable business of raising wool and processing the wool fibers into the best-quality wool clothing and blankets in America. Business suits and logger shirts, jackets, and pants became proud examples of made-in-Oregon products. The Hudson Bay striped trading blankets used as barter along the shores of the Willamette River in the early 1800s, including those brought by Lewis and Clark, were, a hundred years later in the early and mid-1900s, the most popular items for beds in America. From home designs in the Portland Woolen Mills "woolothewest" to the authentic Native American designs from Pendleton, the made-in-America wool blanket was the signature of Oregon wool. Clothing was proudly worn by Oregonians to support the wool growers and woolen mills. Retailers such as Filson in Seattle and Eddie Bauer offered Oregon woolens, as did Hirsch-Weis and White Stag skiwear sweaters. Jantzen featured Oregon woolens, much of it from Portland Woolen Mills. Jantzen set up their own knitting to become more vertical, offering products they made from their own fabrics, not just those sewn on their own sewing machines.

Trying to picture how all this history and business from a hundred years ago could come back in today's wool market was the challenge that lay before me in 2001. I believed I was too old to go to work for any of the companies around Portland, and I was dead set against having to travel around the world to do what I had done here in America, mostly between Portland and Seattle. By the end of the summer of 2001, I had the story committed to memory and had figured out my marketing plan for wool—blankets first, then clothing.

I found out about the new super-washed merino wool from New Zealand that was being sold as Smartwool socks. Dealing directly with New Zealand merino wool growers, the owners of Smartwool were making their socks at American sock mills, mostly in the Midwest. Because the knitting and the sewing of a sock are all done at one time on one machine, these sock mills could stay in business despite the cheaper Asian factories. This allowed Smartwool the opportunity to bring out the new merino wool socks, quickly fill orders, and most importantly, allow for year-round orders with the mills, rather than only once or twice a year with offshore sock mills.

Wool Trading

In early September 2001, I flew to Minnesota to meet with one of the oldest woolen mills in America still operating and making blankets, Faribo Woolen Mills. On the weekend before the meeting, I drove to a historic fort in Wisconsin and learned the history of the voyageurs and trading blankets in North America. The area we know as the Great Lakes was a fur-trading region and a big business in the 1600s for French people, and then continued into the nineteenth century for Canadians, the British, and Americans. Both Indians and white men carved out the trading business that found furs exchanged for tools, blankets, and jewelry. Indians hunted and trapped beavers in the winter when the fur was the thickest. The white men traders, called voyageurs, visited the Indian tepees, bringing presents and articles for trade. Dog sleds were used to carry the furs back to the posts or depots, and then they went by 35 foot canoe across the Great Lakes to places such as Montreal. During the spring, smaller canoes used rivers to get to the Indian tepees, and most of those trips required the canoes to be carried over land and rocky trails. This became known as a "portage," a name used often in the area as years went by. Indians wanted the wool blankets more than anything else, and the weavings on the blankets soon included lines—called points—to help calculate the number of furs to trade for the blanket. This heritage of woolen blankets became a big part of American woolens and the mills that produced them.

My meeting with Faribo was exciting, seeing the mill still working and using water for much of the wool processing before spinning the yarns and weaving the blankets. Orders included a good business with Lands End and L. L. Bean, which helped me believe more in what I wanted to do with Portland Woolen Mills. I learned that the mill had almost gone under and that the city passed a bond to keep the mill going. I laughed to myself, as that is exactly what happened to Pendleton in the early 1900s; they were going under and the town issued a bond that saved them, and of course the brand and company became the best known and most profitable woolen mill in America. The meeting ended with my only opportunity being to sell Faribo-branded blankets, as my company brand was seen as a competitor and the business too small to be part of Faribo. The Faribo folks were not open to merino wool, and I was convinced they would never want to be a part of wool clothing or socks in America.

Flying into Terror

Deciding to get a late-afternoon flight to Newark instead of spending another night in Minnesota, I was able to get the last direct flight from Minneapolis to Newark. A fire near the Newark airport delayed us an hour, and it was almost midnight when I parked my rental car at my hotel in Red Bank. I decided to stay out in Red Bank and enjoy my old stomping grounds and good food and not get an expensive hotel in New York City. Waking the next morning, September 11, 2001, I found a beautiful sunny day for my trip into NYC. I had three options: drive, take the ferry to Wall Street, or take the commuter train to Penn Station in midtown, which was the closest to my meeting. I knew the train schedule by heart; it had not changed in the six months I had been gone.

After boarding the 8:37 a.m. train for NYC, I relaxed and looked out the window at all the green hills and leaves that were just starting to turn fall colors. It was a month too early for the best of the turning leaves, which is a postcard signature for Jersey and all of New York and New England. About fifteen minutes into the ride, we crossed out of the hills and came alongside the saltwater bay that flows out to the Atlantic Ocean and the famous Jersey shore. The tip of that area is Sand Point, the oldest fort that guarded New York harbor in wars going back to the 1800s and a key location during World War II for guarding against German attacks, which, of course, never happened. During the years I lived in Red Bank, 1998 to 2001, I walked the beaches and explored the old fort's tunnels and bunkers, its cannons and guns still in place facing out toward the harbor and ocean. It was fun to watch ships come and go, and see the Statue of Liberty and the famous Narrows Bridge, the longest-spanning bridge in America.

As we got farther along, I saw the Twin Towers and the Empire State Building reaching high into the sunny morning. Dark smoke was coming from the top of one of the Twin Towers, and I thought the famous Windows on the World restaurant had started a kitchen fire that seemed fairly large. The closer we got, the thicker the smoke became, and just before arriving at the Newark station, a larger bloom of smoke quickly appeared. Cell phones were busy and the talk was about a plane that had flown into one of the towers. The engineer kept changing his story about the PATH trains running and not running from Newark into Wall Street. Arriving at the Newark station, I didn't know what to do—stay on or get off—but I knew we were going to Penn Station in midtown at least a mile away from the towers, and the fire, I thought, was caused by a small plane since it was too clear a day for a commercial plane to hit one of the towers. I stayed on the train thinking, okay it's a terrible thing, but it was not something as big as what it turned out to be. After leaving Newark, it would be fifteen minutes to Penn Station, with no stops between.

The smoke was now really thick and black, and both towers were engulfed in the smoke and had flames shooting out from the higher parts. How were both towers hit by planes? It just didn't make any sense. Passengers started yelling that it was an attack and there was more. The Pentagon in Washington, D.C., was hit by a plane and burning. The planes were commercial planes full of passengers, and it was some kind of terrorist attack. I thought about the flight I would have been on that morning from Minneapolis to Newark and was glad I was not in the air. Then I realized we were under attack and nothing was safe. What about the big bridges such as the George Washington Bridge? And what about the tunnel we were about to enter and travel in for five minutes or more under the Hudson River as we approached it?

The train didn't stop, the engineer didn't say anything, and we went into the tunnel not knowing what might happen next. Arriving safely at Penn Station, I got off the train and hurried upstairs, wanting to get out into the daylight and the street and find out what was going on. Approaching a NYC policeman standing on the curb outside the train station, I asked him what was going on. Was I safe or where should I go? He told me one of the Twin Towers had fallen; the other was in flames, and the city was under a terrorist attack alert. I told him I just came in from Jersey and had a meeting by the Empire State Building a few blocks away. He replied that the building was closed and I should try to get on a train back to Jersey before they shut down the train station.

I ran back into the station and scanned the reader board for any train back to Jersey. My line to Long Beach was not for twenty minutes, and the only train leaving right then was going to Trenton. I ran to the platform two stair flights down. Just as the conductor was closing the doors, he saw me and held off until I got safely into the train car. The entire car was packed, and we were standing shoulder-to-shoulder as the train raced through the tunnel trying to get back to Jersey. Nobody spoke, but relief was clearly on our faces when we broke out into daylight.

But the scene was worse than an hour earlier. Only one tower was standing, and it was covered in smoke. The empty space of the fallen tower made no sense. Where had it gone? Did it fall for blocks and kill and destroy thousands of lives? Nobody was talking or asking anything; we just stared in what was a surreal time and place. Then suddenly the second tower was falling into itself, colors of clothes and debris were being engulfed in more smoke, and it all came straight down to the ground. Smoke shot up like a plume from a volcano, and it seemed to never stop reaching into the sky. There was no wind and it just hung there. Then a guy yelled out, "They killed all my friends, those motherfuckers," as he pounded on the glass windows of the train door. It was impossible to believe the towers were gone, that tens of thousands or more were killed and injured. Why was I there? I could not understand it.

My first day back in Oregon six months earlier, I had woken to the earthquake in Portland. Now on September 11, my first morning back in Jersey and NYC, I was in a horrific terrorist attack. The meaning of this just had to be more than coincidence.

I got some help from the train's conductor, who told me to ride one station past Newark, then get off and wait for a local train that would take me back to Red Bank on the Long Branch line. Standing at that train station, there was quiet all around. No explosions and no planes were in the air as I looked toward the Newark airport. Below the elevated concrete train station, store owners were quietly closing their shops, pulling iron gates across the glass doors and windows, and then departing to go home. I had no service on my cell phone, no way to call anyone, and no way to know what else was going on. It seemed the attack was just on that area of NYC and only the towers were targeted.

A guy dressed in a suit stood on the end of the platform, talking on his cell phone. As I approached, he said thousands were dead around the towers, possibly twenty thousand in the towers, and there had been a direct hit on the Pentagon of a commercial plane full of passengers. He seemed almost in shock, gazing over where we were, as he told me he should have been in the Trade Center tower that morning, but left late and was turned around in Newark. He told me of his friends and coworkers, none of whom were accounted for as we talked. Blaming the attack on terrorists and Bin Laden, he was sure only that kind of mind and money could have created the attack. I told him I knew nothing about the people he spoke of and that I saw the second tower fall after getting back out of the city. He was relieved to know Penn Station and the Empire State Building had not been hit by the time I got out of the city.

We both kept listening for fighter jets, but none ever came. Finally a train pulled into the station almost empty, and we got on and were soon safely heading back to my rental car at the commuter train station. The parking lot was full of commuter folks' vehicles, and then I realized that possibly many of the cars would not find their owners by the end of the day.

It was past noon as I drove into Red Bank. I was hungry and had not had a drink of anything since 7 a.m. Sitting in a restaurant, I ordered a sandwich and watched the progress of the attack as it was reported on TV. It just did not make sense that it was over as quickly as it started, and for whatever reason, it was only that part of Manhattan that had experienced the horror and tragedy. The news cameras showed only NYC police and firefighters, as it was too soon for our military to get there. Hearing the newscasters explain that the towers imploded because they were built that way gave me a better feeling that the damage and death was more confined than I thought when I pictured 110 floors of two towers falling over, which would have covered dozens of blocks in many directions.

The brutal scenes of the towers falling and people yelling and running were still more of a movie than reality as I watched them on TV. I had been there just two hours ago, and now in Red Bank twenty-eight miles away, there was not one sign of it ever happening so close. Those signs would come as the day began to shift to evening and candles and flowers and American flags were placed along a wall and on the grounds of a park that lined the riverfront in Red Bank. Pictures of loved ones who had not yet returned or had not been heard from soon filled hundreds of feet and never seemed to stop coming.

Prior to seeing this vigil, I had decided to drive to Sand Point and see what it all looked like from across the bays. Those battle-ready fortresses of old cannons and guns held nothing to stop the attack that was masked as American airliners, common as birds in the sky. Not even radar would have suspected what happened until the plane actually hit that tower. It was clear enough and the land is flat enough that the control towers at both Kennedy, about fifteen miles away on Long Island, and Newark, just across the river, had seen at least the second plane take aim and fly into the tower, exploding with enough jet fuel to bring down the tower in not much more than thirty to forty minutes.

Trying to sleep that night was almost impossible and deciding what to do the next day was unsettling as I turned off the TV in my hotel room. The city was shut down all of the next day and night while the military got into positions at all the tunnels and bridges in and out of Manhattan and around the other NYC boroughs. Every bridge and tunnel from Boston to Washington, D.C., a total of almost five hundred miles, was now under strict military watch and inspection. It was rumored that terrorists had been at the Freeport, Maine, airport before getting to Boston and other airports to begin their attacks. For many years, I had flown in and out of that airport on my visits to L. L. Bean. This was telling me that not one airport in America was safe anymore, from a small one like Freeport to the bigger ones in major cities.

The second day after the attack, I was able to drive into NYC after going through a total search and inspection at the Holland Tunnel on the Jersey side of the Hudson River. Guard dogs sniffed me and my car trunk, as they did every car and truck, before I was allowed into the tunnel. I wished I had taken the train, but came to the conclusion that my rental car was the only protection if I needed the ability to move on should something else start to happen. Most of all, it was a place to sleep and carry food and water. I was happy for the wool blankets I had bought at Faribo, as they assured me comfort and warmth if I was going to wind up traveling and sleeping in that rental car. I had checked with National and was assured I could keep the car as long as I wanted and there would be no mileage charge or drop-off fee, so if I had to drive it all the way back to Oregon, that was okay. The car, a Ford Explorer, assured me enough room to lay in the back with the rear seat down. I was traveling for the first time after my back surgery, which cost me two discs in L4–5, and being able to stretch out was a lifesaver of the more practical sort.

Just what sense did any of this make? Not only was I a displaced American top textile worker, but also I was in the middle of my old NYC homestead, where I had been raised before I went West to college and most of my career in textiles. I rallied around, keeping focused on learning as much as I could about wool in America and also did enough of a presentation to land a consulting job with an old New York State fabric mill to try to create yet another polyester fabric to make a living.

Gehring Textiles was a family-owned business, run by a father and son that made mostly military and industrial textile fabrics. Skip's dad was innocently killed during his lunch hour a few months after 9/11 while waiting to cross the street in front of Macy's in midtown Manhattan, right where the famous Macy's parade performs on Thanksgiving Day. Skip was planning on moving out of New York City after 9/11, and the horrible accident that took his father sealed that move for sure. In the six months that followed my starting to work for Gehring, I tried to find a made-in-America outdoors fabric that could compete, but the outdoor companies then, as now, had little respect for buying American fabrics and sewing here in America or even in nearby places such as Mexico.

There was a spark of "let's bring things back to America" after 9/11, but that spark was not enough to change the financial-quarter counters on Wall Street that now traded the Columbia, Nike, and North Face blocks of outdoor granite. I guess I just did not realize how far these companies had come. For fifteen years, from 1965 until 1980, they were not part of developing or creating polyester fibers or nylon fibers for outdoor products. However, in the year 2001, they were in control of every fiber and fabric created by American textile mills, and they were not using anything made in America or even sewn in America.

Rather than wallow in the pity I knew was lying on my shoulders, I saw the return to wool as the way forward and decided I should start with wool fibers, build my own products, and get back what was in many ways taken from me. I saw the horrific events of 9/11 and the move to offshore textiles as the perfect energy to get it back by doing something totally new: returning to an old fiber in wool with a new technology, super-washed merino wool.

Here Comes the Wool

History shows wool has been around for over five thousand years, and clearly wool defined centuries of wealth and progress around the globe before it came to America and did the same in the early 1900s. Facts and legend and glory from the past were my way into the future, beginning in January 2002, when the popular Outdoor Retailer Show was held in Anaheim, California, because the Olympics in Salt Lake City took precedent over the outdoor show. Finding a diamond in the rough across from Disneyland, I saw Swanndri woolen coats and fabric from New Zealand. Literally carried home from a pilgrim's adventure to New Zealand, the awesome, almost-historic Swanndri wool outerwear was found by two young members of the Mormon church who wanted to set up a booth in Salt Lake City at the Outdoor Retailer Show. Being sent to Anaheim for the show, the duo still believed they had found something worthwhile. I took a deep breath when I was shown flexiwool merino-wool jackets, sensing they were the coming of real wool Polartec. For added insight, I was shown a knitted fabric made from merino wool and FR (fire retardant) rayon viscose that was being developed for smelter workers' underwear. The blend of merino wool and FR rayon viscose was already being used in uniform shirts and pants in every Alcoa factory worldwide.

My fear of flying after 9/11 found me in my car the day before the show, driving on I-5 to Anaheim from Portland. I was not able to face flying again after 9/11. I had for many years become uncomfortable flying, as it all turned into a Greyhound bus experience. Then 9/11 shackled me to that fear, and I was unable to get over it when I woke to fly to Anaheim that morning. Having the car proved a good thing, as I loaded up the trunk and backseat with Swanndri garments and fabrics and New Zealand wool blankets, and drove it all back to Portland.

I had between then, February 2002, and the August Outdoor Retailer Show in six months to sort out my business plan for how to make this New Zealand wool idea work. I was totally ahead in this; only Smartwool socks were being offered in the new washable merino wool that was soft enough to wear against your skin day after day. I began by bringing in fabric, both the outerwear jacket merino flexiwool and the merino wool blended with FR viscose knit for base layers. I used the equity in my homes in Portland and Sunriver to help get the business going. Things were scary after 9/11, and trying to get a loan to build any textiles in America was not possible. Investors wanted 70 percent or more of the business, and I saw no reason to not do it on my own—get to the show and beat out my old customers before they found out about the washable merino wool.

My trick up my sleeve was that I believed all the outdoor clothing makers were so brain-dead on the polyesters I had created and the cheap labor from offshore, that doing something new like wool would not get their attention. I based it on what had happened in the old skiwear industry, which was so full of themselves that they ignored the polyesters, and the fleece and moisture-management underwear knocked them out of the business. Gore-Tex had fired the final shot with breathable outer fabrics that completely protected you from rain, snow, wind, and anything else known to stop you from getting outdoors after you bought that all-day lift ticket. Warren Miller prime theater ski movies created "extreme skiing," and the Gore-Tex/Polarfleece skiwear was going to conquer the slopes, especially the famed north slopes of that namesake North Face. Gore-Tex-trained marketing and sales reps based out of Seattle, Bob and then Steve, became top-level executives at both Columbia and North Face, assuring those brands that the lift into skiwear was never going to stop.

Once again being the underdog in ski apparel, I went to my favorite little sewing shop in Sisters, Oregon, where I had the very first recycled fleece jackets made, and asked Sue, the owner, to make me some samples and redo the Swanndri designs to be more appealing to folks here in America. By the time the Outdoor Retailer Show rolled around again, I had my samples and was ready to meet the New Zealand folks and grind out a business plan.

True to form in textiles, nothing stays a secret very long, and the new washable merino wool from New Zealand was no exception. A team of marketers called NZ Merino came to the show, along with a few New Zealand outerwear companies, including the then-upstart Ice Breaker. My guys from Swanndri did not think much about it since Swanndri was the only brand folks took seriously down under, and the parent mill, Alliance Textiles, was way ahead in development with flexiwool and the merino/viscose blend for base layers. But this was not New Zealand, and 300 million Americans is a far cry from the several million New Zealanders. To put it into perspective, our population of people equals New Zealand's population of sheep in pounds of wool, about 300 million. Marketing super-washed fine-micron merino wool to America was much more appealing than a hundred-year-old New Zealand woolen mill called Swanndri. And I knew it better than anyone, since I was going to try that trick with my hundred-year-old American woolen mill, Portland Woolen Mills. The challenge was really how to beat myself after all the polyester I had developed and sold to skiwear and outdoor clothing makers for over thirty years.

Let me share a story from the Wall Street Journal I helped write in the early 1990s. The story editor was testing an Official Underwear Press Kit for the Olympics. Instead of a fun trip to Aspen and world-class skiing, lodging, and dining he went to Duluth, Minnesota, in January for the ninth annual 475-mile John Beargrease Sled Dog Marathon. Temperatures were 25–35 degrees below zero. Before the author tried out the underwear in the press kit, he wanted advice and called the editor of Outdoor Retailer magazine. The editor confirmed that the stuff was pretty miraculous, but the author wanted a second opinion, so he was sent to me to discuss the claims and the fabric itself. I was written up to be a winter-wear historian. Quoting from the Journal's story:

Layering irony upon irony, Mr. Hoschek explained who was responsible for this winter-wear revolution: hippies.

"Basically Berkeley hippies and mountain climbers decided to make a living, and polyester was the way to go," he said. Actually, he went on, they couldn't find mountain-climbing equipment and clothes that really worked, so they had to invent their own.

From this testimonial, the writer tried the Polartec-based underwear, which was said to be a mysterious fleecelike fabric that had already been atop Mount Everest with Jim Whittaker on his second time to reach the summit during his famous Peace Climb with climbers from the USA, Russia, and China all teaming together. Other comments from the editor were related to wool: "If I were a sheep I'd check to make sure my unemployment insurance was paid up." Clarifying the fabric further, he wrote:

What it is, of course, is plastic. Full Toledo polyester double-knits born again. None of those enviro-wimp "natural" fibers in this stuff. Nothing from free range sheep and organic cotton fields. This stuff is pure petro-chemical cornflakes and fluffed up into cuddly, down-soft underwear, shirts and jackets.

You want to be in harmony with nature, fine. You get a gold star on your forehead. You want to conquer nature, cop some Olympic gold and endorse Wheaties for big bucks, you've got to win in plastic.

The story ended with: "'Remember,' said an Olympic official, 'most athletes who go to the Olympics don't win gold medals.' What they come home with are experiences, feelings, and the kit bags full of official goodies." (This story ran in the Wall Street Journal in 1992. Compare that last quote to what they get today to go to the Olympics.)

Moving ahead to the early years of the new century, the Wall Street Journal was writing about Columbia, Nike, and North Face, now owned by VF Corporation. However, the writings were now counting the quarterly profits of these companies selling that "plastic." I think it is fair to say that no brands of clothing that had made the shift to offshore have come close to what was about to happen to these three brands and their products and profits. (I leave out Patagonia simply because Patagonia stayed private and true to its founder-owner, who wanted to limit the consumption of plastic until a real solution of sustainable business was created for the fiber and fabric made from the plastic.)

Being public brought with it a conglomerate business model of buying up companies and taking the manufacturing of products offshore to cheap-labor countries, which resulted in the outsourcing of more than 190,000 American textile jobs. (See the tables at end of this book.) The top conglomerate award goes to the VF Corporation, which began as a ladies' intimate-apparel maker and acquired such companies as Wrangler, Jan Sport, and North Face on their way to becoming a $3 billion clothing and gear company. Columbia gets the nod for making the most clothing designs without owning any manufacturing— pants, shirts, outdoor wear, shoes, hats, gloves, sweaters, and anything else you could or would wear to cover your body. They bought up brands to help get the designs right as they moved along. As for Nike, well at $19 billion and aiming to double that in five years, you just have to say, Bill Gates eat your heart out; they are what your foundation is trying to create in health with an attitude.

And so it was in the year 2001 and forward to this time that despite the magic of five-thousand-year-old wool and the over five-hundred-year-old merino wool from that breed of sheep, these brands did not get involved enough to lay claim to a sheep station. Closest-to-home sheep award goes to the Columbia breed of sheep, with no relation to Columbia Sportswear. That breed was created about one hundred miles due east of Portland on a ranch known as the Imperial Stock Ranch. Its founder, John Hinton, is said to have owned hundreds of thousands of acres of grazing rights, and his historic ranch, now just thirty thousand acres, still raises the Columbia breed and offers hand knitting yarns from the present owner of the ranch, Dan Carver and his wife, Jeanne. Featured in Portland's 2010 and 2011 fashion week, the hand made clothing seems to be headed into that circle of top designers making the from the ground in America a hint of what is happening from further down under in New Zealand.

The idea of wool returning to American outdoor participants has indeed developed with a very well-planned marketing story from New Zealand. Swanndri dropped out early, selling the historic Alliance Textile Mill to folks in Australia. That left the exciting sock story of Smartwool and a New Zealand country brand, Ice Breaker, to build wool products.

Comparing the customer of the new wool to that of the old wool went something like this: Nowadays you seldom see idiots in the mountains. What I mean
is, not everyone is a famous outdoorsman, but they're pretty well up to whatever
activity they tackle. They wear sensible outdoor clothing, they study the lay of
the land, they ask advice from anyone that knows better than themselves, and
they don't take on something difficult until they're ready for it. In the old days,
before all the education about moisture, warmth, and sweat, things were different. Folks came to recreation areas many times straight from their offices,
wearing city suits and thin shoes. By 2001, outdoor recreation that involved
anything other than walking, bird watching, picture taking, and learning about
nature had expanded into many sports that required gear, clothing, and knowledge. Part of that was a dress code seen as casual even in the workplace.

Most office jobs still had a dress code requiring clothes that were not sloppy.
Much of that clothing was made of fine-quality wool fabrics. Men's suits have
always been high-quality wool and slacks a very fine merino wool, comfortable
and breathable. Sweaters of soft merino wool had replaced the itchy wools of
earlier years. This clash of merino wool vs. plastic was for sure going to bring
out the very best of both fibers. The fear factor in this battle of fibers was clearly
etched into plastic's longevity, vs. the centuries of merino wool and several
thousand years of sheep-raising.

In 2001 and for the rest of this first decade, 60 percent of clothing worn
in America was related to a sports name. The advantage goes to Nike as we
begin trying to get athletes to return to wool baseball uniforms, football jerseys,
and socks. After all, shouldn't that jersey with his name and number be made
of wool, just like the uniforms of the old-timers in those sports?

Under Armour® compression polyester is not the message coming out
of New Zealand woolens. First they wanted to clear up the history. This new
merino was not part of sheep-station workers wearing wool jackets, shirts, and
pants. The iconic Swanni clothing worn by just about every sheep worker in
New Zealand was not the message. Instead, the new merino featured youth
dancing and being active. New Zealand had learned that moisture manage-

ment was part of keeping you comfortable, and sweat plus wool was known to make you itch even more. Science from plastic fibers is measured in micro-sizes of fibers. Thus, the sizes of merino wool, commonly stated in microns, had to be established to assure the same quality of wool in every yard of fabric. A modern technology called super-washing was trusted to keep wool soft and washable and to prevent high rates of shrinkage. The wool industry started to follow the language used by down merchants to grade the quality, and the first step was to identify the area and climate where the sheep were raised. New Zealand has a great overall climate for raising wool. It produces 11 percent of the total pounds of wool raised as merino compared to Australia growing 88% of their wool as merino according to certified grower reports from the American Wool Association in 2000, when I first saw the figures on wool production and grades of wool by breed and micron.. It was at that time merino wool became very important in socks produced by an American start up Smartwool based out of Colorado. Most of the socks were produced here in America by a few leading sock makers. Unlike other apparel socks are made on a knitting machine directly from the yarn thus the labor costs are very small compared to cutting and sewing apparel. The ability to create a high quality outdoor sock with merino wool grown in the famous lands of New Zealand made the made in America sock. I saw this coming on as I was consulting for a patented friction reducing technology using Teflon for diabetic socks which were produced at the same sock mills here in America. It was and still is the fantastic marketing created by New Zealand growers that keeps merino from New Zealand the choice over Australia for outdoor products. Recently Australia has created a powerful marketing plan with an industry leader Stan who pioneered cycling and other activewear including the Pearl Azumi company.

A big part of the marketing for merino wool from New Zealand involved making sure the fabrics and wool growers kept up with the projected increases in demand for the best quality merino for the next generation of underwear—especially after the plastic fiber industries, through the Wall Street Journal, told sheep ten years earlier, in 1992, to make sure their unemployment insurance was paid up. Was it possible, or even probable, that the new merino wool would catch up with plastic underwear? Time will tell, was my thought in 2002. REI alone was selling over a half-million polyester tee shirts, and sets of those plastic long johns from the ten-year-old Olympics never stayed on the racks long enough to get to know each other.

However, there was a big stink (pun intended) in the plastic factory. Yes, bacteria loved that petro-based plastic, and they just never wanted to leave it alone. Chemical after chemical, called antimicrobials, were added, but just like what happens with MRSA, a new bacteria or the old one never got out of the fabric. They weren't deadly infections like MRSA, but created a bad enough odor to move out a line of drinkers at an after-ski happy hour. Instead of asking someone how long they had been backpacking, a quick sniff as you passed them on the trail gave you a good clue if it was more than a few days. This don't-tell-you-smell approach was adopted as compensation for the comfort and warmth from the polyester microfibers. Thus the stage was set for microfiber with smell vs. merino wool without smell. Next came itch. Most folks accepted the merino feel as almost like cotton, but not as smooth or soft as polyester.

I figured out how to make the merino wool/FR viscose fabric I had been given from New Zealand before that mill sold out. Then I was ready to start up my own campaign to sell merino-wool underwear. Calling on my old friend and former Malden associate, Tony Mazzenga, owner of Wickers Sportswear, the issue of finding the wool/FR viscose yarn was solved when we traced it to a very high quality yarn spinner in Switzerland named Flasa. I knew the Swiss made very good textiles, from machines to yarns and fabrics. The best ski brands in America, such as Roffe and Sportscaster, had imported Swiss nylon fabrics to their sewing factories in Seattle and other Washington cities.

Yes, in those days before the Nike route to Asia started, the best fabrics in the world were shipped to America to be sewn into very high end skiwear and outerwear. That inspired the American weaving mills to do better and would usually require buying machines made in Europe to make an equal fabric in an American fabric mill. Going further back to the early 1900s, the building of quality woolen mills in America, especially in Oregon, also required machines from Europe. The history of sheep in Oregon shows that sheep were first used for their wool to make socks on home spinning looms carried across the country on the famous Oregon Trail in the mid-1800s. Thomas Kay is credited with being the wool engineer who brought the European machines and updated knockoffs made in New England to Oregon, and the quality of Oregon wool and that machinery made Oregon a leader in woolens, as we have seen. With this history, plus Thomas Kay marrying into the Bishop family, who are credited with creating Pendleton, I began to build a story of "it can be done again," and I thought about what to make to sell in Oregon under my Portland Woolen Mills brand woolothewest. I realized how fortunate we were to have great outerwear companies making outdoor clothing prior to my plastics. They had built the factories, including cutting tables and sewing machines, full of wool and then plastic nylons and polyesters.

The era of nylon, fiberfill, and fleece covered about forty years, from 1960 to 2000. Wool in America dated back to our founding fathers and even further, to the days of Dick Bell's family in the 1600s. Sheep-raising covered millions of acres of land from northern California to Oregon and Washington state in the early 1900s. Getting sheep out of the national parks was a big concern of John Muir's, once the parks were established. On the flipside, listening to the folks from New Zealand as we discussed the merino-wool marketing plan, they could not begin to think of their country without tens of millions of sheep

From the Ashes of 9/11

At an Outdoor Retailer Show in the summer of 2003, my longtime friend Jerry Wigutow set up a meeting with key U.S. military folks from Special Forces and the Army development labs, called Natick Labs. Jerry was a salesman for skiwear fiberfills when I was at Celanese selling the Polarguard fiberfill to the military in the late 1960s. The company where he worked was picked to create our Polarguard fiberfill, and Jerry went on to use Polarguard in sleeping bags for the military. His company, Wiggy's, makes the warmest, longest-lasting sleeping bags on the planet. Testimonials from the military keep proving it today, almost forty years later. I learned from the meeting with Special Forces that they had purchased and tested Smartwool merino underwear and liked the fabric, but that the sewing was not right and the garments were falling apart after washing. Assuring the Special Forces that the merino wool/FR viscose we had made up would not fall apart and had better fire resistance than 100 percent wool, orders were placed to try out our Wickers underwear.

Yarn had been ordered from Flasa in Switzerland and fabric was made in North Carolina at Beverly Knits, allowing me to begin making cycling jerseys under the Portland Woolen Mills brand to sell locally in Oregon to cycling retailers. Once again, Challenge Designs in Sisters, Oregon, with its owner, Sue, who had sewn up the recycled soda-bottle fleece ten years before, was now sewing my newest fabric, merino wool blended with viscose, for bike jerseys. Helping in the design and field testing, another good friend for many years, Bob Woodward, the SNEWS ("Woody"), was more than impressed with the wool/viscose and its comfort and how it keeps you from sweating or getting tired. Wool has a long history in cycling jerseys, especially in Europe, and racers have always favored wool to keep up their endurance. The Portland Woolen jerseys featured a wide white chest stripe for men's in a retro look that caught on quickly. Sue designed the women's with side stripes and a very clean and comfortable fit. Both Sue and Woody rode long bike outings of hundreds of miles and knew that we had a winner with the new fabric for cycling.

The question of how was I ever going to build this wool business was now answered by the simple reality of my bank account. Thus the goal was to sell to the U.S. military and use those profits to build my wool cycling and underwear business before the New Zealand-based companies beat me to it. To get the funds for the military underwear, I simply had to mothball the Portland Woolen Mills cycling jerseys. I just did not have the means to build a business against my former customers, and plastic fibers were making them too much money to see a seat at the table for my wool. From 2003 through 2007, the use of plastic fabrics in the outdoor performance apparel had gotten bigger than anyone could have ever projected in a business plan. Even today, it is a bubble that has yet to burst. Of course, polluted water bubbles from China might change that at anytime from now on.

New Zealand came on strong, getting financial support from their wool growers, and the Ice Breaker brand began to put serious cracks (pun intended) in plastic fibers. By 2010, Ice Breaker had a flagship store supporting their Portland headquarters, announcing that plastic was now going to have a face-off with merino wool. The perks of merino wool began with a no-contest ranking of odor free compared with plastic fibers, and especially polyester. This was the best approach to the military, as I'd heard story after story during Outdoor Retailer shows about odor in polyester and polypro fiber underwear. The best story I had to post on our Wickers.com website was that the smell gets so bad, guys don't want to ride in tanks with each other. Wickers supported the fabric and yarn financing for building my Portland Woolen Mills products. Owner Tony Mazzenga committed to creating the merino wool products for the military to keep his own business and sewing factory alive in America. Tony was approaching age eighty, and only his devotion to making textiles in America kept him out of a deserved retirement.

From our yarn supplier, Flasa, we learned about the testing and development of the merino wool/FR viscose blend. Flasa had joint-ventured that with Alcoa and Alliance textiles. Alcoa, a wise and smart company, supplied their workers with wool/FR viscose blend safety uniforms that reduced injuries from heat stress and improved worker performance. The industrial factory workplace fears molten splash and heat stress more than the electric-arc flashes common to many other workplaces. DuPont's Nomex, another form of plastic treated to be fire retardant (FR) was the fabric of choice. However, heat stress increased and Nomex soon became a big cause of the heat stress—quite simply, plastic does not breath, and Nomex is a plastic material. It also has a melting point, while wool has no melting point. Wool also will not burn or ignite or melt. It simply chars without holding high temperatures—you can touch the char almost as fast as it appears. Wool fiber actually breathes and absorbs almost a third of its weight in moisture. By absorbing moisture, the fiber supports evaporative cooling, and workers in extreme heat do not get heat stress. Today's fine micron merino wool from New Zealand, Australia, and America allows faster evaporative cooling within the fiber.

Thus the fabric and yarns made of merino wool today were ready to compete with all the plastic fibers, including microfibers. Wearing merino wool of this quality after it is super-washed to be extremely soft and not shrink has become the foundation of the new natural underwear for outdoors and anyplace else.

Layering, as we know, is created by using three layers of fabrics in a total system of comfort, warmth, and protection: base layers for comfort against the skin, middle layers for warmth from changes in temperature outside and inside, and outer layers to protect against wind, rain, snow, and cold. Alcoa carried this a step further, blending a new FR viscose, which is a tree-pulp fiber, for the added fire protection required to resist molten splash and heat stress while working in smelters and aluminum factories. Tree-pulp fiber is commonly called rayon, and the viscose processing technology greatly improves the sustainable scorecard of that wood-pulp-based fiber. The chemical added to make the wood pulp fire retardant is a very good antimicrobial and assures the wearer that odor associated with any other man-made fiber does not happen for the life of the garment.

With these features, boxer briefs made with the merino wool/FR rayon viscose and sold under the Wickers brand became the most popular underwear of the Special Forces warriors. After wearing it for weeks at a time without washing, our troops were so impressed with the underwear, they refused to give it up for laundering, and quickly accepted their next mission. They were safe from fire and melting, but more importantly, comfortable while in combat. Tee shirts followed, and the Army was ready to seriously begin a plan to use the merino wool/FR viscose in every combat uniform for the nearly 500,000 troops worldwide, including those based in the USA during training. But what appeared to be a rewarding business turned into just a trickle of orders, as we found out about the military's policies for buying clothing.

I was excited to get this opportunity again with the military. My first time was back in the late 1960s with the Polarguard fiberfills that were picked for sleeping bags and liners in all military field jackets. That event started my career in plastic polyester fibers, and now I was trying to go back to natural fibers with wool and tree pulp. In the late '60s, the military was trying to get beyond down insulation, an issue that was not easy to accomplish since the down clothing and sleeping bags had been issued since Eddie Bauer's patents in the late 1930s. Down was used during the entire World War II, when the military took all the production Eddie Bauer could make. A shortage of down found sleeping bags being filled with chicken feathers.

In the 1960s, fiberfills meeting military specifications were only allowed to say virgin polyester fiber, which meant a polyester fiber that was produced for the first time. But the specs for crimp, fiber length, and denier (size) were not easy to keep focused in one brand of fiber. There was a well-known waste fiber business that dumped quality virgin polyester fibers into fiberfills, and the military was an easy target since they were not allowed to specify a brand, such as DuPont Dacron 88, which was the best quality at that time. Only when another identity, such as the number 88, was added to Dacron did the user know that it was fiberfill-quality fiber.

The military heard about the new patented fiberfill from Celanese. The continuous-filament fiberfill assured the same quality of fiber for each garment and sleeping bag, something that could not be controlled with the broader ranges of staple fibers. I literally walked into a set-up by a top-level corporate vice president at Celanese, which was doing a great deal of development work with the Army testing facility, Natick Labs. Convinced that the quality was assured, Natick Labs sent the continuous-filament fiberfill to J. C. Penney's corporate offices on Sixth Avenue and Fifty-fourth Street in New York, where Penney's had their testing lab for all the fabrics used in everything from clothing to home furnishings. One of the most important tests was for warmth, and Penney's had a new state-of-the-art testing procedure called clo. The Army wanted them to do the warmth testing on the continuous-filament fiberfill. Penney's did the testing, and the results showed superior warmth by weight, compared with any other fiberfill. That remains true to this day, forty years later. Nothing is as warm as down, ounce-for-ounce, and nothing made of polyester or any other man-made fiber is as warm, ounce-for-ounce, as continuous-filament polyester fiberfill. This is because the long filaments never break apart to create cold spots for the life of the product, especially sleeping bags.

Penney's outerwear and sleeping-bag buyers got wind of the test results and called our office at Celanese to set up a meeting to find out more about the new fiberfill. The military, immediately upon getting the warmth tests, decided to write specifications to only use the continuous-filament polyester fiberfill, and Celanese was assured millions of dollars in orders. I had a very big customer with the Army and other branches of the military. Penney's had me meeting with their top outerwear and sleeping-bag buyers, and soon the continuous filament was branded as Polarguard by Celanese's Madison Avenue advertising agency. I began offering Polarguard to skiwear and outerwear makers across the country.

Polarguard was named after Right Guard, as the need for protection found the word guard to be a smart way to get that message across. Right Guard deodorant was very popular at that time, and the household word "guard" assured Polarguard an easy way to let the consumer understand its benefits for warmth without getting wet like wool and down. National ads were run on the Johnny Carson show, and everyone in outdoor clothing was after me to try out Polarguard, which led a few years later to the invention of Polarfleece.

Now the military was going to once again allow me to bring out a new technology, only this time it was going to be merino wool/FR viscose. What seemed impossible after the Malden fire and everything going offshore was now coming true: a way back to made-in-America textiles, with the military's support. The

Special Forces' acceptance of the Wickers merino wool/FR viscose underwear found me back in full-time dialog with that old Army testing center, Natick Labs.

Immediately the issue of the Berry Amendment came up. The Berry Amendment is a federal law requiring the military to give preference to supplies of products manufactured in America. That requirement is very difficult to get around. Folks at Natick told me they could go to jail for violating it, and getting the Austrian FR viscose tree pulp fiber waivered would be impossible. The yarn was being spun in Switzerland, and the super-washing of the wool was being done in Germany. I kept pointing out to the Natick folks that these textile processes did not exist in America and that since we were at war, with the conflicts in Iraq and Afghanistan in full swing, the Department of Defense should allow the waiver.

It didn't take long for me to find out my big competitor was a program called Generation Three, which was full of polyester fabrics, including those used for underwear. Quite a few years of development had been invested in the program, and most of the seven layers of clothing used fabrics developed by the new owners of Malden after it was bought out of a final bankruptcy by private investors. Thousands of troops had tested the fabrics in garments in combat and loved the performance of the popular outdoor fabrics and plastic polyester fibers. I was literally staring the twenty years of my success with polyester in the face, trying to get this program moved over to wool and FR viscose.

My largest problem now was complying with the Berry Amendment, since only the fabric and the sewing of the underwear was manufactured here in America. The American merino wool going to Europe for super-washing and yarn-spinning was my biggest hurdle. Orders from Special Forces were, by law, limited to $100,000, although since we were at war, they could go as high as $250,000. That was not nearly enough for the 75,000-strong Special Forces, not to mention the Army and Marines, with their hundreds of thousands more troops needing FR underwear while training and in combat around the world.

Malden had strong lobbying and the senators named Kennedy and Kerry, both from Malden's home state of Massachusetts, made the challenge much more difficult. Natick Labs was also based in Massachusetts and had put years into developing the Generation Three program, much of it with Malden. A year passed and the demand from elite troops in Special Forces became stronger; they wanted more and more of our Wickers merino wool/FR viscose underwear systems, which now included a boxer brief, tee shirt, long-sleeve top, and long-john bottom.

Meanwhile, the outdoor marketplace was trying out Smartwool wool underwear, and the company kept improving the fabric quality to get a garment that did not fall apart after washing. The prices of merino-wool underwear were far above those for the best fabrics in Patagonia Capilene. The most popular REI, L. L. Bean, and Cabela's polyester underwear competing with Patagonia was sourced offshore. Most importantly, the water pollution in Asia, especially China, was ignored. Shortly after knowledge about pollution in China surfaced in 2006, REI began trying to bring back the polyester underwear program. Malden, with its Power Dry® fabrics produced in America under proper EPA regulations that had been developed for Generation Three, was going to go after that business when REI failed offshore. Back in 2004–05, honest workers in America serving the needs of Wickers customers REI, L. L. Bean, and Cabela's saw the reality of uncontrolled and unreported water-pollution practices price Wickers out of the business. The retail prices did not drop with the savings from pollution-ridden materials.

Attention

I remained focused on the military. I knew what had to be done to make sure the Generation Three polyester underwear, Power Dry and all, did not go to actual contracts and orders. That also meant putting a stake in the heart of all polyester underwear. Polyester fibers melt and burn and can easily cause second- and third-degree burns on your skin from fire and flash explosions. I had known this since the late 1960s, when children's sleepwear was not allowed to use any synthetic fibers of polyester, nylon, or acrylic until a fire-retardant treatment was found for the fiber. It had been years since I was at Malden. I was somewhat shocked to see the underwear going to the military being made out of polyester. Roadside bombs played such a big part of the injuries in Iraq, it was too much to think that Generation Three, featuring polyester fibers, was going to all military troops in combat. Troops were using their own polyester underwear from the top brands, including Nike, and the newly popular Under Armour was selling bigger than anyone else. Despite the melting and burning, the polyester fiber, yarn, and fabric could be made in America—and that was the deciding factor that stopped my merino wool/FR viscose under the Berry Amendment laws.

A bigger issue arose when a Navy captain who was a surgeon in Iraq issued a letter saying he was not going to keep treating troops with burn injuries from polyester and polypro underwear being worn next to their skin. The military had in place at that time strict orders that did not allow any warrior flying to wear anything but FR underwear made of Nomex or wool or FR cotton. This provided more support for the Marines to stop any Marine in combat from wearing synthetic underwear made of polyester, polypro, nylon, or acrylic. The Army paid attention, but reacted more slowly to the warnings and orders from the Marines.

With personnel changes in the Army, I began to work with a new officer in the Army while the Marines were thinking of another FR fiber, mod acrylic. The funding for Generation Three was held up, at least for the base layer underwear, by the melting issues with polyester, and Malden lobbyists were very upset but unable to get any contracts signed. While all this was playing out, tens of thousands of Army and Marine warriors risked their lives in daily combat. Those ever-too-frequent roadside bombs kept causing more injuries and deaths. Letters from Marines told us that the merino wool/FR viscose was far more comfortable to wear than the polypro they were issued.

Polypro is the same fiber used in the Lifa underwear from Helly Hansen. It is man-made from polypropylene and melts at less than 200 degrees Fahrenheit. How the fiber was being used in Iraq was a story nobody in the Marines wanted to hear about after the Navy surgeon let everyone know it was time to stop allowing that material "outside the wire," which to us means in combat. This issue was on track to a bigger corporate agenda in military purchasing.

Mod acrylic fiber is not made in America, and it was going to run into the same issues of not being Berry-compliant; thus it would not get into bids and contracts. Mod acrylic fiber was used in children's sleepwear fleece called bunting back in the early 1970s. However, DuPont workers in the factory that made mod acrylic fibers tested a high rate of cancer, and around 1977 the EPA and DuPont quietly shut down the manufacturing of mod acrylic fibers in America.

The Army decided to move forward doing their own testing and called their program FREE, while the Marines developed under their program, called FROG. Nomex created too much heat stress, and they moved on to the merino wool/FR rayon viscose. In the military, Nomex stayed in a soldier's or airman's locker and was worn only by requirement when they were flying. Mod acrylic fibers remained in the FROG Marines' FR underwear, despite what had been discovered by the EPA and DuPont. There is also a fire retardant chemical used in mod acrylic—antimony oxide—which becomes a poison when heated. It should have been a simple decision to allow waivers for the FR viscose being produced in Austria and the merino wool/FR viscose yarn made in Switzerland for the FR underwear. Instead, a lobbying battle of wills, politics, and high-ranking officers in both the Army and the Marines finally resulted in an agreement to support waivers for both FR viscose (rayon) and mod acrylic fibers. This should have set up a timeline of few months until the 150,000 troops in combat got the best FR underwear. Instead, a few years was going to consume the minds and wallets of many companies, including mine. Price was also a big issue; mod acrylic fibers were the cheapest of the three—merino wool, FR viscose, and mod acrylic.

In fire and flash explosions, FR viscose was rated the best in that it did not melt or burn, had the least amount of char, and the char was instantly cool to the touch. Merino wool charred, but did not melt or burn. Mod acrylic did not burn, but it melted somewhat and charred. In addition, mod acrylic was the only fiber found to release gas from heat and flame, and the odor easily made you sick and could be even more harmful. Nobody was willing to accept the EPA reports, since no Marines wearing the mod acrylic were found to have cancer from the fiber. All the industrial and safety-clothing markets in the world were using FR viscose, mostly blended with Nomex to reduce heat stress and be assured of no melting from molten splash. Wool was seen as too expensive, and not everyone felt comfortable wearing wool, even the new super-washed merino.

Mod acrylic had a reputation as a cheap alternative and the off-gassing odor kept it out of industrial and safety-workers' clothing. Both the Army and Marines were well aware of these facts. Pressure from lobbyists kept pushing the made-in-America-only Berry Amendment. A $2 million earmark for more polyester tee shirts made in America found Congressman Wu of Oregon shaking hands with waiting Marines, while claiming to save many workers' jobs in Oregon. I was featured on the front page of the Seattle Times in a story about the earmark and the melting tee shirts that were purchased with that $2 million in earmark funds.

Those funds come out of taxes paid by American citizens. Commonly called "pork," this earmark money is better known as barbequed pork. In fairness to the polyester tee shirts, so long as you are not doing something that gets you too close to a flame or an explosion, everything is fine. REI hikers, climbers, and skiers know about the melting issues and respect that shortcoming of the polyester while enjoying its many benefits of comfort, warmth, and quick dry-ing of sweat. Thus thousands of troops who wear those polyester tee shirts, including Nike running shirts, wanted them during combat missions after they were sent overseas to Iraq. There is no question that the Nike, Patagonia, and Wickers polyester tee shirts and thermal underwear sold by many great retail-ers, including REI and Cabela's and running shops across America, have made clothing with better performance than cotton.

There is also no question that not one running brand or outdoor brand of underwear or clothing uses mod acrylic fibers. Why this mod acrylic fiber was purchased in underwear by the Marines and sent to tens of thousands to replace the highly flammable polypro begs the question: what did the Marines know that nobody in the entire outdoor sports and running market knew? Part of the answer comes out of why the Marines were still using polypro after poly-ester had replaced it twenty years earlier in all outdoor underwear. The second part involves a tricky maneuver related to the Berry Amendment.

Mod acrylic had been used for a fake fur hood ruff in a cold weather parka worn by the military, and a waiver was granted for that application years back. The Marines relied on that waiver to get their mod acrylic fiber underwear approved and not be at odds with the Berry Amendment. Now that seems logi-cal until you understand that a three-inch-wide by less-than-two-foot-long hood ruff is not the same as a full set of thermal underwear. That hood ruff is a very small part of the garment, and the rest of that cold-weather parka was full of materials and fabrics made in America, including nylon linings, shell fabrics, zippers, buttons, and insulation. The sum of the parts was clearly made in America, which helped win that waiver on the hood ruff. Now the entire under-wear garment is using a foreign-made fiber and top military officers say that's okay, ignoring the real facts that the fiber has been proven to cause cancer and was outlawed from manufacturing in America over that issue and other issues of toxicity and off-gassing. In the spirit of deal-making, which was confirmed to me in an e-mail, the Army and the Marines agreed to support each other's waivers for FR viscose from Austria and mod acrylic from Japan.

Time is an endless asset for the Army's Natick Labs. Job security is based on continuous development of products and years of testing new materials and products. When I first started reviewing our FR underwear fabrics and garments with Natick after Special Forces purchased more than a hundred sets for testing on troops in combat, I was told the timeline is usually six years. By the time the Marines and Army were trying to buddy-buddy with the waivers for FR viscose and mod acrylic fibers for the FR underwear, the better part of three years had gone by. Head-to-head testing was done in different locations by the Army and Marines, and every test report I received showed that our merino wool/ FR viscose was the winner.

A key meeting with an Army officer assured me more testing opportunity, and I was able to get the Alcoa merino wool/FR viscose shirt and pant in front of him, suggesting that the Army seriously look into the woven fabric for combat uniforms, as well as underwear. I saw this as a big plus in the push to get our underwear into contracts, since both the combat uniform and underwear would have 50 percent FR viscose. This seemed to assure a waiver for the FR viscose, and indeed one was signed by President Bush. The Marines' mod acrylic waiver got high-ranking signatures from officers but was not in keeping with language President Bush added to the Berry Amendment that required the president's signature on any textile waivers.

A delay followed the offering of FREE, and paperwork was blamed for the delay. I sensed trouble ahead and I was right. The Marines got tens of thousands of long-sleeved shirts made with mod acrylic and sent to their Marines in combat to settle the issue of melting polyester. This set up the opportunity, along with the delay in FREE, for mod acrylic to be in production when FREE came out for the Army bidding. More things evolved, and blaming lack of manpower for contracting awards, the FREE program was organized into a system of products. Bids were allowed only by companies that grouped six or seven items together into one bid. These companies are called prime vendors and are new to the military since the Iraq conflict began. Made up of retired officers and enlisted men and women, these vendors were building companies from a few million in sales to hundreds of million in sales during the Iraq war years. Why should we, as an underwear company now with over four years of selling our FR underwear to Special Forces and supplying underwear sets directly to the Army for testing, be cut out of bidding directly with the Army?

The answer was simple. The powers that be in the military were creating big corporations to supply the military, rather than keep the small-business system going and allowing each supplier to directly offer their product to the military. The catchall was the delays in R&D that keep opening the door to purchasing from the prime vendor, rather than an approved product put out to bid by DOD. For me and for Wickers, we had put several years into the military and were now being cut out of a direct path to DOD purchasing. There are no intellectual property rights when you sell to the military, and the Alcoa-created merino wool/ FR viscose yarns and fabrics were not patented. Thus our ability to win was now dependent on other layers of outerwear collectively assembled by a prime vendor. From socks to the outer shell, it all had to win in a winner-takes-all bidding. My best ally was that the uniform for combat was being created separate from FREE, using FR viscose fibers blended with a Nomex-type fiber. I was simply keeping the FR viscose and using merino wool in the underwear because any Nomex-type fiber was too uncomfortable to wear against your skin.

As the bidding got closer, only one out of four potential prime vendors decided to use our merino wool/FR viscose underwear. One of those four, ADS based in Virginia, demanded that we exclusively offer our underwear only through them for the FREE program. That was clearly not in our best interests at that time. The other two prime vendors had deep ties to mod acrylic and I suspected were part of the Marines' FROG program. Politics and lobbying for the polyester were, I'm sure, putting a lot of pressure on the Berry Amendment, which was making it tougher to get waivers in place for the wool's super washing and the Switzerland yarn spinning.

The not-so-funny part of this is that we were the only company offering American fiber (wool) in the underwear. Our American merino wool was sent out of America to get super-washed and blended with the FR viscose and then spun into yarn. Then the wool, as a yarn blend, came back to America, where we knitted and finished the fabric and completed the garments in our sewing factory in America. Both the FR viscose and mod acrylic fiber came into this country as imported fibers, which were made into yarn and fabrics and sewn into garments in America.

So what is the logic of the Berry laws requiring everything be made in America of American materials, and the Defense Department playing traffic controller over which way it flows: fiber flowing in or fiber flowing out for processing into yarn? The answer to that was twofold. First we were offered a $100,000 development contract to teach a U.S. yarn spinner how to make the yarn. We knew from other trials using a patented wool-processing technology that belonged to the Department of Agriculture that it was not possible given the equipment and knowledge of the wool yarn-spinners left in America. We decided that taking the money just to show good faith by trying was not in anyone's best interests, and we did not want a failing development to hurt us during the FREE awards We opted for option two, which is that we were simply told if our underwear wins FREE, we will get a Berry waiver to move forward with production.

FREE was broken out into levels of awards. Win all three, and you win the solicitation. We had strong support based on our performance with Special Forces and other Army tests as the round-one bidding started. We were uncertain about Natick and the mills running polyester in Generation Three, as well as the issue of foreign fibers and processing being submitted in FREE. Our biggest known concern was that the Marines had already put out orders for mod acrylic underwear. No prime vendors were used for these purchases. The same suppliers and bidders now going into FREE had to work through a prime vendor.

Round one came in with us on a winning team from a prime vendor, assuring us the move to level two. Most importantly, our FR underwear was approved as a good, useable product. This was very important to the GSA purchasing opportunities that existed outside of FREE and general bidding from the Defense Department. There were only two awards from level one, and we were one of them, assuring us a run for the final award.

That happy time became a challenge when one of the prime vendors that lost filed a complaint and was allowed to move into the second round with the two of us who had won the level-one awards. Now it was clear that one of us was going to be out before the final-level award. Most importantly, as we went into the level-two shake-out, we were the only underwear system not using mod acrylic fibers.

It was getting clearer all the time that this prime vendor system was really not fair to the individual products in each system. Why should we lose out because our vendor didn't have the best socks or cold-weather parka or any of the other components in his system? Now it was possible, despite our winning the Army tests pitting our wool viscose against mod acrylic many times in wearing trials, that we were going to lose out to mod acrylic because the other two prime vendors only had mod acrylic underwear.

The nightmare happened. We lost round two, and it was not our underwear that was the component that lost it for our prime vendor. Told we had no appeal rights because we were a subcontractor and not the bidding contractor, the chances of getting this turned around were slim to none. Our prime vendor had appeal rights, but it was clear they did not want to get into issues when other contracts are always coming out. We were left on our own to try to get back into the FR underwear program. Four years of getting orders with Special Forces, winning every test outside of FROG and FREE, the solicitation jumbled into a winner-takes-all grab bag of components, and it was over.

Using the Internet, I researched and confirmed the stories about mod acrylic fibers and cancer, and DuPont and the EPA. I organized chart after chart of government agencies and contacts, and contacted whomever I could find in the Department of Defense about the waiver for mod acrylic that was not signed as required by President Bush. It was September 2007. Living in Seattle, I was not able to drive a few hours to Washington, D.C., as I had done during the years of working with the Department of Agriculture and fee-demo programs on public lands. There was no outdoor industry to support wool vs. mod acrylic.

As much as I wanted to just move on to the outdoor marketplace with the wool viscose and forget the military, I was out of funds to keep trying to build the business. Wickers shut down the factory in New Hampshire and let all its workers go. Faced with shutting down the company, Wickers decided to keep going by selling its underwear on the Internet. The good news/bad news is that FREE wasn't funded and few troops got any FR underwear. That is a good thing because in my opinion, they are better off wearing polyester with FR uniforms over it and never having mod acrylic on their bodies at all.

The Seattle Times earmark story sparked good attention for me, and I did a live thirty-minute TV show in Seattle that allowed me to present the entire story of polyester and mod acrylic and the wool/FR viscose. Part of Comcast public broadcasting, the Stan Emerett show and clips are on youtube.com under my name. The publicity helped me get my own U.S. Senator Cantwell in Washington state to support an earmark for me, but the military refused to accept the offer. Developing wool now means supporting the building of a super-wash facility in America, since everyone seems to agree that the Department of Agriculture's washing method is not going to work.

Military combat uniforms all have in them 50 percent or more FR viscose. The FR underwear seems to have fit the six-year time line as we are getting out of Iraq, and are said to be facing only one more year in Afghanistan as I write this in October 2010. Polyester continues to be allowed in training so long as it is not worn "outside the wire" in combat. The Marines have purchased a fancy polyester training suit much like warm-ups used by athletes, and the lure of polyester that started when Nike made running apparel from ladies' loungewear is now seen as tough-guy wear, including brands such as Under Armor hosted by athletes around the globe—if the lack of a Nike logo permits its use. On a positive note, the Marines' running suits are made in America with American fibers and fabrics. Everything meets the EPA regulations for water and air pollution to be at zero emissions. This proves that things are still done here and begs the question: why do companies like Nike and Columbia buy textiles made in catastrophic pollution and contribute to the deaths of Chinese citizens through premature aging. Laws were created to protect the military supply of textiles. Why not protect all of us and citizens offshore from pollution and death caused by American corporate wrongdoing? Full disclosure and transparency will keep data open for all textiles being brought to America. Will this be part of the trade talks and foreign policy positions of our Congress and president?

It is more than obvious that chemicals used in textile processing cause serious harm to water, land, and humans. In China at the end of 2010, the United Nations believed that fifty million citizens were environmental refugees as a result of pollution to water, land, and air. Textiles are being reported by folks like the National Resources Defense Council (NRDC) after extensive evaluations of dye houses found them to be the leading polluter in China. The last part of this book honors the brave citizens in China who have become the victims of this horrific corporate greed and environmental catastrophe. I believe it sums up with facts and conclusions that America needs to stand up to the pollution and demand transparency of the processing of textiles. We should demand that textiles coming into America meet the same EPA regulations for textiles that are processed here.

Fibers such as wool that are grown in America owe their survival to the Berry Amendment. The same is true of all made-in-America textile materials from fibers to yarn, fabrics, and trims. At I write this in the early months of 2011, Congress is trying to put a 25 percent tax on imports from China. Opponents say that tax will create inflation of 25 percent. Tied to China's questioned valuation of its currency, experts say prices from China are artificially lower because China produces without environmental regulations like the EPA requires here in America.

There is an old story about oats going into the front end of the horse and oats coming out the back end. It has to do with quality, not quantity. Polluted textile water reused from wastewater follows the back end of the horse. Possibly the proposed tax on Chinese imports should be more focused on the pollution caused in making the products, just as pollution from automobile exhaust carried with it special taxes and per-mile taxes unless certain miles-per-gallon and air emissions limits were met. Here in America we are required to have our vehicles tested to keep them legally licensed for driving public roads. Textile production that uses polluted water in places all over Asia generates an unknown issue of toxic chemicals. Greenpeace calls it their "dirty laundry program" and asks all brands of textiles to "detox." What is left in the fabric that is worn by children and adults? Most agree, and the EPA confirms, that you cannot call textiles made from oil environmentally friendly. We are also learning that natural fibers using high levels of chemicals such as fertilizers are not environmentally friendly, either, which is resulting in strong sales by consumers shifting to organic fibers in clothing and organic food in their diets.

Beyond this issue is the limited supply of water on our planet to feed us, clean us, and allow us to continue as a highly industrialized society living in a global supply chain. Water issues today are an issue of access. Globally, women spend thousands of hours each year collecting and carrying water. It is said on the website water.org that 3.5 million people die each year from water-related diseases. Of those deaths, 84 percent are children between birth and fourteen years in age. Some 98 percent of the deaths occur in the developing world. The developing world is where textiles flow.

When it comes to the U.S. Department of Defense, however, everything is required by law to be produced here in America, using American-made materials and processing. Here is one of my favorite questions to the teams developing military apparel about using only American-made materials, especially in polyester and nylon: where does the oil come from that makes the fibers? Progress was made in military clothing when mod acrylic fiber development was stopped. The prime vendor that bundled the FREE system of seven layers of apparel that included mod acrylic underwear has simply moved on to join in the development of apparel made of wool and FR viscose and a small blend of nylon. Today two mills in America are making a wool/FR rayon/nylon fabric for the underwear. A yarn spinner has developed a yarn for the fabric, and the super-washing processing is being set up here.

The military's practice of bundling products for bidding by a select group of prime vendors has wiped out the opportunity for small, single-owner businesses such as myself and Wickers to supply the military directly. Most importantly, the development of important products seems destined to not happen again without the inventive minds and passions of single-owner small businesses. Employees at prime vendors lack the knowledge and experience to create textiles from the fiber stage into a fabric. Without a bigger base of textile mills, the few military suppliers lack the knowledge to develop products, as we did with FR underwear. Textile innovation is shackled to pollution in China and the questionable value of their currency.

After September 11, 2001, I tried as hard as I knew how, within my financial means, to give our troops the best possible protection for fighting the terrorists and Bin Laden. The Special Forces elite wore Wickers underwear into missions nobody talked about and few ever knew the results. Names such as "delta" and "the black force" were used during conversations with us, but nothing beyond that was given out. These same names for Special Forces have been offered in media reports about the shooting and killing of Bin Laden on May 5, 2011. Back in 2003–2007, our Wickers FR underwear was worn on many missions by elite Special Forces, as they were our sole customer. Knowing of their operations then and my appreciation of their devotion and timeless energy to get Bin Laden, along with the accomplishment of being the first to offer an FR underwear system those troops wanted to wear in combat, finally brought closure to the attack I saw on 9/11.

All I can hope for now is that the issue of corporate takeovers in the military's buying will finally show up in the halls of Congress and the Oval Office. Without a small, highly trained team of specialists (small-business owners) who live and work in America, whether in uniform, overalls, casual clothes, or anything other than a suit, the ability of America to be the strongest and most respected country on the planet seems in a serious fight to avoid extinction.

Chapter Thirteen:

Who Are We Today

While American citizens are starting to say we are a third-world country, the line in the sand of returning to a strong working class, including small-business owners seeking green living, has yet to reach the youth of America, or their parents.

Years ago at an Outdoor Retailer trade show in Salt Lake City, I attended a conference on getting the industry to go green.

The question of recycling was passed around the room and when it came to me, all eyes were on me as everyone was anxious to hear my thoughts, knowing I had made Polarfleece into a bottle-based fabric by recycling plastic bottles to make the fiber. I smiled as I looked around at thirty-plus people all sitting facing me, each with a plastic bottle of water in front of them. I had a glass of water in front of me. The table nearby was full of glasses of water. I simply pointed that out and told everyone that if they want to change things, start by not carrying so much water in those plastic bottles. The table full of glasses of water was there to be drunk first.

The issue of plastic vs. nature is not about corporations and their products. It is about what we as consumers and citizens choose to do with our energy, water, and money, and how we live our lives. The number of water bottles sold in outdoor recreation stores is now a major business unto itself. No fewer than fifty brands of water bottles are seen at trade shows featuring outdoor products. While this is a good sign for the disposable PET bottles that can reduce the amount of waste going into landfills, it has sparked a great deal of controversy about the safety of the plastic used to make these durable, washable, and refillable water bottles. Of course Starbucks is right behind this with their coffee mugs, and professional sports has them for beer drinkers and tail-gate parties. What is amazing is that folks easily pay over $10 for these plastic mugs—and of course metals get into the act, as well—and now with the chemicals that may or may not leech out, more scientists are trying to figure out what happened to the old skins of hides that carried our water before metal and plastics.

Did all this attention to water bottles get started from my recycling those bottles into fleece in 1993? I know it can't be proven, but here is a replay of a story I wrote for SNEWS,

Updating to the year 2011, 5 percent of landfills are full of textiles, with an average of sixty-eight pounds per year for each citizen of America. The fabrics without a mill in America are simply left in the landfills. Plastic bottles in all shapes and sizes comprise the largest bulk-to-land-mass of landfills. Earlier in this book I wrote about Nike and how their football uniforms worn in South Africa were made from recycling millions of plastic bottles. The CEO of Nike is reported to have followed that trail of recycling to attend the 2011 events in South Africa. He was quoted as telling Wall Street investors that Nike is getting stronger while others are starting to weaken, pointing out that Nike's increases in sales were projected to bring in $1.9 billion from products sold in China during 2011-2012.

The Rag Man Speaks

A little over a year ago, a photo-shop employee/ **SNEWS** tester was quietly testing a fleece pullover made partially from recycled plastic polyester soda bottles. This year's bravos at the Reno OR validate what that tester confirmed after only two weeks of wear. ▲ In the ensuing year, the media has raised questions about the price /value issue in recycled fibers and fabrics. Another angle getting lots of play is the company's report cards, ie., just how green are these companies using the recycled fabrics, fibers and apparel. Lost in all the percents, names, and who's who, has been the original goal of making this fiber from polyester bottles. That goal, in my opinion, was to stop the bottles form being dumped into landfills. ▲ 2.4 million bottles an hour are thrown away every hour of every day. One third, or 833,000, are recycled into polyester fibers. The other 1,666,000 are left in the landfills every hour of every day. Have we no choice but to wait 2000 years until they turn into fossil fuel for future generations, or can we do something about this now? ▲ Of those 1,660,000 bottles still going to landfills, let's convert that to textile products for our industry. It takes an average of 25 bottles to make a fleece jacket, or fiberfill for a

jacket or sleeping bag. With 2.4 million thrown-away per hour, that's about 100,000 textile products per hour being thrown into landfills every hour. ▲ We know for sure that bottles make great fibers for carpets and home furnishings and industrial fiber fills. This has been going on since the early 1980's. Now we know that outdoor fabrics, especially fleece and pile, look and perform just as well with blends of recycled fibers as with virgin ones. ▲ According to one fiber supplier, only 24% of their total fiber production for textile products is made from recycled bottles; another isn't saying, and the third has yet to do anything with recycled polyester from bottles, and has announced no recycle plans for its bottle sales. Yet over five times as many cities have curbside recycling now than did in 1988 (there are now 5400). ▲ If costs are to have a chance to come down, surely supply needs to be increased. If bottles are to be kept from going strait into landfills, which by bulk take up more space than anything else being dumped, the fiber companies need to hear from us in the outdoor industry to get more recycling going right away. Making recycled fibers from P.E.T. bottles was easy; it was already being done. The challenge is to create the incentive to get the rest away from the landfills. ▲ We shouldn't have to wait the 2000 years to see if those bottles really turn into fossil fuels. By that time, no doubt they will have built a Jurassic Park for the fiber companies that made P.E.T bottles from raw materials. ▲

P.E.T. erupts, spewing hot molten plastic bottles into the last of the ancient textile factories

Where was Nike when I offered recycled Polarfleece in 1993–1994? From memory, I believe I was told they only buy fabrics from Asia, as made-in-America fabrics are too expensive. An item on the popular TV show Jeopardy stated that in 2009, Nike had committed to endorsements of $4.2 billion. Clearly, saving money by producing textile apparel and shoes in polluted waters and air in China helps support those endorsement funds. For an analysis of costs to produce clean, environmentally healthy textiles using a synthetic microfiber, I offer the following experience I had in 1996.

As part of my effort to keep microfiber pile fabrics alive in America, I visited the acrylic microfiber plant Cytex in Florida, which had created a nature habitat from recycling and reusing water. The environmental facility had created a wildlife water feature surrounding the fiber-making plant, as well as a forest on its grounds. When the plant was built in 1958, its wastewater system consisted of a lagoon water-treatment area and a direct discharge into the Escambia Bay not far from the Gulf of Mexico. By 1975, the plant had created a system that met requirements of the Clean Water Act of 1972. During my visit in 1996, the fiber plant was devoting $2 million a year to the operation and maintenance of environmental control and protection of the plant. In addition, $5 million was spent to improve water-treatment operations, and $3 million more on waste minimization. I saw the plant, walked the aisles while water rushed through open pipes to help make the acrylic microfibers, and enjoyed viewing the wildlife in the lagoon. The promotion of my branded Glen Pile fabrics from the plant's microfibers was hailed as "gotta have it," with an old mountain climber holding a rope wearing wool clothing and reaching out to touch the fabric. Shortly thereafter, in 1998, a knockoff of the fiber and fabric started up in Asia. Are the Asian lagoons being properly treated by the brands of activewear and outdoor-clothing makers using those mills? Glenoit Mills made the fabric and other pile fabrics for over fifty years in North Carolina, but went out of business in 1998–1999; the last I heard was that the employees bought it and are trying to save it.

Water Boy at Nike

Water is, of course, a major part of processing fibers and fabrics for textiles, regardless of whether the fibers are plastic or from nature. Some 2.4 trillion gallons or more a year are used. The challenge that Nike is getting stronger and others weaker is like the water boy sitting on the end of the "sustainable" bench on the Nike campus, guarding endorsements and tackling anyone who tries to sit on the bench of polluted textile-processing and cheer to change it.

Turning the clock back, away from the battle between polyester microfibers and organic cotton since the mid-1990s, there are older fabrics that have endured over time and through water, weather, and war. Woolens have been associated with fullers for centuries. The finishing of fabrics by fulling came from the desire of weavers for a cloth that is windproof, waterproof, and warm, and that will not ravel when cut. Gee, did I just describe Polarfleece? Not really. Early fullers finished their cloth by beating it in a manner whereby the fibers would entangle and spaces between the yarns, commonly called the warp and weft, would fill in. I believe Egyptians fulled linen by beating it with some kind of a wooden club, a bat was used in Mesopotamia, and the Old Testament says that in the fullers' field, fabric was beaten with sticks, hand-rubbed, or trampled by feet. Usually water was used with some kind of alkaline agent. Fermented urine was used as an alkali due to the ammonia that formed.

Wools Endurance

Sturdy fabrics that have been used for hundreds of years in many different ways are made of wool, nature's premier fiber. Geiger wool is from Austria. Duffel is named for a small town in Belgium. This fabric is best described as a twill, heavily fulled, with a dense nap on both sides. Now that gets as close to Polarfleece as possible. Melton, which comes from a fox-hunting area of England, is usually a twill weave of wool, with a cotton warp and wool weft. It is best known for uniforms, including today's military dress uniforms. Portland Woolen Mills, which made the fabric for fifty years, from 1910 to 1960, twice received Military E awards for excellence during both the first and second world wars.

There are many others, and these fabrics that rely on wool do not have to worry about there being no oil in fifty years. Native Americans took wool blankets and replaced their fur robes with them, and soon even the traders called voyagers were wearing the trading-blanket coats the Natives created. We all know these blankets today as Hudson Bay Trading blankets. Nobody has changed the signature points of that famous blanket in terms of fiber, fabric, or design since 1779, just a few years after our nation was created.

Back then, the master weaver bought and blended wool and delivered it to the farms in the area. The yarn was taken back on a return trip to the area where the blankets were made. Packhorses were used because the tracks were too small for wagons. Men did the carding and women spun the wool. The master weaver at his home did the weaving with helpers and men in training to be weavers. Compare this to today, with folks flying all over the world buying fibers, yarns, and fabrics, and then going farther to have the fabrics sewn. In this age of global business, water is wasted and polluted. Air is scraped up in miles of airplane pollution. Freight usually crosses the oceans in containers on super-sized vessels, each of which consumes as much or more fuel than the oil used to make the plastic fibers, fabrics, and clothing. Is it any wonder that outdoor recreation clothing and backpacks all look like giant Nike running shoes with enough compartments to be away for years? Plastic water bottles are sitting on kitchen counters while glasses and cups stay put away. Simply go to the Patagonia website and click on their global footprint to see the supply routes of each of their garment designs.

How will history record this infusion of plastic, industrial-strength endorsements into the timeline of humans on this planet? It might be gone as quickly as it appeared, if some folks are correct. What is more important is the use of water to process textiles. Not just for Patagonia, but for all the clothing makers chartered as companies in America and Europe. Each and every one bought Polarfleece as a way forward from natural fibers and other synthetics, which leads me to wonder if history will say it was all about "getting fleeced the American way."

Where in all these smart minds did the four Rs not become part of their most important goals? I know many dropped out of college before sustainable business was offered in a master's degree program. Instead of three Rs like in my days at school, we are now up to five Rs: Recycle, Reuse, Reduce, Renew, and Recreation in the outdoors, which was started by hunters and gatherers who went into the woods for food, picking berries and killing for meat, while others fished.

A very important Native American tribe is the Tlingits, known in the Northwest for their beliefs in Raven and the higher calling of Nature. Their homes faced the sea while they waited for the tides to bring them food like spawning salmon and clams. The rear of their homes faced the forest, where the Raven lived and the sacred

Mountain Goat blessed their lives. Weavings of baskets were used in designs for the weavings of their ceremonial robes made of mountain goat fleece and cedar bark. Named Raven's Tail weaving, the robes were not worn like point trading blankets, nor were they slept in. They were for birthing, marriage, and death. The Tlingits made cedar into protective hats and clothing that kept out the rain.

This Land is Our Land

There has always been trading in America, moving from generations of gatherers and hunters, to farming, and to industrial economics. Since the early 1900s, America's vast amount of lands and waters have been divided into private and public lands. Nearly one-third of the lands and waters in America are public, protected by laws as a heritage to be preserved and passed on to future generations. An alarming number of streams on these lands have no water at all at this time. The issue of water rights has compounded those taking from rivers, and the supply has simply run out, leaving thousands of miles of year-round empty streams in many states such as Montana. These lands, led by nonprofit activist groups such as the Sierra Club and Wilderness Society, were formed so that citizens had an active voice in making sure the lands and waters stayed protected.

The mix of clothes, shoes, and gear for being outdoors in what is called recreation has always come from those same items used in the workplace and on the farm. Just as gathering gave way to land for industry and cities, outdoor recreation has moved on from centuries-old fibers of nature to recent decades of plastics. The pattern and evolving seem to be the same. Riches follow new materials, as did the wool fibers into many new woolens.

Each of these natural fibers has always been recycled and reused, from point blankets to coats and woolens shredded into new fabric. The collection was once done by folks called ragmen, who pushed carts and rode in horse-drawn wagons filled with the scraps from mills and holding stations for old clothes. Cottons were also among the rags collected. Compare this time-honored system of reusing natural fibers to today's plastic fibers, which are barely recycled and/or reused.

Doug's Ragman's Story Written in 1992 The Rag Man

THE RAG MAN

Strolling the streets with his horse drawn wagon in search of clothes, the Rag Man collects for free and sells at a profit. In many ways, today, he would be a roll model environmentalist for the outdoor industry. Why? Simple. What he sells is shreaded and recycled into other products; not dumped into landfills. Labels in the new products said " made from recycled fibers".

I have personally spent the last 12 months searching old fabrics and clothes looking for a new product to sell to the outdoor industry. What I found is that, repeatedly synthetic fibers, (artifical fibers) can be made to mimic a given property of a natural fiber; Wicking, non odor, wrinkle free, warm when wet to mention a few. Nylon fabrics replacing cotton, polyester fiberfills replacing down and wool insulations, and polyester fleece replacing wool sweaters. These all happened because the synthetic fiber was capable of mimicing a given property of a natural fiber, without taking on other, less desirable attributes.

Sadly, as these artifical fibers have grown, the Rag Man has disappeared from our industry.

About two years ago the environmental stewards of the outdoor industry gathered us all and preached their views on how we must all contribute to cleaning up, and especially, protecting the last of our outdoor spaces and waterways. Somehow, the Rag Man either slept in or knew there was nothing for him to shread and recycle from that gathering.

Today, our industry recyles everything but the products they sell. The polyester fiberfills of today are run on the same fiber opening machines that made wool and cotton insulation from recyled clothes in the era of the Rag Man.

Nylon fabrics and polyester fleeces are dumped, rather than recycled. It is most upsetting that this cry of concern from our industry is being smothered by another new artifical fiber, micro fiber. One could say these microfibers will take up less space in the landfills which really means, more can be dumped there.

Industry media approaches the front end of the cycle by talking about the chemicals to grow cotton and plans to study the actual processes used by the mills to make the fabrics for the non recycled products. Thus, the finished products will stay in the landfills for thousands of years.

The fiber industry knows it's cheaper to make new than recycle used. Profits and the American way, of billions sold on the McDonalds sign, is the Good Housekeeping seal of approval.

It is, at this point, that the lessen of the Rag Man should be studied by all fiber producers, mills, and product makers in the outdoor industry. Becoming a Rag Man is an exciting way to be a better environmentalist. Today, the Rag Man lives and works many miles away from 7th Avenue. He or she is, in fact, you.

Now, I want to share two true stories with you, one about a modern day Rag Man who tried, and the other of a man who didn't even know he was important for being a Rag Man.

About ten years ago, I was contacted by a company in New Jersey. They had tons of polyester film and wanted to make it into a recycled fiber. Their business was removing the silver from the x-ray and photo film, and selling the silver at a very good profit. They had approached the fiber producers, but soon found these chemical giants could make new fibers faster and cheaper than by using recycled film.

In the true spirit of the Rag Man this aggressive and risk taking company made their own fiber. They approached several leading carpet mills. Unable to compete competitively with the bigger fiber giants they were unable to get a start up order. My own attempts to introduce their fibers to the fiberfill industry failed, mostly because the Rag Man wool and cotton batting machines had fallen prey to the corporate ownership of bigger blue chip companies.

One last effort was made using cheaper polyester bottle film. Soft drink companies cooperated but this effort failed too. Again the fiber giants out marketed this modern day Rag Man. Some say it would have worked except the labels in the recycled bottles came out upside down.

The obvious moral to this story is: Recycling your product catalog, and most everything in your office you consume and use, and not recycling the products you make puts your credibility upside down.

The other story I want to share happened just this year. I was asked to review some new products being made by a company

that is, mostly industrial in nature sells a small amount of
product in our industry. As it turned out, he is the son of an
original Rag Man. His company recycles and uses all kinds of
old fabrics and fibers to make new products. He was speechless
to know that his recycling could be the biggest selling point he
could offer the outdoor industry. I said, yes, recycle could be
more important than hollow or micro.

While the longterm goal of this industry is the dream of a
biodegradable fiber, short term, right now recycle should be put
at the top of every speck sheet of every product you manfacture
and sell.

 Sure we know artifical fibers are needed, as there isn't enough
land to raise cotton and feed sheep. But, we also now know
there is not enough land to dump artifical fibers.

And now we know how to be a real Rag Man while we still have
time to make a difference for the future.

From this story back in 1992 I went on to create recycled polarfleece in 1993.
An enormous amount of support came my way when I visited a book store in
Bend that hosted many books on going green. Beyond the famous A Sand County
Almanac by Aldo Leopold many authors were bringing forth books about business
and going green. Silent Spring was becoming much more than the attention to
nature and the environment. Tucked away amongst the green technology books I
found the book Call Of The Rainbow Warrior by Twyla Dell. Reading it through the
teachings showed how a business man in the logging business moved forward to
balance his business with the environment extracted for his logging. I knew I had
found a path to follow with my plan to bring recycled soda bottles back into a polyester fiber for polarfleece. Little to nothing happened after the recycled polarfleece
came out to change the ways of sending millions more bottles to landfills compared

to the consumption that followed. We have reviewed those numbers and events earlier in the book. My biggest point is there it was 1992 and I was about to create recycled polyester fiber into the most popular fabric on the planet. Travelinmg through the next 20 years which ushered in the massive offshoring of textiles in Asia the entire recycled textile fabric issue has been ignored. We do find hints of it every time Nike gets into a big sports promotion as they did with the Olympics around year 2000 with a non woven fabric for apparel made from recycled bottles. And Again recently in this year of 2011 with the football jerseys for the world class soccer games in South America. Today in the year 2011, natural fibers are not seen as products to go into landfills. Clothing from natural fiber is used and reused globally but little is recycled into new fibers or fabrics. Levis are collected and shredded into a fiberfill-type batting, covered with reflective Mylar polyester film, and used in home insulation. Yet why were the American factories that made the denim fabrics and jeans shut down after over a hundred years of workers doing it in America? Worse yet, the American middle-class workers are losing their jobs, health care, and retirements, and their homes are being foreclosed upon. Plastic products, whether films or bottles or fibers, are expected to be dumped into landfills after being collected by several garbage companies whose stock has placed their owners among the two richest men in America. Trying to get fleece recycled put me out of work in the mid-1990s.

People running businesses do not like things changing unless they create the change, which is why I believe they hire lobbyists to control change in our government. America's calling to the Great Outdoors, especially aimed at youth, does not carry the message of landfills and plastic waste, whether it's their soda or water bottles. The numbers of tonnage of plastic and bulk area used by waste collectors is best left to others to write about. One number to think about, though, is the billions of pounds a year of textiles (mostly clothing) that gets dumped into our landfills: sixty-eight pounds per citizen, of which we number 300 million. Not much Nike, North Face, or Columbia apparel is being saved to be vintage like White Stag and Bogner. At least 60 percent of the clothing and shoes worn in America are logo- and color-inspired by outdoor sports.

Before it's sent to America, it is swooshed around Asian factories, where the water is so polluted that even the highest officials in China admit it has happened sooner than expected.

Greenpeace in August/September, 2011 takes it a step further asserting that our home washing machine could be sending toxic chemicals into our sewers and even the clean waters that find that treated water presently safe. The toxic chemical has been discovered and identified in dye house waste water in China and said to be carried forward in the finished fabric and apparel to us and our washing machines. Look it up on the internet under greenpeace/nike / adidas to get the full story.

Outdoor Mega Bucks

Outdoor trade associations hold lobbying days and present our government with big numbers of dollars for recreation and sports: $700 billion in sales and over 6 million jobs. The landfills are all outdoors, waiting for the clothes and shoes. Can we assume the reality of plastic vs. natural is determined by the minds and consumption of citizens? Or is it a presentation given out to corporations to make as much as they can, get as rich as they can, and then finally buy up the stocks of garbage-collection companies to assure the space to keep building landfills.

Distracted by the economy based on oil and gas profits, outdoor recreation drives itself into an area that threatens the healthy supply of clean water on earth. We in America give up the history and lessons of our culture from Europe and from the native habitats of our lands for thousands of years. Inventing plastics, we gave away the manufacturing because we cared more about the consumption and ease of buying things made in cheaper labor worlds.

Brands are everywhere, new and old. Bundling them up seems popular today, as Wolverine Worldwide, a company dating back to 1863, collects new footwear start-ups such as Merrell and Chaco. Chaco was especially creative, but its owner, once established in places like REI, faced the exit timeline to sell out because the demand became bigger than his funds available to supply it. Just another of the many that pollute in China and do not give a hoot.

Industry veterans tell me that China has changed, and increasing prices and issues of labor and production are the reality of the long road traveled since the 1970s. Meanwhile, at home here in America, we are learning that the calling to natural requires our foods to be organic and our economic consumption beyond food to be sustainable. We hide the horrific wastewater pollution of textiles in China, ignoring what we were taught and how we obeyed EPA regulations to create our products and processes.

Sustainable Education

A fully credited master's degree program in sustainable business is now available across Puget Sound from Seattle, on Bainbridge Island. The Bainbridge Institute was founded through family funding from Gifford Pinchot, the first head of the U.S. Forest Service, a great leader in conservation and establishing public lands. Pinchot saw public lands not only as lands to be protected and preserved, but also to be used by citizens and even corporations to help create funding for maintenance of the lands and waterways.

Recreational access owes much to Pinchot's devotion to bringing his views to reality. He differed with John Muir over the uses for public lands, as Muir wanted the lands to be excluded from any extraction, grazing, and other businesses that would take away from the wilderness theme he worked so hard for during his lifetime. One of the most important struggles was over water rights after the fire that destroyed San Francisco. Getting water from the Yosemite area seemed unfair in Muir's eyes, but necessary for the good of the people according to Pinchot.

Pinchot won and the good of the public became a permanent part of conserving and protecting public lands. From this ruling, the Forest Service and the BLM have administered the uses of public lands other than national parks. After one hundred years, present-day practices find very strict regulations for logging, mining, and grazing. Muir's Sierra Club is credited with a great deal of the wins in getting those uses to be reduced or eliminated. The strongest voices have come from citizens and grassroots organizations that have organized under nonprofit laws. Funding comes from grants, donations, and the goodwill of citizens and businesses. Sustainable business brings forth conservation ethics fostered by our public lands. Environmental practices combine science and conservation, especially when trying to protect habitats and flora and fauna.

Today, more than all the issues of logging public lands for profit, the issues of water are a primary concern of pollution and waste management. Smarter minds, such as those in NRDC, take the advanced platform that the water issue is really about consumption.

Wilderness ethics and laws were passed to ensure that millions of acres of forests were left to Nature to be untrammeled by humans and passed on to future generations the same way. Visiting old shut-down logging towns, there are many photos of a logger sitting on a fallen tree stump that is big enough to be cut out and used as a cabin. In the redwoods of California, a tunnel was cut to allow folks to drive through the tree itself, as part of educating people about the importance of allowing these giants to stay as long as Nature allows. Muir and Pinchot taught us about stewardship of the forests and advocating for the good of the people.

Point Theme for Trading

Using the point theme today, textile clothing and footwear are shipped across oceans, mostly the Pacific, on very large vessels called container ships, which are as long and wide as a football field. Oil, not wind, powers these vessels. Today's regulations for these vessels owes a great deal to a group of activists for the environment called "river keepers." It was out of their devotion and courage to clean up the Hudson River around the port of New York City that the EPA was created. One of the big issues was the dumping of ballast water full of pollution.

Vessels refilled the ballast with fresh Hudson River water for the return voyage to a foreign port, where the fresh water was sold for commercial uses such as filling swimming pools in posh hotels. Far more than vessel water was causing the death of habitats such as the famous striped bass fishery in the Hudson River. Striped bass was the East Coast's pride, comparable to West Coast salmon.

From the EPA came regulations for all textile mills, both plastic and natural fibers and fabrics, weaving, knitting, dyeing, and finishing. Millions of dollars were spent by each textile mill to stop the dumping, as we showed in the example of the Florida microfiber acrylic mill that met the EPA regulations by 1975. These regulations were mothballed during the building of offshore textiles in the 1980s. A total disrespect for water and its health was replaced with technologies of moisture-management (known as sweat, rain, and snow).

Outdoor clothing and gear today pretends to be technology that allows you to go exploring and be comfortable, fit, and safe.

Real Time Exploring

In reviewing real exploring, the best example I can find was an expedition that started in 1914. Sir Ernest Shackleton set sail for his second adventure in the South Atlantic. Hailed as one of the most astonishing feats of exploration ever recorded, the expedition took two years before Shackleton and his crew reappeared and were able to communicate again.

His ship, the Endurance, was surrounded by ice, which forced him and his men to leave the ship as its timbers were being crushed and sunk; its massive beams from Norway's forests could not withstand the pressures of the ice. Left on land, his men and dog teams, carrying their supplies, began to walk in a two-year survival race against the coldest place on earth. They survived through the seasons, with warmer weather melting the ice enough to get food for both men and the dogs. At no time were they able to reach anyone anywhere to get advice or report their position. They used several small boats to sail through ice-cold waters, and often were attached to floating ice stations. Although the weather changed over the season, from cold to warmer melting, the temperature always was below what anyone would want to survive in.

Picture Shackleton and his twenty-seven men in a nylon Gore-Tex jacket with a layer of Polarfleece and Power Dry polyester underwear. Of course for that to be real today in any so-called exploration, you need to add in the safety of communication by cell phone and helicopter availability, among other choices. But for Shackleton and his crew of twenty-seven men, it was 1914, not 2010. In 1914, thousands of miles away across America, woolen mills were making outdoor fabrics, and folks were fishing and hunting and exploring in much safer places. Shackleton's men were embedded in nearly one million square miles of ice that shifted with the clockwise winds and current of the Weddell Sea. That sea reached out to both the Pacific and Atlantic oceans through the Scotia Sea.

From many books about the expedition, we know their survival kit in 1914 included the clothes on their back, two pair of mittens, six pair of socks, two pair of boots, a sleeping bag, a pound of tobacco, and two pounds of personal gear. Doctors kept more, and men with diaries were allowed to keep them and write in them. Their sleeping bags were woolen or made from reindeer skins, and they slept on planks of wood from the ship or the bare ice. They all dressed the same, wearing heavy wool underwear, woolen trousers, a thick, loose wool sweater, and a pair of light gabardine Burberry overalls on the outside. Their heads were covered by a knitted woolen helmet and Burberry outer helmet, which tucked in at the neck. A Burberry parka was worn as the outer shell.

Since these were all natural fibers, they were soaking wet from the weather and water and ice. The layers would freeze and dry, and the difference between the gabardine outer layers and the wool inner layers absorbing and drying kept them alive. Today this same freezing and drying is promoted in more words than anyone ever used for toothpaste. Gore-Tex film keeps developing into a better this-and-that while it covers nylon and polyester fibers that do not breath, absorb, freeze, or relax enough to be anything but another story for another micropore to prevent decay.

Shackleton's team also hunted seals and used the skins for further protection—skins soft enough to be worn as boots. Compare that to soft shells today in Polartec Power Shield, which is three layers of panty-hose fabric combined with a polyester double-knit, held together with bonding chemicals or, for more money, Gore-Tex films. Polyester and nylon are also layers, with polyester hating moisture and nylon loving it. However, neither of these fibers can absorb moisture into the fiber itself like gabardine and wool can. Thus moisture is suspended between the fibers and runs off or freezes, depending on the conditions and time out there.

True exploring, like what actually happened and was recorded in the Shackleton Expedition, has yet to be tried or even considered in today's performance outdoor clothing and gear. For sure, today the gear would have the communication features of the North Face parka and rescue by helicopter would be part of the exploration. My point in this is that fabrics like Polarfleece and merino wool have been created for comfort in daily outdoor activity. Wool goes back hundreds of years before it arrived in America in skiwear clothing. Skiwear started out in wool and gabardine and gave way to nylon and down and then to polyester fiberfill and nylon, before finally ending up in polyester Polarfleece and nylon Gore-Tex.

Being outdoors is a wonderful way to find ourselves in nature and enjoy the freshness of air and water and the lands around us filled with trees, snow, and fields of grass and flowers. Do we really want to bring the electronics with us and be chatting and reading dials while we are out there walking, biking, rafting, and running? Or sending e-mails and googling about the function of the storm vent in our jacket when the storm comes up? We can take gabardine and wool and Polarfleece and enjoy being outdoors, knowing that others have explored beyond the limits and returned safely.

Jim Whittaker summited Mount Everest the second time in a Peace Climb with American, Chinese, and Russian climbers. I donated a red full-zip, two-pocket fleece jacket for each of the climbers and was told it was the one item they would not climb without. Today's Everest summits flow like a tramway, and climbers use base camps to read the air flow for wind resistance and water resistance dials of soft-shell polyester and Gore-Tex nylon, adding seam-sealing and enough designs like the North Face summit style to be able to call a high-tech vacate when it leaks. Make no mistake, that plastic will not freeze and thaw and freeze and thaw while you cross the coldest place on earth for two years.

Today only a Burberry-branded coat has endured what is shown in the catalogs and ads of the newest brands like North Face and Patagonia. REI is not going to put Burberry and Pendleton on the racks next to all that plastic. Burberry and Pendleton took the oldest and most trusted fibers in the world, cotton and wool, to the extremes of exploring, as well as to daily workers' lives in America and Europe over the past hundred years. They made their outerwear and other clothing in their own factories until the plastic warriors found a cheaper place to just do it, far away from the homes of those workers and mills. A stitch in time should show us all that plastics are not going to create a society that will pass on hundreds of years of clothing, or any other want and need that is now made of synthetics.

Can You Here Me Now

No one person in America or anywhere on this earth can change something. But he or she can light a candle, and showing that light brings things to those who are open to look into that light and think about what they see and believe. Then they will act on what they believe in and ask another to light another candle. Today, what shines in America are the faces of youth trying to understand what they are to do as they become old enough to realize that mom and dad fear losing their jobs.

Others who are better off live in denial of the corrupt pollution in places like China, from which flows their money. Our government starts to fear too much regulation from the EPA, while China ignores the one they wrote in 1993 to show good faith to get into the World Trade Organization.

Looking around the winter blasts in America this winter of 2010, wool coats without a brand logo and high-tech fabric vent quietly keep folks warm and happy. Fibers proven over hundreds of years do not need space-suit comics and polluted-water makers far away from our own backyards. The costs of environmental cleanup now facing China will equal out the reason to produce in America once again that which was taken by polluters.

Now outdoor makers are formed into a coalition for sustainable apparel. Launched in March 2011, many of the coalition's members are presented in previous chapters of this book. They claim to be the biggest and most influential companies in the apparel and footwear marketplace. Giving them that standing, one can also say they are collectively the biggest polluters of water and air in China and other parts of Asia. However, they are not kneeling and admitting responsibility for that obvious situation. Rather, from SportsOneSource.com on March 2, 2011, speaking as a collaborative approach, they state they will reduce the environmental and social impacts of apparel and footwear products sold around the world. They suggest creating an industry wide index to measure and evaluate product sustainability performance.

One can only ask whether these companies are selling apparel using chemicals and natural fibers produced under the same EPA regulations as when they purchased textile chemical supplies and natural fibers made in America? After all, the press release further states that academic experts and the U.S. EPA are members of the coalition. Missing is the equivalent of the EPA of China or of any other country where they currently have their textiles produced. They have a goal of a shared vision using tools from stakeholders and including words like "metrics" to ensure full transparency—big words that come down to chemicals used to make their products with both natural and synthetic fibers, as we have learned in this memoir. The denial of the pollution reported in this book and the cover-up of their polluting via offshore production make these companies slicker than the oil companies. Of course, given all their moisture management and inventions of chemical treatments, from chips making fibers to garments of household plastics, nobody would think the cloak of their garments is that simple to find.

College students in China rally around more than a thousand activist organizations, the oldest and best-known of which is called Green Camel Bell. With their help, we can close these memoirs with a transparency that has been sent around the world by the brave students and farming villages of China since 2004.

Green Camel Bell (gcb) founded in 2004 is trying to anchor to the culture and life of China: respecting nature first so that what they are lent by their children today is there for them tomorrow. Many of the workers and volunteers are avid outdoor recreation men and women. Others simply want their village to stay healthy as the economy of China moves across rural lands and waters. Given the year 2010 statement from the United Nations that 50 million citizens in China are now considered "environmental refugees" these brave young men and women deserve our attention and support. Speaking out and exchanging emails as I do with gcb makes the call to action to end the catastrophic pollution to return the refugees to their homes and villages safely.

Chapter Fourteen:

Transparency

A documentary film titled Warriors Of Qiugang was nominated for a 2011 Academy Award. The film is about real village life in China's industrial beltways, where a rural village of 1,900 people suffered from pollution for decades from nearby factories. Major factories with few or no pollution controls pump out polluted waters filled with textile dyes, pesticides, and chemicals. Local rivers turned black. Fish and wildlife were killed. Air filled with fouled pollutants burned residents' eyes and throats and sickened children. Since 2007, as reported in the New York Times, the residents have been trying to do something about it. Getting records and data from the factories in China is not easy to do. The Chinese government in 1993 established their EPA-like agency, which is controlled by the government without transparency or oversight, a move that looks more like a cover-up to get into the WTO than an honest pledge to control pollution and waste, which the American EPA has done for forty years.

Tomorrow's history of today's outdoor and activewear textile brands, especially American brands using offshore production, will, in my opinion, record that outdoor recreation used plastic as a sign of wealth and intelligence. Assuming that humans are still here in a thousand years to find the plastic, what else will they find? For sure, the abuses to water and the stupid travels to find cheap labor and unused water are the most deploring behaviors to simply make clothes to protect two arms and two legs, totally ignoring the gift between the ears. We know who these companies are as they beat their brands in logos across the garments and footwear. Today's outdoor gear is covered in easily seen trademarks for both the brand and the technology used to make the item. The design universe for outdoor gear lives in our lifestyles but somehow seems less tasteful once the truth about its pollution abuses is known.

The beauty of nature and its violent changes in weather make sense to a person on a horse wearing a fiber material that actually came from the natural world. Today that rider into a base camp would be thought of as an intruder in the adventure of rubber tires, rubber-sole shoes, and plastic-fiber clothing and gear. On the street, the simple fashion of a black sweater and black coat, both made out of wool, do not need a technical logo or the company brand or the designer's name to tell the story of why it is being worn. Neither Ernest Shackleton nor any of his expedition's survivors went on to build outdoor gear.

The famous Burberry fabrics used in the expedition are trenched into outerwear without micropores, assuring wearers that they'd keep dry and warm during a day in the cold of winter in their hometown. No branding logos covered the beauty of the fashion design of the coats. When Edmund Hillary returned from the summit of Everest, he did not create a co-op of mountain gear that would later find a path to catastrophic wastewater pollution trickling down from the snow melts of his famous climb to the summit. In those same mountains, rivers, and valleys, today's climbers are polluting enough drinking water to put a guilt trip on every citizen in America.

China is slowly allowing its citizens a voice in this destruction of their lands, waters, and people. The origin of the Green Camel Bell activists alludes to how the Silk Road caravans that once traveled the region were called "camel bells." Green Camel Bell's founder, an environmental activist named Zhao Zhong, seeing his country turning to ruin, is climbing the wall of China step-by-step to save his country's natural landscapes and water.

In China at this time, 320 million innocent people, including more than 100,000 working in the outdoor textile and sportswear supply chain, have no clean drinking water. The solution to this has been ignored for over a decade while American businesses educate themselves about being a sustainable business. Training at a masters degree level in sustainable ways is a mere thirty-minute ferry ride from the Seattle-based REI corporate headquarters, to the Bainbridge Institute on Bainbridge Island.

Instead of facing the truth about warriors like those from Qiugang and the voices of young-adult volunteers and interns of Green Camel Bell, outdoor and activewear brands ramble and scramble around the protected lands of America and Europe.

Pictured above are GCB logo tee shirts made in the USA by Doug Hoschek. Does their plastic gear really work? Brand-for-brand, item-for-item, the answer remains unknown without an expedition such as Shackleton's to support the product claims. When extreme weather blows hard enough to tear your arms off and trees lean over as the landscape gets wet and cold, does the crackle of nylon laminated with plastic films make you feel like it's going to crack open? Can a soft-shell polyester and nylon stand up to that? Are all those seams and pockets the design of an industrial matrix tested for wind shear and water and snow? The simple truth is, sewing thread is not as durable as the fabric itself. So count the patches (seams too) and pockets in things like a North Face or Columbia ski parka and be extremely prepared for the threads to break and pull out. The static of plastic polyester makes fleece crackle for warmth until it gets really wet. Dwarfed in this reality is the impression that your mind is living in a space suit while you are still attached to Mother Earth. The branded logos are required to show the difference between the older natural fibers and today's plastics. Today's adventure gear uses the trickery that claims only plastic fibers and modern technology will keep you safe from the weather.

Making outdoor apparel, shoes, and gear a "logo land" of the same things from the made in China manufacturing. Marco Polo...the "polar pollution" is going to wipe it all out.

I believe that by the time I need new clothes, they will be made here, and pollution in China will be under control as they make clothing for their own population and clean up their water. To clarify, I have enough merino wool/viscose underwear made in the Wickers sewing factory in America to last me twenty years, washing one set each week and wearing them for at least two years. My old unworn, real Polarfleece vests and jackets made in America are ready to be allowed a time outdoors. I have the special one-time-only merino flexiwool, which was custom-made for samples by the little shop in Oregon, assuring me an outer layer when it gets to the point where I need my wool to release that moisture but hold it frozen to keep me warm. I have wool/alpaca socks of good quality made in America, as well as boots. I'm assured clean, healthy air and water. America has already rid itself of the manufacturing pollution that came with black-magic textiles: EPA, not WMCA (Why Make China Accountable).

Nester Hosiery in Mount Airey, North Carolina, received an environmental award in 2011 for wastewater treatment in the town where they manufacture their popular socks, employing more than a hundred workers. This proves that we are free to innovate and invent new fibers and technologies, and we are free to return to stabilizing our needs to the balance in nature that is as old as time and creation. Voices call for government led by citizens and a new order of protection for making things here, to assure our children that what they build will stay here for their children, as well.

Melting sets apart the sustainable creations of nature from the black magic and its bottle of dumping and pollution. Remember this if you remember nothing else from this book: America has always risen to the wants and needs of our citizens and our lands, water, and air. Our democracy allows freedoms that cannot be found anywhere else in present or past times and countries. We control the ability to create sustainable materials and meet our needs from them here, in our clean and healthy waters and air. The will to get that done was created by the devotion of American factories to admit their wrongs and do it right. That challenge was my life's work during the 1970s. It anchored my values to always believe in making things here in America.

Today as we enter the year 2011, the fashions of the '60s and '70s are showing up in quilted down, cotton chamois shirts, woolen plaids, and even quilted polyester fiberfills. These designs were etched under the best environmental laws ever written in the history of the world. Each and every citizen had a job and the means to buy what was made here in America at that time. The investors and bankers telling us we cannot make things here is a simple corporate business ploy to avoid responsibility for fair wages, benefits, and collective bargaining, which built the middle class of America. The top 1 percent wants to keep all the money, while a farce of outdoor corporations pretend that their giving 1 percent of profits to the planet is what the average citizen of America needs to pay attention to. BSBB (Bull Shit Baffles Brains). We already have the environmental regulations to assure our children safe water and places to get outdoors. Jobs created by making things here will rebuild the losses to our homes, assure funding for education, and protect America's natural resources so they are sustainable for future generations. The costs are easily adjusted into wages that will allow the comforts, recreation, and security of retirements. The money is here in America. It simply has to be redistributed into a healthy working class of citizens.

As citizens and stewards of the Earth, we do owe a debt to the innocent villages and people of China who were forced to accept the American corporate greed wanting an escape from the EPA regulations here in America. Today in China there is a new transparency on government pollution data. American citizens, journalists, and many other professionals working through the NRDC and Environment360 (E360) from Yale University are supporting and reporting the activists' progress in China to change the practices of pollution. Warriors from Qiugang have faced the fears of their government's supreme control, saying the next generation cannot live this way.

Nickel-and-dime efforts by the leading American brands (Sustainable Apparel Coalition) act as if this kind of pollution never existed on the planet before they started using China as a supplier. This is simply a farce. Every name in this book that has gone offshore knows about the EPA in America and what it stands for and why. They accepted my double-faced fleece and then acted in double-faced ways, creating alliances for funding environmental protection from polluting corporations such as oil companies. Now it is those same tactics, photos, and groundswells of warriors that are standing up to them.

What history will record remains to be seen. But today for sure, the journalists and photographers are standing shoulder-to-shoulder with the innocent warriors of China. Their lands and water are polluted to the core with carcinogens. Green Camel Bells ring louder than the liberty bells of America. For the thousands of importers of textiles not mentioned in this book, they are easy to find. Just look at the label of origin. Made in China really means made without EPA regulations by those who know and live a doubled-faced life, fleecing citizens around the globe. The article "In China, a New Transparency on Government Pollution Data" should be read on E360's Internet site, e360.yale.edu.

Basic education teaches us that everything in this world requires water to survive. Our own bodies are made up of just over 80 percent water. The Earth itself stores water and makes water every minute of every day. Over five thousand years ago, sheep became a very important part of the world's ways and means. Today we see the sheep shiver on the ice cap (cover of this book), not sure if there is any land left to walk on or eat and drink from. We, too, are facing exactly that place. Beyond the greed of pollution, we are failing at every turn to save water and create proper consumption practices for ourselves and future generations.

Textile dyeing evolved in factories dyeing millions of yards of fabrics made of synthetic fibers, woven and knit. A mere hundred years ago, before synthetics,

wool fibers were dyed before they were made into yarns for weaving and knitting. Most cotton fibers were dyed in the yarn stage, not the fabric stage. As
demand increased for more and more textile products, mills found it most efficient and profitable to weave and knit what is called greige goods, meaning
fabrics that are not dyed. Inventories could be created in very large production
runs and stored until actual orders were placed for a specific amount of fabric.

Abundant supplies of water in America, especially in areas where textile mills
were built, found rivers flowing with an endless supply of fresh water. American
history has lived and recorded and accounted for the pollution and wasting of
water in textiles and all other manufacturing. Data for all our drinking water is
reviewed daily. During one of my recent walks in the five-thousand-acre Forest Park within the Portland city limits, I saw a team of water testers collecting
samples from very small streams to check for chemicals and other possible pollutants. The streams run through vast acres of woodlands and natural plants.
Challenges arise from recreation's desire to expand the uses of the lands to
allow for more mountain-biking trails. This is a common theme across America,
fueled by the mega retailing of outdoor products by the big billion-dollar retailers. Virgin streams in national parks face the same kind of demand from users
of plastic boats, helmets, and clothing who paddle over white water preserved
to be pristine for nature and for viewing by we who own our public lands.

In America, we have the safest drinking water on the planet for our population of 300 million plus. Yet, when it comes to the outdoor corporations using
suppliers for textile dyeing in China, the issue of pollution is not and has not
been part of how they do business. As the Chinese develop their country to be
as modern as America, a plan to relocate 900 million people from rural farms to
urban living places and work areas challenges the officials to find healthy drinking water. In the middle of this transformation, complete with photos of desert
areas to be regenerated like our own communities, is the broken and polluted
water system of factories supplying textiles and plastics for computers. Raw
numbers show China with 20 percent of the world's population and 7 percent of
the world's useable water supply. Why does a multi-billion-dollar outdoor textile

industry steeped in environmental protection believe their supply of products is safe and secure in this challenge for production of fiber, yarns, fabric, dyeing, and sewing? A polite answer is that just about every CEO and worker in these companies never owned or worked in American textile mills to understand the importance of controlling waste and pollution. Put into simple numbers, the outdoor textile industry created a Conservation Alliance in 1989 to protect the environment, and especially water. Twenty-one years later they have raised through donations $9 million and have used those funds exclusively to protect natural lands and waters for their so-called natural playground.

Recall the story from earlier in this book about a microfiber synthetic-fiber plant in Florida in 1996 that spent an average of $10 million annually to meet or exceed EPA regulations to produce their textile fibers. By the year 2000, the fiber plant was out of business, since its customers—many of them Conservation Alliance members—had offshored production to the uncontrolled pollution of producing textiles in China. The Florida microfiber plant was spending $5 million a year for water-treatment compliance, $2 million a year on maintenance for environmental controls, and $3 million on waste minimization. The grounds hosted a forest and a very large freshwater lake. Water from the fiber processing was taken from and returned to both the forest and lake. Compare this to the outdoor industry funding access to waterways and forest for recreation in what they call their natural playground of public lands. The other face of this double-faced outdoors industry is responsible for polluting so much water in China that a village (Qiugang) became warriors to save themselves and their children from death and starvation. Today the environmental movement in China fights the same polluters that present themselves as environmental stewards of their favorite rivers and trails, with a logo for their brand in bold letters for easy purchasing on Amazon and eBay. This is the real footprint of today's outdoor brands—complete with enough plastic water bottles to survive for about two days away from home; wrapped in plastic that is always bound for a landfill. Google the Conservation Alliance and then google the Chinese organization, Green Camel Bell.

Of course, sooner or later, this name will be chased after by the corporate CEOs who hunt and gather up authentic outdoor brands, as we have discussed in this book. This time it won't be so easy for them to bag their trophies. I own the rights to the Green Camel Bell logo for apparel in North America. China owns and controls everything in their country. My common sense says we should keep helping groups and citizens in China. Our knowledge and experiences with our own EPA are the guidelines for cleaning up the pollution before it is too late. To accomplish this, I have a written authorization from the owner of Green Camel Bell to make and sell apparel using the GCB logo "Camel" for three years. Profits will go to improve the welfare of lands, waters, and habitats in China, supporting GCB in becoming their own vision of our Sierra Club. Some of the proceeds from the sales of this book and Green Camel Bell tee shirts will be donated to GCB.

The simple fact that China has ignored the environmental issues and regulations since they created their own EPA in 1993 clearly puts the blame on the country's rulers. The shame goes to the American textile brands, as I've written, as well as bigger bounty, such as Apple in computers. If you are not convinced that our own health is at stake from the pollution in China, consider these facts: Acid rain has claimed 220 cities in China. South Korea pollution is horrible and comes directly from China. Premature deaths from pollution in China are climbing to nearly 750,000 a year. In some areas, streams are so polluted that even cows cannot drink the water. In America, outdoor textile-led activists fight to keep cows out of prime fishing and rafting streams. Of course, in China if the cow can't drink the water, the fish are dead and a rafter is in the hospital critically ill. It makes you wonder what the North Face is talking about when they tell their Wall Street investors that their brand in China will get Chinese youth outdoors to rivers and trails.

The United Nations predicted that at the end of 2010, the degraded water and soil in China will have created 50 million "environmental refugees"—innocent citizens forced to leave their homelands in search of potable water and safe farmland. A humanitarian crisis looms. Yet the Nike, North Face, Columbia,

Adidas, and Timberland brands promote selling to China as a way to double their billions in five years. They brag that they are at the top of the list to get the cotton, polyester, and nylon fibers as needed.

Green Camel Bell is reported to be one of the first environmental groups active in China today. Its founder, Zhao Zhong, left his job as an educated engineer to try to save his country from the pollution brought about by many American businesses that did not stand up for the environmental regulations the Chinese EPA created in 1993. The Chinese government maintains the right to jail activists. Yet activists such as Zhao say "the mountains are dying." Warriors from Qiugang speak louder about people dying. In America, our own wilderness is attacked monthly by someone in Congress. Activists led by Scott Silver and his organization, Wild Wilderness, keep the cover for wilderness protection, decades after the act to protect it. In America, we simply cannot ever give up to the most-to-lose-have-done-the-least.

In my opinion, China faces a big truth when the focus turns to the country's water supply. Cleaning up their pollution should save the citizens of China and allow them to build a life that promotes education, clean air and water, and a means to be safe and compete globally. However, that leaves very few resources to provide 300 million people in America with textile products. While 50 million in China leave their homelands because of pollution, one in five Americans faces losing their home or home equity because their jobs have been sent offshore to pollution hellholes in places like China. Whatever the banks have done in mortgages, the corporations using pollution-riddled products from China are guilty of a bigger crime, in my opinion. In China, breaking their EPA regulations and laws is not punishable with jail sentences, nor can a lawyer sue the polluter. Here in America, breaking EPA regulations and laws is punishable by the government and also by lawsuits brought against the polluter. Herein lies the truth about "doing it," "never stop polluting," and "one tough life."

Until textiles are properly brought back to the EPA-regulated factories in America, the "polar pollution" of my doubled-faced technology seeks landfills and destroys the ability of American citizens to gain the respect of making things here in America. Those currently making textiles off the shores of America are simply not paying respect to the thread and fabric of life. Allow me to offer this explanation for what I mean by not paying respect. The outdoor and activewear brands presented in my book moved offshore their sourcing for fibers, yarns, fabrics, dyeing, finishing, printing, and chemicals for treatments like wicking, moisture management, antimicrobials, bonding, and laminating—many known to be toxic—without requesting or demanding that the manufacturing and processing follow the EPA regulations they were supplied by American and European sources.

Today China, the prime source of textiles, reports a rapidly growing wealth with a total economic growth of 9 percent in years 2009 and 2010, according to the World Bank. This 9 percent matches the unemployment rate in America of 9 percent for the same two years. It is widely accepted that manufacturing in America, especially in textiles has been moving offshore and especially to China since the mid-1990s. China's population, reported to be 1.3 billion, is the largest on earth and more than America and Europe combined. Some 72 percent of the Chinese population is between the ages of fifteen and sixty-four, with a median age of thirty-five, according to reports from the Central Intelligence Agency. China's middle class is now larger than the entire population of America. What China calls their second-tier cities will grow by 900 million more people in the next five years to fill the labor demands of their industrial areas.

The big outdoor and activewear brands, as reported in this book, are targeting a doubling of their billions of dollars in sales during the next five years, much of it going to China. In what can be called an orgy of workers in China's middle class, both the big American brands and the rich and wealthy in China see this gold rush of plastics produced without environmental regulations as a miner's boom and water-pollution bust. Panning for synthetic and cotton textiles finds the waters so polluted that dyeing must be done several times to get the color shade correct. The polluted water is put back into veins of the land and then brought back to be used again, with dirt and chemicals attached to the murky water. Metals and other toxic chemicals are shifted in a miner's metal box called a dye kettle. Skimmed off the top, the valuable plastics and cotton move on to fabrics and sewing factories.

It is reported that the rich from the upper and middle classes are purchasing luxury items like Burberry and Hugo Boss, bringing the value of the luxury market in China to just over $14 billion in the next five years. The larger second-tier cities and citizens—all 900 million—make up the target marketplace for many American brands to sell what is made for them in China. Not one of hundreds of American brands has become honest enough to demand the pollution stop in the processing of their products. Instead, the biggest ones report increases in sales and profits to waiting investors on Wall Street. These massive corporations have bundled up hundreds of brands and are passing themselves off to the American consumer as triple-A for the environment and pledging more sustainable components as profits grow during the next five years. I can only sense this is one more trick-for-treat to the wealthy in America and a million-dollar lifestyle for more than millions in China. Simply put, Wall Street is doing it again, only this time with polluted textiles and other plastics manufactured in China to avoid EPA environmental regulation of American manufacturing.

What does the middle class of the new China look like as a consumer? Urban Chinese women are spending more and saving less, pouring 63 percent of their incomes into consumer spending. Women are reported to be the spenders in the Chinese middle- and upper-class households. Is this picture starting to look like American women before our recession came in 2008? Well here is more "dish" from the women's side. Spending jumped from 30 percent of income in 2006 to 63 percent in 2009. Asked what they expect to buy in 2010, 63 percent of the urban Chinese women said they would spend it on clothes and accessories such as shoes, 75 percent on travel, 22 percent on cell phones, and 41 percent on cosmetics. The income spent in U.S. dollars equals $3,200, or 21,900 yuan. The primary reason for the reversal in spending vs. savings since 2006 is stated to be for a better life. On the guy's side, Playboy owner Hugh Hefner said during a recent TV appearance on CNN that China now hosts 220 retail stores under the Playboy brand and is a leading item for Chinese men to own and wear.

To this luxury lifestyle, add on a big green board the numbers for water and air pollution, and the deaths of 100,000 from water pollution and 750,00 from air pollution. Factor in 90 percent polluted groundwater and 320 million people without safe drinking water.

In recent years, the words "cheap cashmere sweaters" have been seen across the aisles of retailers in America, from Saks to Costco. Taking the luxury out of cashmere I believe really puts the truth on what China is all about, The area of prized grasses on the famous Alaskan Plateau, which is rich in history dating back to Genghis Kahn, produced the cashmere goat, whose downy undercoat we know as cashmere wool. Cashmere is valued at six times the price of merino wool and is often referred to as the diamond fiber. In 1949 there were around 2 million goats grazing that land. By 2004, the herds were up to 28 million goats and the lands were turned into a dust bowl equal to the famous 1930s dust bowl in America. This breeding produced over-grazing, and the goats not only ate all the grasses, but also the roots and the bark of seedlings. Relying on other feed sources, such as corn and hay, the goats are failing to stay healthy. On the plateau now, winds commonly create giant dust storms that are reported to swallow over a thousand villages and push the citizens out. Most alarming, the dust and sand blow east over the coal plants, adding their pollution to the mix. This air pollution reaches the shores of North America, especially Washington state, Oregon, Idaho, and British Columbia, in about five days. In 1998, a public warning was issued. Now, over ten years later, the status has not changed for the cashmere goats or the pollution sent along with the cheap prices.

So far that might be considered their pollution problem. However, once you comprehend what I have presented in this book about America losing its manufacturing in textiles for so-called cheaper prices, you realize the cheaper prices come with hidden costs. The fact is that environmental protection, which started the companies presented to you, was simply left on the shores of America as the shoes and clothes went offshore for profit and glory, to become the next wave of insiders to be used and abused by investors, bankers, and Wall Street.

On top of Mount Bachelor in Oregon, where I tested out Polarfleece, the weather observation station recently captured the pollution. The sunny skies of California, home to the Patagonia footprint of open environmental disclosure, find almost 30 percent of their air polluted from Asian, and especially Chinese, textile manufacturing. Getting fleeced the American way is now a bigger game of polar pollution. Boreal forests are putting more and more carbon into the air as the planet warms from all the pollution, and energy and water use are the biggest polluters.

Come on, America, that big white polar bear is begging you to become a bull and kick some butt, not stuff your face and bodies with plastic wrappers of fibers that make you sweat and stink. Go indigenous, be natural, Nature will take care of the rest. Still not a believer? Just how is China getting so rich manufacturing what we are giving up? Cheaper is based on what the American brand uses for an excuse to move out from under EPA regulations, so a woman in China buys the shoes and clothes you can't buy because you lost your job and we as a county lost our middle class. BSBB, as my New York roots know, doesn't work.

Today's textile products using synthetic fibers (plastics) are chemically made and thus become chemically "dependent" on the brand selling them. Natural fibers such as cotton and merino wool need chemicals for processing. Brands are promoting the use of organic cotton as a means of creating a sustainable business model. However, in my opinion, all are failing to advance out of the chemically dependent dyeing and other chemical processing used to create the materials that make their finished products.

The purpose of organic cotton is rooted to the Esprit Company, to the best of my knowledge. From that company, which was discussed earlier in this book, a new company emerged from one of the Esprit employees when his son Scotty was traveling in South America. Named Indigenous Designs, the company uses organic, natural fibers of merino wool, silk, and alpaca. The fibers are all produced in South America. Using environmentally friendly dyes and hand-made eco-fashions, a network of artisans make men's and women's apparel that is hand-woven and hand-knit with needles and hand-held knitting looms.

We have learned about the textile industry moving from home to factory during the Industrial Revolution, and the resulting development of machines that use vast amounts of energy, water, and chemicals to mass-produce today's apparel, footwear, and gear. Indigenous Designs is a competitive company with sales just over $5 million—doing it by hand. I point this out because in the early years of my career, $5 million was the average annual sales of most outdoor and skiwear clothing companies, including Columbia, North Face, White Stag, and hundreds more. And they had the advantage of industrial manufacturing to build with. More importantly, without asking for or wanting it, regulations for controlling the chemical parts of their manufacturing process were established for them by the EPA in America and were honored by myself and their other American suppliers. Likewise, the artisans used by Indigenous Designs to create their millions of dollars in sales also protect their communities from pollution and chemical health and water issues. Fair wages are a pivotal part of the Indigenous Designs plan, and they meet or exceed that goal with 75 percent of the costs of manufacturing going to labor, vs. 50 percent of the costs for labor in industrial factories.

The solutions to the issues of chemically dependent textile products is, in my opinion, the responsibility of you and I as the consumer. This includes all our purchases of apparel textiles, footwear, and gear that use an assembly-line basis for manufacturing. This base of assembly-line manufacturing evolved from Europe to America and most recently has been set up in Asia, especially China, without transparency into the pollution and catastrophic results. At this time, the brands owned by big corporations such as Jarden, Nike, VF, and Columbia do not have control or ownership of the manufacturing, so they cannot control the pollution. Two things stopped me from wanting to be a supplier to them or work for them the past fifteen years. First, I had no desire to travel to Asia and rebuild what I had created here. Second, I knew that the environmental regulations necessary to produce man-made fiber textiles were not being used in Asia and would cost too much for the factories there to change over.

The Asian market at that time was a cotton-rich textile marketplace, not capable of properly dyeing and finishing polyester fibers and fabrics. I could have pioneered that challenge, but I saw into the future that the growth created at that time was the result of ignoring EPA regulations by manufacturing offshore. I did not believe any company in America, especially the outdoor and activewear apparel industry, would allow such pollution in the processing of their fibers and fabrics. And finally, the Microsoft dot-com economy did not exist yet to support investors getting into the outdoor marketplace. Thus I opted to create recycled polyester fleece, and then moved on to merino wool and truly sustainable fiber-dyed viscose tree-pulp fibers. Today the pollution of chemical plastics in textile fibers and fabrics and in computers and other electronics goes hand-in-hand with the growth of China's economy. It is also my opinion, based on all the facts now disclosed, that the resulting pollution is catastrophic to water and lives in China and other places, such as Indonesia.

At some point in each of our lives, we face the truth about who we are and how we fit into the natural world of this planet. During the 1990s, I learned about myself when my Polarfleece was taken from me and I was given the chance to move offshore. I had moved to Seattle in 1973 because I fell in love with the lands and waters of that area. Oregon, just a few hours' drive away, offered me the wilderness that I did not understand as a college student in Missoula, Montana. My journey was clearly to stay here in the Pacific Northwest and do as I did, which I have written about in this book. Today seeing the deaths of hundreds of thousands in China each year from textile water pollution, I know that the real face of outdoor products consists of chemical products without proper, chemically responsible manufacturing to protect our global environment.

I sincerely hope that sharing my story and the undisputed facts about textile chemicals and pollution to air and especially water will bring us closer to a natural way of living. I believe our future is not about science and math. I believe it is about living in balance with Nature, about finding a path out of being chemically dependent and the behaviors it has brought to us.

I learned textiles from the chemical side when I began my career in the chemical company Celanese Corporation, as I shared earlier in this book. Once the chemicals were made into fiber, the processing to make yarns and fabrics required more chemicals, many of them toxic and extremely dangerous to our health if allowed into our air and water supply. Each and every company that uses natural and man-made fibers has, in my opinion, no excuse for ignoring and/or not following the EPA regulations that created safe processing of textile chemicals for both natural and plastic fibers in the 1970s. Daily we see claims of many chemicals being added to the fibers and fabrics to enhance performance. This clearly shows that the brands understand they are in the chemical business. Chemicals are used for waterproofing, windproofing, breathing, moisture management, and antimicrobial applications. Few if any of these chemicals are used with natural fibers.

The final conclusion, in my opinion, is that chemical textile products must be regulated globally under the same regulations and laws. Today any brand of outdoor, activewear, fashion, sportswear, or other type of textiles cannot "hide in the closet" about the pollution they have created by sourcing and manufacturing offshore instead of staying in America.

Chapter Fifteen:

Textile Profile of America

The Office of Compliance in the EPA completed and published a "notebook project" in September 1997, containing charts of data obtained from various 1992 Census of Manufacturers, Industries Series, for SIC's 2211-2299 U.S. and the Department of Commerce Census, Bureau of the Census, 1995. Allow me to share my opinions from these charts, which follow my comments.

In 1992, the products called Polarfleece and Polartec were made on knitting machines at Malden Mills.

According to table 2, Summary Statistics for the Textile Industry, knitting is listed under Industry SIC Code SIC 225. There were 2,096 establishments, making up 1,911 companies, employing 193,300 American workers. The value of shipments from the knitters was $16.9 billion. The value of Polarfleece and Polartec known to me in Malden knitting mills, including dyeing and finishing dollars, was just under a half billion dollars in revenues annually.

Table 4 shows the 1995 sales for the top ten textile mills in America, with number ten being Guilford Mills at $783 million. Had the 1995 fire not destroyed so much of Malden, the plan to become number ten would, in my opinion, have happened by 1998, or no later than 2000. Not until after 2000 did Asian mills and American brands and retailers achieve a quality of fleece fabrics to compete with, but not equal, the technology of Polarfleece and the Polartec fabrics. They did all of that without following the environmental regulations used by and required of Polarfleece and Polartec by the EPA in America.

Going back to table 2, we find a total of $70.5 billion in the value of shipments produced yearly and sold by American textile makers from 1992 through 1995. Eight of the top-ten textile companies reported $1 billion in sales, and two reported over $2 billion in sales a year. Nearly $17 billion of the $70 billion total was reported by the top ten textile companies. That leaves $50 billion spread over the rest of the textile companies. In 2010, China reported textile exports of $200 billion.

Comparing China's 2010 figure of $200 billion to the 1992–95 figure of $70 billion shipped from American textile companies, an important point is that the American $70 billion was textiles, not sewn garments and accessories. China's figures are based almost entirely on finished sewn products that include textile materials. We have learned from the 1913 American wool textile report about the value of woolen fabrics and finished products vs. just wool fiber. That accomplishment pushed wool values to be second to steel in the economy of America at that time. I believe it is reasonable to say the value of the $70 billion in American textile companies produced at least another $250 billion in finished sewn textile products, giving made-in-America textiles, from materials to finished products, a total value of $320 billion a year in 1992–1995. During those years, an imported cotton sweatshirt hoodie retailed for $29 and an imported knockoff of Polarfleece was about the same price. Today that imported cotton hoodie retails for $49 from the brands we have reviewed in the book and is made offshore, mostly in China. A knockoff of Polarfleece retails for at least $49. Adjusting for inflation, the China $200 billion in textile exports in 2010 reflects the cheap, slave-labor costs of sewing.

Only by ignoring the EPA regulations in textile materials and processing has China, in my opinion, kept the pricing from being equal to manufacturing here in America at this time. After 1995, we had a diversion from making textiles in America with the boom of computers and electronics that brought in revenues not seen since the gold-rush years at the end of the nineteenth century. After that boom, the riches of America found an unregulated banking system falsely building up the values of real estate—especially citizens' homes with the mortgage fraud. In between these two bubbles of wealth, textiles slipped offshore, mostly to China. I believe that easily a trillion dollars a year of revenues in textiles has been lost in actual consumer income and spending dollars because of textiles not being manufactured in America. Our unemployment rate also reflects the reality of not manufacturing textiles here. Unregulated banking here and unregulated manufacturing offshore is the reality of the polar pollution that engulfs America today. All of it is the responsibility of Americans and their companies. As the EPA notebook project says, "Most textile mills are small, specialized facilities. A large percentage of establishments in the textile industry have fewer than 20 employees" (table 3, Summary of Establishment Sizes within the Textile Industry). Table 2 lists the number of establishments at 5,500.

Every time we hear a political statement or a news-channel expert talk about small business being the heart of the American economy, it appears they are talking about coffee wagons in a parking lot, not an establishment that makes textiles in America. In China, the water pollution caused by producing textiles has polluted the water to the point where they do not have clean water for coffee. As for the textiles themselves, just how safe are the fabrics in our clothes from that pollution? In terms of jobs and deals in textiles, do the math in the four tables that follow, and the next bad guys are the brands selling them to you.

TABLES

Table 1: Standard Industrial Classifications within the Textile Industry (SIC 22)

3-digit SIC code	4-digit SIC Code
SIC 221- Broadwoven Fabric Mills, Cotton	SIC 2211 - Broadwoven Fabric Mills, Cotton
SIC 222- Broadwoven Fabric Mills, Manmade Fiber and Silk	SIC 2221 - Broadwoven Fabric Mills, Manmade Fiber and Silk
SIC 223- Broadwoven Fabric Mills, Wool (Including dyeing and finishing)	SIC 2231 - Broadwoven Fabric Mills, Wool (including dyeing and finishing)
SIC 224- Narrow Fabric Mills: Cotton, Wool, Silk, and Manmade Fiber	SIC 2241 - Narrow Fabric Mills: Cotton, Wool, Silk, and Manmade Fiber
SIC 225- Knitting Mills	SIC 2251 - Women's Full-Length and Knee-Length Hosiery, except socks SIC 2252 - Hosiery, not elsewhere classified SIC 2253 - Knit Outwear Mills SIC 2254 - Knit Underwear and Nightwear Mills SIC 2257 - Weft Knit Fabric Mills SIC 2258 - Lace and Warp Knit Fabric Mills SIC 2259 - Knitting Mills, not elsewhere classified
SIC 226- Dyeing and Finishing Textiles, except wool fabrics and knit goods	SIC 2261 - Finishers of Broadwoven Fabrics of Cotton SIC 2262 - Finishers of Broadwoven Fabrics of Manmade Fiber and Silk SIC 2269 - Finishers of Textiles, not elsewhere classified
SIC 227 - Carpets and Rugs	SIC 2273 - Carpets and Rugs
SIC 228- Yarn and Thread Mills	SIC 2281 - Yarn Spinning Mills SIC 2282 - Yarn Texturizing, Throwing, Twisting, and Winding Mills SIC 2284 - Thread Mills
SIC 229- Miscellaneous Textile Goods	SIC 2295 - Coated Fabrics, not rubberized SIC 2296 - Tire Cord and Fabrics SIC 2298 - Cordage and Twine SIC 2299 - Textile Goods, not elsewhere classified

Source: *Standard Industrial Classification Manual*, 1987, Office of Management and Budget, Washington, DC.

Table 5: Geographic Distribution of Textile Mills in the United States

3-digit SIC code	Major states (based on employment)	approximate % of employment in 3-digit SIC code category, attributable to major states
SIC 221	NC, SC, GA, AL	87
SIC 222	SC, NC, GA, VA	79
SIC 223	VA, GA, ME, NC	69
SIC 224	NC, PA, RI, SC	52
SIC 225	NC, KY, LA, NY, GA, PA, TX, NJ	40
SIC 226	NC, SC, GA, NJ	63
SIC 227	GA	64
SIC 228	NC, GA, SC	70
SIC 229	NC, SC, GA, AL, TN, MA, OH, NY	40

Source: adapted from various 1992 *Census of Manufactures, Industry Series*, for SICs 2211 - 2299, U.S. Department of Commerce, Bureau of the Census, 1995.

Figure 1: Distribution of Textile Establishments in the U.S.

Source: 1992 *Census of Manufactures, Industry Series*, for SICs 2211 - 2299, U.S. Department of Commerce, Bureau of the Census, 1995.

235

Table 2: Summary Statistics for the Textile Industry (SIC 22)				
Industry SIC Code	Establishments (No.)[1]	Companies (No.)[2]	Employment (000's)	Value of Shipments (millions of dollars)[3]
SIC 221	323	281	55.9	5,814
SIC 222	422	321	87.4	8,793
SIC 223	99	87	13.7	1,612
SIC 224	258	224	16.8	1,314
SIC 225	2,096	1,911	193.3	16,968
SIC 226	481	440	50.8	7,077
SIC 227	447	383	49.4	9,831
SIC 228	598	372	92.2	11,277
SIC 229	1,160	1,071	54.5	7,829
Totals	5,584	5,090	614	70,518

Source: adapted from various 1992 *Census of Manufactures, Industry Series*, for SICs 2211 - 2299, U.S. Department of Commerce, Bureau of the Census, 1995.

Note: The shaded rows highlight the SIC codes which contain the largest number of establishments, employment, and value of shipments.
[1]An establishment is a physical location where manufacturing takes place. Manufacturing is defined as the mechanical or chemical transformation of substances or materials into new products.
[2]Defined as a business organization consisting of one establishment or more under common ownership or control.
[3]Value of all products and services sold by establishments in the industry sector.

Table 3: Summary of Establishment Sizes within the Textile Industry (SIC 22)				
Industry SIC Code	Percentage of Establishments[1] with 0-19 Employees	Percentage of Establishments with 20-49 Employees	Percentage of Establishments with 50-99 Employees	Percentage of Establishments with 100 or More Employees
SIC 221	64	4	4	28
SIC 222	40	8	6	46
SIC 223	45	22	9	23
SIC 224	49	14	14	22
SIC 225	44	21	14	21
SIC 226	32	22	15	31
SIC 227	53	12	9	26
SIC 228	24	11	13	52
SIC 229	58	18	11	12

Source: adapted from various 1992 *Census of Manufactures, Industry Series*, for SICs 2211 - 2299, U.S. Department of Commerce, Bureau of the Census, 1995.

Note: The shaded column highlights the large percentage of facilities that have fewer than 20 employees.
[1]An establishment is a physical location where manufacturing takes place. Manufacturing is defined as the mechanical or chemical transformation of substances or materials into new products.

Rank[a]	Company	1995 Sales (millions of dollars)	3-digit SIC code
1	Springs Industries, Fort Mill, SC	$2,233	221
2	Burlington Industries, Greensboro, NC	$2,209	223
3	WestPoint Stevens, West Point, GA	$1,650	221
4	Unifi, Greensboro, NC	$1,555	228
5	Dominion Textile, New York, NY	$1,429	221
6	Collins & Aikman Corp., Farmville, NC	$1,291	221
7	Triarc, New York, NY	$1,128	221
8	Fieldcrest Cannon, New York, NY	$1,095	221
9	Cone Mills, Greensboro, NC	$910	221
10	Guilford Mills, Greensboro, NC	$783	225

Source: This chart has been adapted from data in *Fairchild's Textile & Apparel Financial Directory* 1996 with assistance from ATMI.

These tables show that one hundred years of textile manufacturing in America, from the late 1800s through the 1990s, brought America from a developing nation of farming to the leadership of industrial manufacturing with a safe and healthy plan and laws for environmental protection through the EPA. I believe my book has walked us through that period of time, proving that we had a sustainable textile industry making things here. Most experts agree that sustainable business and lifestyle involves economics, the environment, and social responsibility. Polar pollution as presented brings with it a disturbing change in how humans access the water of our planet and our own bodies.

Looking at social responsibility, water.org reports that 884 million people globally lack access to safe water supplies. Reports about China show 320 million people, or just about one-third of their total population, lack access to safe water. Water issues, including sanitation, are reported to claim more lives through disease than any wars with boots on the ground. Add to the issue of sanitation the alarming amounts of water pollution from textile manufacturing, especially the dye houses, and the ability of people in developing countries to access clean water becomes more than a catastrophic issue for economics. Without healthy people, there are simply not going to be healthy workers to hold down jobs in textile manufacturing.

Adding to this so-called labor shortage in China today, based on issues of wages and collective bargaining, the bigger global picture seems to be saying sanitation and access to healthy water. In Bangladesh, the water continues to be reported using the classic phrase "water, water everywhere, and not a drop to drink." The water in slum areas, according to ABC News, was contaminated with E. coli bacteria. Bangladesh is a targeted area for more textile manufacturing because of its cheap labor of under $100 a month, compared with Chinese wages of $300 to $400 a month.

India has said they are closing hundreds of textile dye houses until they are reopened with zero water pollution and waste controls. Sourcing conferences that I listen to here in America say that leading brands are complaining that production is too slow in India to take the country seriously as a prime producer of textiles for today's apparel and shoes. In America, where we once manufactured most of our textiles, as shown in the map on the previous pages, an economic return of $8 is gained for every $1 invested in water and sanitation. On a per-year basis, an investment of US $11 billion a year in sanitation yields a payback of US $84 billion in economic value (water.org).

With only 62 percent of the world's population having access to modern sanitation—meaning a facility that separates human excreta from human contact—how can these sweatshop labor factories, both sewing and textile processing, assure consumers like us here in America that the fabrics and products are clean and healthy.

The stated goal of the textile brands in their supply-chain meetings, which are held on public webinars, is to keep pushing for a new developing country to sew their apparel and shoes and build water-sucking machines and chemicals to color the fabrics. In the developing world where these supply-chain managers point their products, 24,000 children under the age of five die every day from unclean water, leading to 1.4 million deaths a year as a result of diarrhea. At least half the hospital beds in the world are occupied by people with diseases from lack of access to safe drinking water and inadequate sanitation. Compared to the sanitation return of $8 in the United States for every $1 invested, according to the World

Health Organization (WHO), the return on investments in safe drinking water and sanitation globally is $3 to $4 dollars, depending on the region and technology. Areas that need safe drinking water find two out of three people living on wages of less than $2 a day. Thus, where will the textile supply chain begin to create another catastrophic base of manufacturing in developing countries—Africa?

Yes, Africa is now the next target, and of course Nike, showing up for a world-class football event there with a limited supply of recycled bottle-made uniforms, is trying to settle the area first. Water consumption and sanitation flow from the ice packs of outdoor-adventure mountains to streams that feed rivers for irrigation for growing food and producing textile cotton fibers. In what is commonly called trickle-down, less water is flowing out of the mountains due to global warming. Then the streams wash out in silt. Once water makes it to the rivers, it is polluted with fertilizers and carried on into the towns' and cities' water supplies. That alone, without proper sanitation treatment, causes diseases in humans, fish, and plants. Bring on the new textile makers, and their chemical pollution fouls the water further, including groundwater, and the clean water is lost. In real numbers, 70 percent of freshwater goes to irrigated agriculture. In America today, the average citizen uses 100–175 gallons of water a day. That amount does not include water for drinking and making our clothes and shoes.

Today's textile brands in America are talking more about moving farther in to the poorest developing countries in search of cheaper labor. To a tee shirt and shoe, they have no plans for water conservation and consumption. Putting together names like Sustainable Apparel Coalition, they are enablers who count gallons of water rather than cut down the consumption. The enabling in my opinion requires a double-faced step program: First they should admit how they got to where they are today, obsessed with sweat and rain and snow to the point of using enormous amounts of water to mix their toxic chemicals of oil-based brews. Second they should admit that flushing and clean hands are only possible with clean water free of chemical pollution, thus requiring them to greatly reduce their gallons-per-minute of water processing, from growing natural fibers to adding colors, and to substitute clean, toxic-free, man-made materials.

The UN estimates that by the year 2025, at least forty-eight countries with a combined population of 2.8 billion will face freshwater stress and/or scarcity. At this time I predict, based on what I know about textiles and water consumption, that only twelve countries on the planet have the access they need to clean drinking water and enough left over for agriculture and sanitation.

Wastewater is extremely costly to treat and requires continuous investment. Most important is the commitment to stick around and be there to keep the water as clean as possible. Daily stories are reported on the Internet about pollution and a town not having clean drinking water in China and other countries in Asia that make textiles and electronics. My biggest hope is that within a few years of publishing this book, the readings will be outdated by the cleanup needed to save our water and the lives of hundreds of millions of people.

12138437R00140

Made in the USA
Lexington, KY
27 November 2011